PATHS OF THE CHRISTIAN MYSTERIES

From Compostela to the New World

Virginia Sease and Manfred Schmidt-Brabant

TEMPLE LODGE

Translated from the German by Marguerite V. Miller and Douglas E. Miller

Temple Lodge Publishing
Hillside House, The Square
Forest Row, East Sussex
RH18 5ES

www.templelodge.com

Published by Temple Lodge 2003
Reprinted 2009

Originally published in German under the title *Compostela, Sternenwege alter und neuer Mysterienstätten* by Verlag am Goetheanum, Dornach 1999

A catalogue record for this book is available from the British Library

ISBN 978 1 902636 43 6

Cover by Andrew Morgan Design
Typeset by DP Photosetting, Aylesbury, Bucks.
Printed and bound in Great Britain by Cpod, Trowbridge, Wiltshire

Contents

Illustrations

Preface to the English Edition

Since this book appeared in German there have been repeated requests for a translation into English. Because of other responsibilities, it has not been possible for me to undertake the task, therefore my gratitude to Marguerite and Douglas Miller is indeed great. The accuracy and the knowledgeable finesse which they applied to this work extends far beyond the normal mandates for translation. They connected with the themes presented in such a manner that even complicated subtleties shine through and maintain their vigour.

Some changes were made for this English edition, especially in regard to dates. The book was published in the last year of the twentieth century and in various cases it was necessary to reflect the fact that we are now in the twenty-first century.

Manfred Schmidt-Brabant travelled and lectured extensively in the English-speaking world. Since his death in February 2001, many friends have expressed the hope that his lectures would become available in English. The subjects covered in this book include aspects which he brought in his lectures; therefore a small portion of the wish achieves fulfilment at this time, for which I too am grateful.

Virginia Sease
Goetheanum
January 2003

Preface to the German Edition

The 13 lectures that form the basis of this book were given in Santiago de Compostela in Spain at the invitation of Manfred Kraus for a vacation course sponsored by the Studienhaus Rüspe in September 1997.

Years of research on the place of the Camino in the entire context of the more recent history of the Mysteries went into these lectures. The extensive literature about Santiago de Compostela, the Camino, and associated themes that we used for this research could only be partially reflected in the notes.

We are in large measure indebted to Elisabeth Bessau for the editing and proofreading of the transcripts of the lectures. We also thank Hanna Dändliker and Heinrich Muhler for the typescript, and Mr Muhler in particular who showed great patience in continually rewriting the manuscript to include its many revisions.

Virginia Sease
Manfred Schmidt-Brabant
Dornach, August 1999

Lecture 1

The Cosmic Origin of the Grail Mysteries—Hiram, Solomon and the Queen of Sheba

Manfred Schmidt-Brabant

During the last twenty-five or thirty years an enormous interest has developed in the Camino, the pilgrim's route to Santiago de Compostela. Where does this interest come from and what does it mean? It almost seems as though primal memories are rising up in people. We live in a time of spiritual quest. In the last few decades alone, human beings have become more sensitive; as a result, something like a memory of what this route meant in the high Middle Ages may be emerging in many human souls.

This growing interest may also be related to a kind of need that lives in many people, a need Rudolf Steiner points to when he says that we should live not only with external history, but we should also learn to live with what lies behind external history, with the history of the Mysteries.[1] Now, at the beginning of the twenty-first century, it may become vitally necessary to live consciously with this history of the Mysteries of mankind, because our time places us in a mighty Mystery battle, a battle on the soul-spiritual plane.

Turning-points in the History of the Mysteries

We often look at the history of the Mysteries in a way that leads us to say: There were the old Mysteries which died away, and new Mysteries will be arising in the future. In 1924, Rudolf Steiner summarizes this approach in more detail, noting that it actually has four major steps. There were the old Mysteries, when it could be said that human beings and gods lived together. Then there were the half-old Mysteries, during which human beings could continue to experience the activities of the gods in and around themselves. Following these, there were the half-new Mysteries, when human beings began to assume an independent place, apart from the gods. And then there will be new Mysteries.[2] He places the beginning of the half-new Mysteries at approximately the same time as our theme, at the time of Hiram, Solomon and the Queen of Sheba—about 950 years before the turning-point in time. The portion of the history of the Mysteries we refer to as the history of the newer Mysteries extends from that point to the present. We intend to present here some of the critical turning-points of this period.

Three themes form the basis for grouping these turning-points in a particular way. The first is that Rudolf Steiner called the whole of anthroposophy 'a science of the Grail'.[3] He described the book *Occult Science, An Outline* as 'containing the outlines of anthroposophy'.[4] He says that what is presented in this book is 'science of the Grail', and modern initiates 'can be called the *initiates of the Grail*'.[5] The second theme he points to—he actually pointed to it throughout all of his works—is that the earthly Grail Mysteries were established in northern Spain. And the third theme is that this Camino must be viewed as closely connected to the Grail Mysteries.

This approach should suggest something quite specific—that a powerful and sudden change takes place in the whole history of the Mysteries, but especially in the half-new and new Mysteries. The guidance of humanity is changing from being determined by the nature of wisdom to becoming an inner seed growing within the individual nature of the human being in the future.

This is generally characterized in the same way we find described by Rudolf Steiner in *Occult Science*. Beginning with the Earth stage of planetary development, the wisdom of the outer world will become inner wisdom in human beings. And when this wisdom is internalized, it will become the seed of love. Wisdom is the prerequisite of love; love is the result of wisdom born again in the ego. This may be expressed even more succinctly: an old cosmos of wisdom transforms itself on the earth into a cosmos of love in the future. We will attempt to explore the turning-points from this perspective.

The Temple Legend

We will begin with what is called the Temple Legend. This legend did not become known exoterically until the beginning of the nineteenth century. For a long time it was kept secret, many say in the lodges (German, *Bauhütten*); this was certainly the case in regard to the Freemasons as well as other esoteric connections. In the mid-nineteenth century, the secret is brought a bit into the open by the French poet

Nerval. Then Rudolf Steiner begins to lecture frequently about it in a specific form that he said went back to Christian Rosenkreutz, the creator of the true form of the Temple Legend.[6] Therefore, we will present the legend here in a brief and concise form.

The Temple Legend unfolds in seven great steps. In the first step, the legend says that at the beginning of Earth evolution one of the elohim, one of the spirits of light, descended and united itself with the earthly mother, Eve. Cain, the first earth man, resulted from this union. Some legends say that this spirit of light was Lucifer. Then came another elohim—Yahveh or Jehovah—and created Adam from the dust. Adam united with Eve, and their union resulted in the birth of Abel. Cain was the result of asexual procreation, Abel the result of sexual procreation. Cain became a farmer, working the land; Abel became a shepherd and, without labouring, lived from what the earth provided.

Now the second step follows. One day both men make sacrifices to Jehovah; the one offers fruits of the fields, the other the yield of his herd. But Jehovah accepts only Abel's burnt offering and rejects Cain's. Because of this, Cain slays Abel. Jehovah gives Seth to the parents as a substitute son.

We now come to the third step. The descendants of Cain become the people who pursue earthly occupations—the sciences, the arts. They lose the life of the spirit through Cain's deed, but they acquire knowledge of the earth. The children of Abel and Seth live in a dreamy perception of the spiritual world. Because of their sexual origin, they can no longer perceive the spiritual world fully. They become priest-kings who receive through revelations what comes from the spiritual world.

The legend then takes an enormous leap when it says that the greatest descendant of the Seth stream, the wise King Solomon, came next. Solomon conceived the plan of a temple, the Temple of Solomon, in which all the secrets of the universe would be mirrored. On account of his wisdom, he could design plans for this temple, but he was unable to build it. And so he calls upon the greatest of Cain's descendants, the architect Hiram. Hiram builds the temple for Solomon. Now the Queen of Sheba comes to admire the wisdom of Solomon, and she becomes engaged to him.

Next we have the fifth step. The Queen of Sheba comes to know Hiram and suddenly recognizes that he is also a great human being in his own right; he is the greatest child of Lucifer, a new kind of personality. She regrets her engagement to Solomon; while he is drunk, she removes the engagement ring from his finger and considers herself to be free. She joins Hiram and conceives a son with him.

The sixth step follows. The final element in the construction of the temple is the casting of the Brazen Sea. It is an artful casting, made from the seven planetary metals in such a way that, in the end, the whole mass becomes transparent as a crystal. The casting is prepared, but there are three evil journeymen who are envious because they had not been promoted to the level of master craftsman by Hiram. They mix impurities into the casting and, as it is executed, flames shoot out from all sides. From the flames, Hiram hears a voice telling him: Throw yourself into it! You are indestructible! He throws himself into the flames and arrives at the centre of the earth where he finds his ancestor, Cain—Rudolf Steiner says, 'illuminated by the rays of Lucifer'[7]—in a state of innocence, as he was originally. Cain gives Hiram a new hammer; Hiram returns and completes the casting of the Brazen Sea.

Then comes the seventh step. Hiram wants to visit his temple once again. He goes through the temple and, as he starts to leave, the three evil journeymen lie in wait for him. With three blows to the head—to the right temple, the left temple, and to the forehead—they murder him and secretly bury him. The other true master craftsmen look for the body, find it, and when they find it they create a new Master Word. The Temple Legend ends with Hiram's experiences after his death. We will look at those later.

The Queen of Sheba in the Old and New Testaments

There is an interesting question that arises: What was it that people have always encountered in this Queen of Sheba? The legend of the Queen of Sheba radiates from the Old Testament stories about her, and it reaches into India, Persia, Egypt, Yemen, into the Jewish culture, later into Islam and the Christian world. A wealth of iconography, miniatures, frescoes, illuminated manuscripts and statues exists along with the legend! Who is not familiar with the wonderful Queen of Sheba on the north portal of the cathedral at Chartres, standing there next to Solomon, below them a slave with a vessel, Melchizedek nearby with the Grail chalice at his breast? She is portrayed throughout all of Christian art in stained glass windows, tapestries, paintings—by Raphael, Veronese, Tintoretto, Holbein, Rubens—right up to the present, where she can be found in comic books, on playing cards, and in Hollywood films.

This is quite astonishing because the story in the Old Testament is brief and rather meagre.[8] The Queen of Sheba comes with camels, gold and slaves in order to hear the wisdom of Solomon. She poses questions to him—we are not told what they are. She receives answers—which we also do not hear. We hear only that she marvels. Gifts are again exchanged, then she packs her things and departs for home. Around 500 years before the turning-point in time, the Book of Kings was edited by priests in keeping with old court reports. Based on this meagre story, a wave of veneration, admiration and fantasy-filled elaboration of the Queen of Sheba begins to move across the face of the then-known world.

Later, the New Testament is written down and a completely different note is struck. Christ speaks of the Day of Judgment, and it says in the Gospel of Matthew and the Gospel of Luke, 'The queen of the south shall rise up in the judgment with this generation, and shall condemn it: for she came from the uttermost parts of the earth to hear the wisdom of Solomon; and, behold, a greater than Solomon is here.'[9] It is as though a curtain behind this whole folkloric business of camels, gold and slaves were suddenly pulled back to reveal a completely different level of reality. Christ Himself, Who will be the judge at the Last Judgment, says she will also be there and will condemn this generation. This can be understood metaphorically to mean that she will sit in judgment of mankind.

Who is this Queen of Sheba characterized by Christ with these words? What reality emerges from His words? People sensed this reality from the few words contained in the Old Testament; they perceived her through the words. In the Middle Ages, human souls were still constituted in a way that is difficult to understand today. They had an imaginative perception. A phrase like 'the Queen of Sheba' was enough for them to arrive—by way of a half-clairvoyant or fully clairvoyant perception—at a reality that lies behind the Old Testament story.

The Middle Ages and the Queen of Sheba

An amazing image of this Queen of Sheba arises, especially in esoteric Christianity. It begins around the year 1000. At that time, on the border of Spain and France, there were two powerful cloisters, San Pedro de Roda—which was not only a cloister, but a complete university resting high above the Mediterranean—and Santa Maria de Ripoll, a cloister more towards the Pyrenees. Today both lie in ruins, but Roda is still recognizable because of its size. Both of these cloisters conveyed to the rest of Europe the Arabic wisdom that was flowering during that period—

mathematics, astronomy, language, music. And so around the year 1000 one of the most beautiful illuminated manuscripts of the Bible is created; it is still in existence. In this illuminated manuscript the Queen of Sheba is portrayed as she is described in the Koran. She is striding through the water in order to come to Solomon. People at that time could still read such pictures: she came through the water, through the ether, to the earth, to Solomon.

Thus wonderful descriptions spread in the West, especially in esoteric connections. We will look at only a few. In *Aurora Consurgens* [Rising dawn], which is ascribed to Thomas Aquinas, it says:

> It is the wisdom, the Queen of Sheba, that came out of the Orient in order to hear the wisdom of Solomon, and into her hand is given might and honour and power and dominion, and like a bride adorned for her bridegroom she wears upon her head a royal crown of the rays of twelve shining stars. And on her garments there is a golden inscription: As queen I will rule, and my realm is without end for all who find me and look upon me with discernment, an inventive spirit, and steadfastness.[10]

Then a further step follows, one that makes many researchers a bit uneasy. In his book *Mirror of Mysteries*, Honorius von Augsburg from the Rosicrucian milieu refers to it:

> As the Queen of Sheba herself surrendered her body and her blood to her disciples, there lay John at the breast of Jesus, and drank there of the well-source of wisdom.[11]

We will find more such aspects where we sense—as with the Last Judgment—that the Queen of Sheba is placed in close proximity to the Christ Being.

We find an entirely different image in the work of Isidor of Seville, the great teacher in the Church of Spain:

> The queen from the south must be understood as the Church which gathers itself together from the far reaches of the world in order to hear the voice of God. But the Church is Mary who is the bride of God.[12]

Within alchemy there are many references to the Queen of Sheba. Johannes Graceus says in his *Arca Arcani*:

> The radiant white dove is contained in lead, called the salt of metals. This salt is that chaste, wise, and wealthy Queen of Sheba, clothed in a white veil.[13]

Penatus a Portu writes:

> You already have the virgin earth within an alchemical process; she is the Queen of Sheba.[14]

Hugo St Victor takes up another theme and says:

> The Queen of the East, Solomon's divine wisdom, came hither. Black is she, but lovely, blackened by myrrh and frankincense, a Black Madonna.[15]

The Black Madonna

This is a continuing tradition, but one which should not be taken in a merely superficial way by saying: Well yes, she came from Yemen, from Sheba, so naturally she was dark-skinned. Something else is meant here. It is possible for someone to be blackened by frankincense, but not by myrrh. And we should recall momentarily that three kings came from the land of Sheba and brought gold to the King of Mankind, myrrh to the Saviour, the healer, and frankincense to the God. An old Catalonian map depicts the countries of the earth known at that time. Everywhere across the map there are pictures of grim kings, but in the Land of Sheba the Queen of Sheba sits, smiling graciously with numerous rays streaming out from her to all the other countries; one of these rays points to the Three Kings riding towards Jerusalem.

Black is the secret of the Black Madonna. Throughout Europe you will find the White Madonna and the Black Madonna. In esotericism this always means that the White Madonna is the one who conveys wisdom from heaven; the Black Madonna is the one whose wisdom comes from the earth. Hence the legends connected to the discovery of the Black Madonna say she can be found in caves, in a tree stump, and so forth. The Black Madonna is the Madonna of Hiram; the White Madonna is the Madonna of Solomon.

The Fall of Lucifer

In addition, there was also a secret tradition that Rudolf Steiner takes up and confirms. It claims that the Queen of Sheba had brought Solomon the vessel which later became the Holy Grail. She brought him the vessel said to have been made from the very stone, the most precious gem, that fell from the crown of Lucifer when he was cast out of heaven.

Let us therefore turn our attention back to that point in the cosmic past when the fall of Lucifer began and when the history of the Grail also begins. We look at evolution and can say that the Earth went through earlier stages before it took on its present form. It went through an Old Saturn stage where it consisted entirely of warmth. Then followed an Old Sun phase of Earth, when air and light were present in addition to warmth. Then an Old Moon phase of Earth developed, and water was added as well as what is called the chemical ether, or tone ether. The truly solid mineral element and the principle of life did not develop until the present Earth condition.

Spiritual beings, those hierarchies that go back to Dionysius of Athens and the School of Athens, have also undergone their development along with the earth's development. We call them angels, archangels, archai, as well as the elohim, the spirits of movement, the kyriotetes or the spirits of wisdom, and the highest hierarchy—thrones, cherubim and seraphim. All of these undergo a development that normally ascends step by step; but there are also beings that remain behind, beings that fall, as it were.

Let us look at this pre-earthly progression during a very particular moment on Old Sun. In this situation there was still no mid-point; something like seven planets moved together in balance. Something existed there that corresponds to today's sun, and Christ was the spirit of this planetary state. There was also something that corresponds to today's Venus, and Lucifer was the spirit of that planetary state. There were seven planetary forms in the Old Sun stage of Earth. In esotericism, Christ and Lucifer are portrayed as brothers. Christ and Lucifer were brothers. Rudolf Steiner adds that brothers often behave quite differently from one another.[16] Thus Christ and Lucifer each had a very different relationship to knowledge of the world, experience of the world, and the creation of the world. Surrounding Old Sun was something like a wreath of powerful, ancient beings—the twelve world initiators. Where the signs of the zodiac stand today, there stood powerful primal beings that came out of the past. Together they created the Cosmic Word, the Cosmic Logos. Christ then opened Himself completely to this Cosmic Word, this Cosmic Logos, so that He might penetrate everything in the world because of His bond with the Cosmic Logos. He merged with the Logos. Christ, Who was actually an archangel on Old Sun, becomes the Cosmic Word.

Lucifer's gesture was completely different. He did his best to penetrate everything in the world with the light of his own ego, a powerful cosmic ego. But this insistence on his own ego led to his being left behind in evolution. While Christ ascends by merging with the Cosmic Word—with the Logos—and makes the sun into the mid-point of the planetary system, Lucifer loses Venus, he descends to earth, he falls to earth. But on earth he becomes mankind's greatest teacher of wisdom.

Rudolf Steiner says about this situation, '... all later development flows from what Lucifer and Christ were at that time.'[17] We stand here before the enormous age-old question: Why do beings remain behind in their development and become evil? There are a number of answers that we should consider together.

Beings that are Left Behind

One answer is that certain beings are ordered by the highest deity, by the Trinity—and here Rudolf Steiner uses an odd expression—'to become a detachment' and remain behind, sacrificing themselves in order to make development possible. Indeed, he even says that these beings bring the 'sacrifice' of remaining behind, because they are supposed to prepare '... the way to the Christ'.[18] This is something we will come across repeatedly, especially in regard to the enigmatic figure of Lucifer. It must be said that, next to the Christ, Lucifer is the most enigmatic figure in all the hierarchies. This is related to the fact that there is a multitude of luciferic beings—lower, higher, mighty beings, beings of wisdom, but also demonic beings; we will come to know them later. The divinity of Lucifer lives in all of them. But among them there are real adversaries of the entire evolutionary plan of the gods—and we will encounter them. They work into evolution from the outside; they infect beings within the hierarchies. What must be told here is a secret that earlier (even in the case of Rudolf Steiner) could only be revealed at the highest levels of initiation. In the course of evolution, beings must fall so that other beings can rise. We see the same thing happen around the hypomochlion of a balancing scales—that one side must fall so that the other side may rise. Within evolution, morality consists in the fact that the fallen ones must later be lifted up by the ones who ascended.

We approach such a cosmic riddle cautiously, and yet a history of the Mysteries must touch upon it. We ask ourselves: Did Lucifer have to fall so that Christ could ascend to the Logos, to the Cosmic Word? Or did it happen the other way around—Christ ascended to the Cosmic Word, to the Logos, so Lucifer fell? This paves the way for one of the great themes of cosmic and human evolution—the redemption of Lucifer.

The Nature of the Queen of Sheba

Rudolf Steiner gives certain indications about the Temple Legend. Who is this Queen of Sheba, he asks. She is the 'old star wisdom'; or he calls her 'the soul of mankind . . . the representative of the true human soul', or it is said that the Queen of Sheba is 'wisdom'.[19] We will frequently encounter the fact that real, physical human beings can at the same time be carriers of great, cosmic principles—which, of course, always sounds a bit strange in a materialistic age. The Queen of Sheba lived as a physical, human being, and we will even find her again in a later incarnation; but at that time she was the carrier of star wisdom, the carrier of a powerful cosmic being.

The second question one might ask is: Why does she always have a new name? It is readily apparent that this has to do with wisdom, with Isis, with Sophia. Human names do not measure up to the gods. We always need new names, new situations in order to experience another aspect of such divine beings. In this case, the cosmic being of star wisdom passes from the children of Abel—who until then had been inspired by it in a dreamy clairvoyance—to the children of Lucifer, to the children of Cain, to the Hiram stream. There are passages in the Temple Legend that make the Queen of Sheba seem like a kind of lesser sister of the Cosmic Word—we already saw the proximity to the Christ Being—like an aspect of the Cosmic Word, the Logos, that is turned towards the human being. At the beginning of the more recent history of the Mysteries it comes to pass that the ancient wisdom no longer inspires the old Abel stream because that stream did not have an independent ego. Even the great Solomon had only a reflected ego which could therefore be lost. This is shown in the image of the Queen of Sheba pulling the ring—always an image of the ego—from the finger of the intoxicated Solomon. The star wisdom passes over to the stream that has a self-acquired, enduring earth-ego, and that is the Hiram stream.

The time when this star wisdom passes from the children of Abel to the children of Cain is now—in the present time. Rudolf Steiner says, 'The arrival of the Queen of Sheba points to what is happening now.'[20] The whole story is concerned with what is happening now. In the history of the Mysteries, three thousand years is actually not a very long time. From this time on—from the construction of Solomon's Temple and culminating in the present time—star wisdom passes over to the ego that has become independent in those human beings who have acquired such an ego.

Eve

Now we understand the beginning from another perspective. Who is this Eve who was everything in the beginning? Earth and mankind—not yet ego-humanity, but a pre-humanity—had been prepared on Old Saturn, on Old Sun, on Old Moon. What carries over and begins as our earthly condition, what condenses from out of the spiritual element, is something unique. Earth and humanity together, earth and the human being together, that is the earth mother—Eve. She is feminine because the feminine element had already arisen on the Old Moon. The feminine element is the oldest, while the masculine element first arises on the earth.

Thus there are three unique stories. We know two of them from the Bible; and this third one—which tells that Eve came first—has always been known as well. When the great initiate Trevrizent teaches Parzival, he tells him, 'The earth was Adam's mother.'[21] Adam came to life as the bodily fruit of the earth; but the earth was a virgin. Only two human beings have been born of a virgin—Adam and Jesus. These traditions that reached far into the past were still known in the thirteenth century! This was humanity at the earliest stage of Earth evolution, during the Polaric epoch; human being and earth were one—the primal mother, Eve. Then comes the second creation story, the one found in the Bible. The gods, the elohim, spoke: 'Let us make man in our image!'[22] And they created him as both masculine and feminine, androgynous. The human being had two genders; that was the humanity of the Hyperborian epoch. The human being did not yet have only one gender. At that time, the kingdoms of nature began to differentiate themselves from human beings. Virgin procreation still existed; human beings and nature each reproduced out of themselves. Only then does the Lemurian epoch begin and human beings receive an ego from the elohim. This is the story of the third creation, the story of Adam and Eve—created from Adam's rib.[23] Now two genders emerge; two genders also arise in the kingdoms of nature. The Adam of this Lemurian epoch is the first ego-man. What is meant by the image of Eve being created from his rib? It means that Eve is an ego-human being of the same substance; that human beings now arise out of egohood.

However, during this Lemurian epoch, when egohood emerges, Adam's soul existence only partially incarnates. A part, an innocent part, of the Adam-soul is held back in the spiritual world and does not participate in the Fall of Man. And as we saw earlier in the words of Trevrizent, knowledge of this tripartite Eve is now in everything that comes into play: Eve, the primal mother, who once comprised the whole earth; Eve, who was part of Adam, Adam and Eve as one human being; and Eve who, like Adam, emerges from a substance—the ego-substance.

Doubt, Fear, Hatred

Now, for the first time, we can understand who these three evil journeymen actually are who murder Hiram. The human being originally lived in the spiritual world. He was as one with the spiritual world; he lived in spirit. This was the earliest origin of the old Mysteries that go far back into Lemuria. But then incarnation began. He drew into the astral body with his ego, into the ether body, into the physical body. And even to this day, he receives a mortal blow each time he does. When he draws into the astral body, doubt befalls him—doubt of the spirit, doubt of himself. In the spiritual world, the human being does not know doubt. He lives in everything; he lives in the truth. He receives the second mortal blow when he enters into the ether body. In occultism, this blow is called superstition. We understand this to mean that the spirit would have to appear in some particular form. Everything learned through education—that this is correct or that is false—all of it is superstition. And then comes the worst of these, the truly mortal blow. When the ego enters into the physical body, the illusion of an individual self-identity develops. In the spiritual world, the human being does not know superstition. He knows the nature of the spirit. In the spiritual world, the human being does not know the illusion of personal individuality. He knows how he is interconnected with everything; although he is an individuality, he is bound up with all other spiritual beings. He lives in everything, and everything lives in him.

Superstition leads to hate. If I hold the opinion that the spirit must appear in some particular cultural, religious, artistic or other form, then I begin to hate everything that differs from my opinion. If I am convinced that I exist only as a personal individuality, I would have to fear that the spirit might absorb me. Then I am filled with fear of the spirit. The three evil journeymen are also doubt, fear and hate. Time and again, they kill spirit-consciousness; they kill the ego.

The Asuras

The Queen of Sheba has not only been honoured; from the earliest times the Queen of Sheba has been subject to terrible slander. This begins already in Judaism and radiates out even into the present. These slanders are based on the mistaken notion that she is a demon, a spectral being that strangles children, ensnares men—a terrible sexual demon; that she is the notorious Lilith, 'Adam's first wife'.[24] But knowledge of Lilith has existed from as early as the year 3000 BC, two thousand years before the Queen of Sheba.

In the second epoch, in the Hyperborian epoch, the human being was an androgynous, bisexual being. Legend says that Adam and Lilith had grown together, so to speak, back to back. This does not suit Lilith. One day she tears herself loose, grows wings, flies into the wilderness, and becomes a demon. It is said that every day she has hundreds of children with Lucifer, but that she immediately strangles them all. What remains of Adam sits there and laments. God takes pity on him and creates Eve for him from his rib. Now Lilith becomes jealous; leaving Adam is one thing, but his having a new wife is another thing entirely! Thus she unites herself with Lucifer, and together the two of them slip into Paradise in the shape of a snake. They tempt Eve and, through her, Adam as well. This is the legend as it exists.

Extraordinarily complex and significant facts are concealed behind this legend. When the human form came over from the Old Moon, one might say it had already developed the physical body, the ether body, and the astral body at an earlier stage. As the Earth now begins, the activity of particular spirits—the archai, the spirits of personality—enters into the picture. They take a portion of the astral body, separate it off, and create the foundations for the current members of our soul—the sentient soul, the intellectual soul, the consciousness soul. They create these foundations of the soul so that from the Lemurian epoch onwards the human being becomes capable of incorporating an ego into this soul foundation. However, at the time of the Earth's beginning there were archai that had been left behind, that had not ascended during the normal development—the so-called asuras. These asuras also create human astrality, also create a soul structure, but this soul structure cannot incorporate a human ego. It can live in human bodies, but it is incapable of incorporating an ego. These egoless soul forms, these soul forms that cannot be used by an ego, have a particular affinity to sexuality. Rudolf Steiner says this quite emphatically. The highest spirit of the asuras is

Lilith. Lilith is the all-inclusive name, the consciousness name, for these asuras.

Sexuality

Since the concept of sexuality will emerge of necessity from the theme of the Grail, what follows here can effectively bring clarity to this matter. In 1923, late in his life, Rudolf Steiner says that in the present time we confuse everything about the following concepts—nevertheless, we still have to differentiate among them. We have to differentiate the love between ego and ego, the love between human being and human being, the spiritual genius of love from the lower handmaid of love that is eroticism. As a result we must see that there is an opposing demon that counters love, and that is sexuality.

> We recognize the spiritual genius of love; we have spiritualized love. We recognize the lower servant, eroticism. However, we fall to the demon of love. And the spiritual genius of love has its demon in the interpretation of sexuality—not the real form, but the current civilization's interpretation ... The greatest misunderstandings can arise precisely in this area. Because what originally lives in sexuality is permeated by spiritual love.
>
> However, the demon of love arises when what otherwise is at work in human beings through the divine will falls prey to human thinking, when it is torn away from spirituality by intellectualism ... I would even say that it is in the power of the human being to be capable of denying his own nature. He denies it when he sinks from the level of the genius of love to the demon of sexuality ...[25]

Sorat

Now it is simply not the case that we are continuing to postulate a confusion between the Queen of Sheba and Lilith merely as an intellectual exercise as is done even in modern literature. Something is actually taking place in the spiritual world. The fact is that the Lilith-Asura figure continually tries to put herself in the place of the Queen of Sheba, which is to say in the place of the being for whom the Queen of Sheba was the bearer. How is this possible?

The Queen of Sheba is a lofty being, one of the kyriotetes, a spirit of wisdom; Lilith is only an archai, which is a much lower level within the hierarchies. And here we speak of the secret that will permeate us right into the present time, permeate us into our soul-physical and spiritual existence.

Lilith can place herself at the same level as, and in opposition to, the Queen of Sheba because she (Lilith) is permeated by the most powerful force of evil present in our universe—Sorat, the sun-demon. He is a being that comes from outside our time and space, a being from beyond our universe. Sorat is a spiritual power that denies the entire meaning of our evolution from Saturn to Vulcan, and wants to negate this evolution. The meaning of our evolution rests in the possibility of beings acquiring the ability to say, 'Not I, but the Christ in me.' However, in order to accomplish this an ego must have become so strong that it can make of itself a vessel, that it can withdraw itself so that it surrenders its egoism, and yet remains an ego that carries the Christ. Sorat wants to destroy all egohood.

Lucifer wants to possess the ego for his own purposes; Ahriman wants to win the human ego for himself; the Sorat-being wants to demolish egohood. The Sorat being works principally through what the demon of love is—the opposing demon, sexuality that has turned demonic. When Rudolf Steiner once spoke of this, he said, 'And in much of what ... is now coming to the fore in our large cities as wild orgies of pointless sensuality, we can already see the grotesque flickering of hell.'[26] Imagine what he might say today! We are so influenced by a Sorat-infected shaping of public opinion that we hardly notice any more what is actually taking place. From this we see that the egoless mistress of the soul, Lilith, wants to take the place of the true, ego-endowed soul of mankind.

The Philosopher's Stone

Again and again we are led by these observations to the secrets of the physical body. A secret of the physical body comes to expression in the casting of the Brazen Sea. For this Brazen Sea—had it come into existence—would have made the earth into a transparent, clear planet. The human body was intended to be like this—transparent, clear. The Brazen Sea points to what the human being would have become if it were free of doubt, superstition and the illusion of the personal self. This is the secret of the phantom, of the Philosopher's Stone; we will be accompanied, until the apocalypse of the future, by the image that physical existence should have been transparent and clear, like a crystal. According to Rudolf Steiner, the Cain human being—with his power of ego and in harmony with the planetary powers within him as the harmony of his seven members—would have actually formed such a being, a being that would have allowed the spiritual world to become visible through the physical-sensory world.

The Solomonic Temple

Throughout the Middle Ages people sought to reconstruct the Solomonic Temple—by constructing cathedrals. Just as with descriptions of the Queen of Sheba, the Old Testament description of the Temple of Solomon is not very exciting, especially when we consider what mighty temple buildings there already were in that time, in Egypt for instance. Some historians say the Temple of Solomon was nothing more than a shed—a kind of a longish building, the Holy of Holies closed off in the back, two pillars in front. It would have been impossible for it to have held all the world's secrets—of course this is not so! The Temple of Solomon was never made physically visible. It existed in etheric form. It was Hiram's great art to create the merely physical temple in such a way that it formed the entrance to the actual supersensible temple. But what did this supersensible temple contain?

Let us also look at another structure—Noah's Ark. In wonderful images, legends tell us about the Great Flood, about how Noah built the ark, and how everything was brought aboard. It was an image of how mankind and nature proceed out of the Atlantean catastrophe into the post-Atlantean time. The ark was built by Noah, the greatest of the initiates, so that the bodily structure of our present age emerged through the ark's forms. All of us—no matter if we are tall or short—carry in ourselves the proportions of Noah's Ark. In Atlantis, the physical body was still capable of a certain plasticity and was comprised in a completely different way. There were many Noah's Arks then, models of form that moulded the physical body so that the upright human being, the human being we are today, emerged at the end of the Atlantean epoch.

The Temple of Solomon is what prepares the physical body for the next great epoch, the sixth epoch. For this reason it works continuously into the future, and Rudolf Steiner says about the construction of the first Goetheanum, 'We want to achieve exactly what the Temple of Solomon intended to create—the proportions for the future of mankind.'[27]

The Great Mother

From this, we are also able to understand how the Temple Legend ends. It ends by pointing to Hiram's experiences as his corpse falls away and his being rises up. As Rudolf Steiner describes it, the Temple Legend tells us that when the Master 'experiences himself as born anew in the cosmos, the first thing he senses is the being of the Great Mother, the Earth Mother . . .'[28]

This is a theme that has remained a mystery in the work of Rudolf Steiner. It arises once in the first Mystery Drama, when Capesius says, '. . . we ourselves lack the means to question the Great Mother this way.'[29] There are a few places where the Great Mother is fleetingly mentioned; but within the anthroposophical view, she remains otherwise hidden. Actually, Rudolf Steiner says that after death every human being experiences the Great Mother, the Earth Mother, but we cannot do so as consciously as Hiram. It is clear from this experience of the Great Mother that the human being is experiencing earlier stages of the earth's development during which he was more dependent upon and inwardly more connected with the earth. He experiences Old Moon, Old Sun with the seven planets, Old Saturn with the twelve images of the zodiac. He experiences the historical development of the physical body, because it began on Old Saturn. Then the etheric body comes along on Old Sun, and the astral body on Old Moon. The physical body as we know it today first emerged as the great Earth Mother, Eve, as the Adam-Eve human being which was at the same time an earth that had expelled from itself the kingdoms of nature. We expelled the animal kingdom and the plant kingdom from ourselves. In *Occult Science* it says that 'even the mineral kingdom . . . was created through its expulsion from the development of humanity'.[30]

Hiram perceives how the human form can elevate itself as a result of first expelling from itself the animal, plant and mineral kingdoms. In what follows, we will continue to examine the individuality of Hiram up to the present, and we will see how the great Mystery secrets of the physical body and the human ego circle around him. We will also see how the great powers of evil—like those of the sun-demon—battle against this Mystery of the physical body and the ego. In 1998 a great Sorat impulse culminated for the third time.

Lecture 2

The Mystery of Golgotha and the Founding of the School of Athens

Manfred Schmidt-Brabant

When we speak of the turning-points in the more recent history of the Mysteries, we must of course note that they are all related to the one great turning-point in the history of humanity and the earth, the Mystery of Golgotha. The Mystery of Golgotha was not just a turning-point in time in the whole of evolution; indeed, the sense and purpose of all of Earth evolution—from Old Saturn to the future condition of the planet as Vulcan—come to expression in it as well.

As an imagination, the secret of the Grail comes particularly close to the Mystery of Golgotha. It is precisely this Grail secret that reveals how the whole point of evolution is to make it possible for the chalice of true human existence, the individual human ego, to take the Christ-being into its own being as its higher nature. All of evolution should lead to the human being uniting with his true, divine Ego so that divine existence and human existence become one as a result of evolution.

The entire development from Old Saturn up to the central event of Earth serves as the preparation for this Mystery; all of evolution into the future, up through the Vulcan period, serves to carry out this Mystery, to make it real. Rudolf Steiner once said in connection with the three temptations Christ experiences just after the baptism in the Jordan that Christ—and all of mankind with Him—has to grapple with Ahriman until the Vulcan period. Thus the hierarchies serve this Mystery throughout the whole of evolution. But there are spiritual beings—beings from completely different universes—who want to destroy the purpose of this evolution, who fight against it. We also refer to this as the beast from the depths of cosmic space; this beast is alien, fundamentally alien, to everything that humanity and the gods seek to achieve together.

We now approach an understanding of this Mystery, essentially through a secret of esoteric Christianity. This is not sufficiently well known. Rudolf Steiner formulates it in the following way: 'The one true name of Christ is I AM. Anyone who does not know, who does not grasp this and who calls Him something else, understands absolutely nothing about Him. I AM is His only name.'[1] When, on Sinai, Moses heard resound from Jehovah, 'Ejeh Asher Ejeh,' 'I am the I AM,'[2] Jehovah was reflecting the Christ-being to Moses in the same way that the moon reflects the light of the sun to us. *Christ* is the translation of the word Messiah, and Messiah means *the anointed one.* It is proper that we speak of Christ in the world, but whenever we want to immerse ourselves in the depths of Christian esotericism, we must be conscious of the fact that His name is 'I AM'.

Lucifer as a Teacher of Wisdom

We have already touched upon the cosmic secret that beings remain behind as sacrifices in order to make higher development possible—in fact, in order to prepare the whole of evolution up to the Mystery of Golgotha. Lucifer's role as the great teacher of wisdom in all the Old Mysteries plays a part in this preparation. The wisdom of Lucifer illuminated all earthly Mysteries, as we can see in an image that has come down to us out of the past of the Mysteries.

Lucifer is always the fullness of the luciferic world, a multitude of luciferic beings. Rudolf Steiner once said that it goes against the grain to speak of Lucifer because, in reality, we should speak in the plural of 'the Lucifers'. The collective divinity, Lucifer, who is the brother of Christ, is made of a multitude of beings. In this fullness there are the lowest, most abominable luciferic beings, beings that are demonic; and there are great, infinitely lofty beings of wisdom. A circle of beings that cannot be considered evil makes up a portion of these powerful luciferic beings of wisdom; even today we refer to them with the old designation 'the circle of the twelve Bodhisattvas'. They are superhuman beings and, personified in them, the entire all-encompassing wisdom of our world shines. In the midst of the twelve is a thirteenth member, and that is the Christ. He is neither the teacher of wisdom nor the carrier of wisdom; He is life itself. Life—the life of the world—radiates from Him. And the great Mystery teachers of the past come from this circle of twelve Bodhisattvas.

We look at this image in which a twelvefold chalice, a chalice of wisdom, is modelled in the cosmos, and see that in the middle of this chalice lives the Sun Mystery of the Christ. The image of the Grail will appear to us in many forms. It is also a cosmic, primal image—the chalice of the twelve, and the thirteenth filling the chalice with life.

Manu and Zarathustra

Now let us look at the Sun Mysteries in Atlantis. During the old Atlantean period the Mysteries were arranged according to the planets. There were Venus, Mercury and Moon Mysteries; there were Mars, Jupiter and Saturn Mysteries. At the centre, however, the Sun Mysteries were at work. They were led by Manu, a superhuman being, one of the great Mystery leaders of this pre-Christian era. Manu administered not only the Sun Mysteries, but he also directed something like a preview of the Mystery of Golgotha. Manu had a favourite pupil and he initiated this pupil into the Sun Mysteries. This pupil bore the name Zarathustra in later incarnations. Zarathustra became the greatest pre-Christian herald of the Sun Word and the Sun Logos. The post-Atlantean epoch began with the Indian culture, which was a purely spiritual culture. The leaders of this culture were the seven Holy Rishis, seven great Mystery teachers. Manu himself initiated these leaders. Each Rishi was initiated into one of the planetary Mysteries, and all seven together embodied what can be called the fundamental teaching of our evolution, the teaching about what takes place between Old Saturn and the future and final Earth condition, Vulcan. One could say that what we have today in a book like *Occult Science, An Outline*, written in the dry language of our time—otherwise it could not be expressed—lived as powerful cosmic imaginations in the seven Holy Rishis. Zarathustra was initiated into these secrets of the Rishis; in each of his seven great incarnations he experienced one of the planetary Mysteries.

This great world of imagery prior to the Mystery of Golgotha can be seen in the ceiling murals of the Goetheanum. There are images of Adam and Eve, the seven Holy Rishis, Zarathustra placed opposite the Sun Mystery, the Egyptian Mysteries, the Greek Mysteries. The history of the Mysteries is there to be seen in a mighty cosmic panorama—the development of the physical body during Lemuria, during Atlantis; the secrets of the development of the physical body are even illuminated in the coloured glass windows of the Goetheanum.

In these seven initiation incarnations—from the Sun Mysteries of Atlantis, in the middle of the Atlantean epoch and throughout the entire post-Atlantean epoch—Zarathustra prepares himself for his great mission. In one of his last incarnations, he becomes the teacher of Pythagoras (580–500 BC), the founder of the Pythagorean School. By and large, we only know about the Pythagorean Theorem, a significant step in mathematics and geometry. But it could be said that this theorem was only a by-product of the Pythagorean School, a powerful theosophic-esoteric school in which not only mathematics, music and astronomy were taught, but reincarnation as well. Pythagoras had assimilated all the Mystery wisdom of the Egyptians, and now this Mystery wisdom was transformed in him through the influence of Zarathustra so that it became something like a preparation for understanding the Mystery of Golgotha. We find Pythagoras incarnated again as Melchior, one of the Three Wise Kings. Rudolf Steiner says that these wise men actually existed. Led by karma, these last true representatives of the old star wisdom, these three kings from Sheba, came to Bethlehem to adore the Child.[3]

Plato and Aristotle

In preparation for the Mystery of Golgotha, there are also Mysteries at work in another place. In Greece, there are the Mysteries we refer to as the Apollonian and Dionysian Mysteries. In the Apollonian Mysteries, the veneration of Apollo is like an allusion to the Sun Mystery of the Christ. Through music, Apollo, the great teacher of the arts, paves the way for logical thinking in human beings. In this Mystery period, human beings still live in a world of imagery; but through music, through what he conveys from the cosmos, Apollo lays the groundwork for logical thinking. Everything Lucifer brings to the strengthening of the ego—or more specifically to the soul forces in the ego—lives in the Dionysian Mysteries dedicated to Dionysus the Elder and the Younger. Thus, in the Greek Mysteries the objective sun-quality of thinking and of logic is prepared, as well as the power of the ego to make use of this thinking.

Then comes that point in time that arouses so much interest in humanity—the Mysteries dim, cease, and pass over into the free, independent thinking of the human being. Two names stand at this threshold, Plato (427–347 BC) and Aristotle (384–323 BC). Each was an initiate in his own way, both still knew about the Mysteries; but their innovation was to lead the old Mystery wisdom, the old Mystery perception, over into knowledge through thinking. The School of Athens, the first philosophical School of Athens, comes about through their efforts around 425 BC. This School of Athens lasted 900 years. It creates around the Mystery of Golgotha that point of convergence that leads out of Mystery wisdom into free knowledge through thinking, and that leads upwards again from thinking to the Christian Mystery. The Platonic tended increasingly towards the Apollonian, the Aristotelian towards the Dionysian.

Millennia will pass before all the secrets of what circles around the Mystery of Golgotha are revealed. There will come a time when music will be the means through which the true Christ Mysteries can be experienced.

The Two Jesus Children

We are confronted with a wondrous puzzle in the fact that two Jesus children were born, and that the family tree of one of them leads back to the priest Nathan. We call that child the Nathan-Jesus child. Spiritual research shows us that the part of Adam which came from Lemuria appears for the first time on earth in this Nathan-Jesus child; it is the part of Adam that never went through the incarnation of the ego, nor through incarnations or the Fall of Man, but was instead held back in the spiritual world. We refer to it as the innocent part of the Adam soul. This heavenly being, which completely lacked the quality of an ego because it had never incarnated, entered into a physical body. Everything we experience of this Nathan-Jesus child reflects that infinite innocence, the loving harmony that can only be radiated by a being who was never subjected to the temptations of earthly incarnation. The one Jesus child grows up in this way.

A second Jesus child is born. The Zarathustra individuality is incarnated in this Jesus child whose family tree leads back to Solomon; we refer to this child as the Solomon-Jesus child. That powerful individuality referred to earlier had been initiated by Manu and was connected to the Sun Mysteries since the middle of Atlantis; it enters into a physical body.

Both children grow up; then that cosmic moment occurs that is among the many secrets of the life of Christ-Jesus. In the twelfth year a kind of unification of the two Jesus children occurs. The Solomon-Jesus child, the carrier of the Solomon ego—Zarathustra—leaves his Jesus body and enters into the Nathan-Jesus. The physical body of this Solomon-Jesus child dies soon afterwards. Imaginative reports in the Gospels point to this Jesus child who, suddenly filled with wisdom, teaches the priests in the temple. His parents, who have been looking for him full of despair, find the twelve-year-old teaching wisdom in the temple.

It is one of the peculiarities of our very satanic age that books appearing today heap scorn on this event, saying, 'What was this kid doing in the temple? The priests and Talmudic scholars were there debating the most difficult legal and religious questions, and a twelve-year-old from the provinces comes and suddenly teaches them all?'[4]—this is how materialistic understanding judges things today. There is a well-known writer, Salcia Landmann, who writes this way in her book, a book full of derision about the whole life of Christ. We have to examine such phenomena in order to grasp that people who think this way will never arrive at the Mysteries! Why should a being like Zarathustra, who was prepared throughout lifetimes, not suddenly manifest all of its wisdom through the body of a twelve-year-old?

The Three Wise Kings from Sheba knew who was incarnated there—they were wise and they were initiates. They approached the Solomon-Jesus child, and it was Melchior who immediately felt a close connection to the secret that flows from Sheba over into the Mystery of Golgotha. Hieronymus Bosch, who portrayed quite a number of secrets, painted an *Adoration of the Magi* as they kneel before Mary and the Jesus child. In the front is Balthazar, the old king; behind him is Caspar, the black king. In the middle stands Melchior, wearing a wonderful large helmet. On this helmet is depicted the scene of the Queen of Sheba bringing the Grail chalice to Solomon. The whole picture is painted so that even in the way Mary sits there holding the Jesus child one senses Grail secrets.

Then comes the moment of the baptism in the Jordan. The ego of Zarathustra leaves the body in which the innocent being of the Nathan-Jesus still lives. The Nathan-Jesus was not an ego being, but rather a being that received its ego through Zarathustra. The Christ-being then enters. And who is making all this happen? The first Adam, who appears again after many incarnations as John the Baptist. It was this ego-Adam from the Lemurian epoch who had first received an ego from the elohim, from the exusiai, and who now lived in John the Baptist. We might say that, through this baptism, John guides the Christ-being into his sister soul. What Zarathustra did during his incarnations was to prepare himself to penetrate down into the bodily nature—even into the breath, into the circulation of the blood, into the metabolism—so that a being like the Christ could draw into such a body. Zarathustra prepared the vessel, the Grail, into which the Christ-being could enter at the baptism in the Jordan.

The Black Magic Mars Mysteries

Because we cannot speak of the Mysteries without looking at what stands in opposition to them, we must now turn our attention to two great crushing events that play a role in this time period. This is one of the first times the counter-Mysteries of the Antichrist become visible. A powerful betrayal of the Mysteries had taken place in Atlantis, the first great betrayal of the Mysteries during the entire course of history; as a result, various Mysteries (but not the Sun Mysteries) had fallen into decadence. It says in *Occult Science, An Outline* that even as Atlantis was coming to an end there were Mysteries of varying degrees of depravity which afterwards became ever more decadent and depraved.[5] The royal dynasty of Herod was connected to such decadent, depraved Mysteries. Its members were not Jews, but Arabs from Petra, the capital city of the Nabateans. The grandfather of Herod the Great had come from Petra. Petra stood at a junction of many caravan routes, so it was also a gathering place for all sorts of Mysteries brought along with the caravans, as well as for the people who settled there. It was a gathering place for great and meaningful—but also quite evil and decadent—Mysteries. When the Herodians ascended the royal throne in Jerusalem, they brought with them these decadent Mysteries.

There are two elements in particular that emerge. First, there is everything connected to Herod the Great who lived at the time of the birth of the Solomon-Jesus child. He was a powerful personality; but according to Emil Bock's description, he was also a half-crazed practitioner of black magic. With his assistants, he perpetrates infanticide. The surrendering of one's own life has been a good and true part of the Mars Mysteries from their very beginning—and remains so. An individual sacrifices himself or, in times past, a human being, a child, would be sacrificed for the deity in the most reverent mood. A portion of this Mars Mystery fell into decay, and black magic, ritual infanticide arose. People murdered and tortured children in order to gain magical powers for themselves through this torture. Herod perpetrated this in dark caves in Bethlehem. Bock describes this in his book *The Childhood and Youth of Jesus*.[6] Herod carried out such murders of children in order to possess the magic power to hold on to his kingdom.

This evil principle appears throughout history; we find it again in Gilles de Rais, the brother-in-arms of the Maid of Orleans, Joan of Arc. He was the Marshal of France, the Bluebeard of legend, who murdered and tortured more than eight hundred children in order to gain magical powers. With these magical powers he tried to obtain gold from the devil, because producing Christmas plays had ruined him financially. As the Marshal of France, he had organized these plays in grandiose fashion; when the Three Kings arrived, they came with a hundred camels. He sponsored these plays until he was bankrupt, and then he tried to raise more money by means of black magic. He went down in history because he sought to obtain magical powers from the devil by means of infanticide.

The black magic Mysteries of Mars appear at the beginning of the life of Christ; they will reappear again with Philip the Fair when he martyrs the Templars.

The Black Magic Venus Mysteries

Herod Antipas, the husband of Herodias, rules more towards the end of the life of Christ. Because Herodias was the niece of Herod Antipas, their marriage was invalid. According to Jewish marriage laws, this marriage was absolutely forbidden and was considered sinful; therefore John the Baptist rebuked it and preached openly against their misalliance. Herod Antipas had him confined in a fortress. But he valued John the Baptist, and it pained him that John spoke openly about this matter. Thus he imprisoned him but continued to converse with him. Herodias had a mortal hatred of John; she wanted to see him dead. Then there comes the moment when Herod Antipas' birthday celebration takes place in the same fortress where John was being held under house arrest. During this birthday celebration, Salome, a daughter of Herodias from an earlier marriage, performs the famous Dance of the Seven Veils. This Dance of the Seven Veils sets the court and Herod Antipas into such a frenzy that he says: 'Ask of me what you will, even half my kingdom.' Salome asks her mother: 'What shall I ask?' She answers: 'Demand the head of John the Baptist!'[7] So Salome makes this request of the king. Since he had given his word before the entire court, he cannot now go back on it. He gives the order to behead John, and the bleeding head of John the Baptist is brought in on a silver salver.

This story belongs here because of Rudolf Steiner's statement that this bloody head on the silver tray is the symbol of the counter-Grail.[8] What had happened? Not only had Salome danced naked; something else entirely had taken place. The decadent Venus Mysteries had been brought to bear here. Something existed in the good Venus Mysteries which is no longer understood today—cultic temple prostitution existed. The priestesses were available to anyone who wanted to unite themselves with the goddess. We refer to this here as prostitution, although the phrase 'temple prostitution' is completely wrong. A portion of these

Venus Mysteries became decadent, and the black magic sexual ritual was what ensued. Salome's dance was nothing other than a black magic ritual dance in which 'the seven indecencies of women' were presented in a way that threw the entire court into a frenzy. We will find these 'seven indecencies' once again in the whore Babylon when we turn our attention to the end of Earth evolution. Thus something emerges at the beginning and at the end of the life of Christ that will create the substance for the appearance of the Antichrist.

The Phantom

Paul speaks of the death and resurrection of Christ. He says with justification that if Christ had not risen from the dead, our entire faith would have no meaning.[9] What took place then was the real meaning and purpose of the entire Mystery of Golgotha. We bear our physical body with us; it has been prepared from the time of the Saturn period, and is at the highest evolutionary level of all of our members. It is more highly developed than the ether body, astral body or even the very young ego that we first received on the earth. As a result of its advanced development it offers the ego the possibility of developing itself. What we see is actually not the physical body; an invisible form made of energy—called the *phantom* in occultism—forms the foundation of the physical body. For instance, people who have lost a limb in war speak of phantom pains. They say: 'I can move my toes. I can feel them. But my leg is no longer there.'

This invisible shape is filled out by matter. This is the result of the Fall of Man. Our physical body ought to be crystal clear; its substance should not have been denser than the scent of a rose. But as a result of the Fall of Man, matter intruded more and more into this energy form. In occultism, one says that it was filled more and more with ash—that this form began to turn to ash. What we actually see are the ash deposits that resulted from the Fall of Man. These deposits led to a growing weakness in the inner plasticity of the invisible energy body, so that the phantom was damaged and its condition grew worse and worse. Mankind was in danger of no longer being able to develop its ego nature within the physical body because it might become unsuited to that purpose. What came to pass as a result of the death and resurrection and the entire life of Christ was the restoration of the original phantom. The Mystery of Golgotha made it possible for mankind to continue developing its ego nature within the physical body.

When the Christ-being united itself on Old Sun with the Cosmic Word, the Logos, He simultaneously took up into Himself the whole process by which Saturn, sun, moon and even earth move. This process was in Him; He Himself was the Cosmic Word, the Logos. The Christ carries the fundamental cosmic gesture of the creation of the physical body into the present. One could say that He renews the energy form of the physical body as an archetype based on the fundamental principles of all of evolution. Rudolf Steiner notes that the alchemists always said the human body is made out of the same substance as the transparent, crystal-clear Philosopher's Stone.

The Roman Empire at the Turning-point in Time

Let us look briefly at the conditions during the Roman Empire. The Roman Empire was not only a multicultural society, but also a multi-Mystery society. Innumerable Mysteries were present in this Roman Empire—African Mysteries, Middle Eastern Mysteries, Asian and Northern European Mysteries. All religions and Mystery paths were permitted, assuming Caesar was honoured as a divinity, too. There were good Mysteries and evil Mysteries among them. In order not to forget any of the gods, an altar was even erected to the unknown god—to prevent him from being offended should there be no Mystery cult for him. People lived in a unique agnostic pluralism. And into this world enters Caesar Augustus.

Caesar Augustus was the first to use his imperial position, his role as caesar, to force an initiation; he gave the order that he should be initiated. Later this occurred more frequently, with frightful consequences. But with Caesar Augustus the results were still for the good. He did not misuse the outcome of his forced initiation. This forced initiation led him to a certain level of perception. He saw how humanity was decaying and he wanted to reverse this. Augustus' great plan was to deal with all of civilization as it had been dealt with at the time of the Egyptian Mysteries—that is to say, to allow everything in the social and human realms to be determined by the cosmos, to be based on the forces of the stars and wisdom.

A second significant phenomenon is found in Apollonius of Tyana. According to Rudolf Steiner, he was a great initiate, the last of the great initiates.[10] Miracles were attributed to him; he engaged in politics and influenced the course of the Roman Empire. He still represented all the teachings of the Pythagorean School, one of which concerns us particularly. He said that a person can only enter into a relationship with the highest God 'by way of the better Logos'. By 'the better Logos' he meant the Logos in us that 'does not go through the mouth', that cannot be expressed in words.[11] It is as though he alludes here to an early form of pure thinking! We recall the words from *The Philosophy of Freedom*: 'What a concept is can never be expressed in words.'[12] Only words can make human beings aware they have concepts. The whole of powerful initiate knowledge still lives in Apollonius. Both Bock and Rudolf Steiner describe this beautifully and in detail. The following thought rests like a seed within this powerful initiate knowledge: The most important thing in us is the highest Logos, which stands above language. After the Christmas Foundation Meeting, Rudolf Steiner said: 'Thinking in words is never a path to Michael; in order to come to Michael, we must reach that place where things can no longer be expressed in words.'[13]

Paul

Now let us turn our attention to Paul. He was born in Tarsus in 10 AD; from childhood he was called Paul, which was his official Roman name. His parents were Roman citizens. He was named Saul because his parents were Jewish. He was not re-christened later, nor was his name changed from Saul to Paul; he was called Paul from the outset. He completed a study of the Torah with Gamaliel in Jerusalem, which is important because Gamaliel was one of the most significant initiates in the Hebrew Mysteries. Paul himself is initiated into the Hebrew and the Greek Mysteries; he is an initiate in both the Greek and Hebrew cultures. He was initiated into the Mystery tradition which taught how to read the Old Testament truly—which is to say, imaginatively. Rudolf Steiner says this was '. . . a tradition which persisted into the last century with individual rabbis'.[14] This was not the Cabbala; it was the way the Mysteries approached the Old Testament.

Through his initiation into the Hebraic Mysteries, Paul knew about the great anticipation of the Messiah. The expression 'the Anointed One, the Messiah', was originally used only for Jehovah. No one but Jehovah could be called Messiah, the Anointed One. Only later would kings also be called Messiah, the Anointed One. The first king to bear this title was Solomon, a title that until then was granted only to Jehovah. The Jewish population waited for this Messiah, particularly during the oppression and occupation by Rome, and the initiates knew what the Messiah would do. Therefore, Paul was sent to Damascus by order of the highest religious council, the Sanhedrin, in order to hold a disputation there with a sect that called themselves Christians, and to ban them if possible.

Now it happens that Paul, while filled with holy zeal to eradicate these heretics, experiences the Christ on the road to Damascus. In that moment he knows the Messiah has appeared! He, for Whom we have waited so long, is here. Paul sees the restored phantom. He knew that the phantom was ruined; he knew that initiation no longer reached down into the physical body in any way. Now he sees the phantom in its temporal form; he looks through this phantom and sees, as it were, its development over time. Today, when a good anthropologist or a good physician observes the physical human being, he can say: Those are old organs, the pineal gland for example, and these are younger organs. At least intellectually, they can see in the physical body that it has developed over a period of time. The initiate sees time. Paul sees, as it were, how the past seems to be renewed in the restored phantom, and he knows the Messiah has come. He is so shaken by the whole experience that he is blinded for a time; later his vision is restored. Naturally this is all meant spiritually; it should never be imagined that he was physically blinded by some kind of light. Instead, we should understand that his spiritual ability to see was extinguished by this powerful impression.

The School of Athens

Paul now becomes the founder of the other School of Athens, the Christian-esoteric School of Athens, with Dionysius the Areopagite as its leader. The Areopagus was a hill in Athens, and the word itself means the mountain of Mars. There was a kind of ultimate authority at the Areopagus for all religious and cultural questions. The most worthy men of Athens—we could also say those who were still initiates—were called to it. The Areopagus originates in the far distant mythological past. Those who were called to the Areopagus took up a lifelong task, making decisions about the practice of the cultus, of religion, of education, and so forth. And one of the most worthy of these men—Bock[15] indicates it was the one who was the most initiated—was Dionysius the Areopagite. He now becomes the actual leader of this Christian-esoteric school. Rudolf Steiner's words guide us even further into the future: '... the path given by the founder of the Rosicrucian esoteric movement, known to the outer world as Christian Rosenkreutz, had already been prepared in part long before Christianity. It assumed a particular form as a result of that great initiate who appeared as Dionysius the Areopagite in Paul's esoteric school at Athens. Dionysius the Areopagite founded the schooling there that led to all later esoteric wisdom and schooling.'[16] In another place it is said that 'in this ... school ... the purest spiritual science was taught'.[17]

Let us look at this School of Athens which endured for nine hundred years. On the one hand, the secrets of the Mysteries stream into it and transform themselves into knowledge through thinking. And on the other hand, based on this knowledge through thinking, an ascent to the secrets of the Christian Mysteries begins. There stands Paul—with him his friend and companion, Dionysius—founding the knowledge of the Christ. Therefore, Heten Wilkins, in his fine book on Paul, calls Paul 'the patron saint of thinking'.[18] We can ask how the two schools stood in relation to one another. I think this Christian-esoteric school was something like a secret subgroup within the great school of philosophy; this will become clear in what we will discuss later. Perhaps those who were awake in this school of philosophy founded the very small circle that began to develop the Christian Mysteries based on knowledge through thinking.

Above all, two elements lived in this school that should touch us at the deepest level. Today we are so abstract; we say that the Christ united with Jesus at the baptism in the Jordan. Human beings at that time were in their own way much more discriminating and exact. For them, the questions arose: How is a cosmos created out of which a god can descend into a human body? And how then must the human being be created so that it can take a god into itself?

Two answers from the Mysteries were cultivated in this esoteric School of Athens. There was a spiritual cosmology and a spiritual anthropology. Rudolf Steiner is more precise and therefore more informative when he says an 'etheric astronomy'[19] was cultivated. People looked out at the planets, at the fixed stars, but what is fixed was not what was important to them, rather what lived etherically, as process. The questions were: What is the Mercury process in the cosmos? What is the Jupiter process in the cosmos? What is the Lion process or the Bull process? People observed etheric activity and found in it the higher beings up to the Godhead. Then they looked at the human being. And here Rudolf Steiner offers an amazingly illuminating thought when he says 'an ancient doctrine of humours' was cultivated there; the processes—like the movement of the white gall and the black gall, the blood and the lymph—were considered, rather than the contours of the organs. The process within the human being was observed.[20] And now people began to understand that a lung process is closely related to a Mercury process, to a quicksilver process. A liver process is exactly like the Jupiter process, the tin process. Today, this is still described in the same way; in every occult bookstore, works are sold that talk about lungs and Mercury and quicksilver, about gold and sun and the heart. At that time, this was living perception! People understood how a god can descend from the world of the planets and the processes of the zodiac into the processes of the physical body. This continued for a long time, up to the Middle Ages—to Paracelsus and Basilius Valentinus. Today all of this should be resurrected—and it is!

The History of the Mysteries as Our Own Existence

The history of the Mysteries is not what is written; we ourselves are the history of the Mysteries! It is at work in us and with us! We have friends among us who work with the interconnectedness of matter, and with what is cosmic in the field of medicine. We have friends among us who work in curative eurythmy, in which an attempt is made to rediscover this harmonizing in the gesture of eurythmy, this healing between our organs and the cosmos. We have among us friends from curative education. They ask: How do I help the handicapped human being, the handicapped child? I can do this in so far as I am able to see how etheric astronomy and the doctrine of humours work together, and to the extent I can bring them into harmony.

We do not look back to what has been written; we look instead to our own existence. There may be some among us who helped build Solomon's Temple, some who were masters with Hiram, some who were magi accompanying the Queen of Sheba; others may have heard Plato and Aristotle or, later, Dionysius the Areopagite in the School of Athens. Others may have travelled the Camino, obtained the secrets of the Grail, fought as Templars, heard Bernard of Clairvaux or Thomas Aquinas, experienced Christianity as a Mystery in connection with Gnosticism, or, as Cathars, endured the difficult fate of heretics at that time. Although each of us has a different experience, this is nevertheless our shared past!

What we actually see in Compostela is Roman Catholicism; but what is hidden behind the walls is still Christianity as a Mystery.

We begin in all humility—in Rudolf Steiner's words—as forerunners of the forerunners. Just as even the greatest genius begins with the ABCs, we stand before the ABCs of the new Mysteries.

Constantine—Julian the Apostate—Justinian

This School of Athens suffers a peculiar fate. Constantine—a great, significant personality—founds Constantinople. Under his rule, Christianity becomes the state religion in 313. He knows that the Mysteries exist. It no longer happens that he is initiated simply because he is emperor. On the contrary, he sets out to destroy, root and branch, everything that still exists from the old Mysteries. The religions of antiquity are forbidden; the penalties are barbaric. Children who happen upon the head from a broken statue of Zeus and play with it are immediately put to death. This rabid policy is ostensibly for the benefit of Christianity. But Rudolf Steiner says that under Constantine a second crucifixion of Christ takes place.[21] Another emperor, Julian the Apostate, rebels against this. He is emperor for only a short time. From the beginning, even as a child, he revered Helios, the sun. He is initiated into the Eleusinian Mysteries. He sees how Christianity has been rigidified under Constantine, how Roman law moulds the life of Christianity, how faith is forced into dogmas. He wants to return to the Christianity of the Mysteries, and he is murdered for it. We will find him again at the time of the Grail. Rudolf Steiner says, 'Had the times been favourable, had the right conditions existed, he could have created out of the old Mysteries a direct connection from the pre-Christian Christ—from the genuine macrocosmic Logos—to the Christ who was to work on in humanity after the Mystery of Golgotha.'[22]

And then comes the malefactor Justinian. He is filled with hatred for everything that remains from the old spirituality, including Greek culture and philosophy. He causes the School of Athens to be closed in the year 529. With that, the almost nine-hundred-year history of the School of Athens comes to an end.

Gondishapur

Those philosophers of the School of Athens who could not connect themselves to Christianity go to the academy of Gondishapur in Persia. There they place all their knowledge, their lofty spirituality, into the service of the greatest adversary of Christ, Sorat, who in 666 reaches his first great culmination in human history. A very fine scholarship, but one that gave no consideration to the Mystery of Golgotha, connects itself with the sun-demon Sorat, the greatest adversarial impulse to the Christ. Taking on bodily forms as a teacher in Gondishapur, Sorat becomes the counter-teacher to the Christ. Gondishapur strove for a pure culture of reason on earth. Human beings were to become clever; in all respects they were to become clever about earthly things. Around 666, or by the year 1000 at the latest, human beings were to have become what they will in fact become only around 2493. This has been investigated and it was found that mankind in the year 1000 could have developed to the level we are now in the beginning of the twenty-first century; all the technical conditions were there. Just think of how we have developed the phenomenal technology of today in such a short period of time! When the first flight to the moon took place, an elderly lady came to me in Berlin and said, 'You know, as a schoolgirl I always helped Lilienthal pull his glider up the mountain so that he could sail down again.' In the course of one lifetime, the development took place from that clumsy gliding—he broke his neck in the process—to space flight! Therefore we can imagine that if Gondishapur had become a reality, a technically civilized world without a heart would have arisen. The entire inward character of the Middle Ages would have been lost. It was intended that these people who became so clever in earthly things would no longer return to the spiritual world, but would instead preserve themselves within the earth.

Now a peculiar thing took place. This powerful impulse coming from Gondishapur was thwarted by the fact that Mohammed appeared, bringing Islam with him. In reality, the mood of Gondishapur was totally atheistic. Now a strict fundamentalist religion appeared and, so to speak, took away Gondishapur's main thrust. Nevertheless, much of it remains. Rudolf Steiner once said that as a result of Gondishapur the whole of humanity had 'received a blow right down into its bodily nature'.[23] Gondishapur was still hidden away in the skull of even the lowliest peasant. As a result, the impulse of Gondishapur continued to work into the West, even though its evil power had been thwarted. It sent its influence towards southern Europe, Africa, powerfully towards Spain, towards France, England, and into the Continent.

Dionysius the Areopagite

The writings of Dionysius the Areopagite suddenly appear at this time, as the School of Athens is being closed. These writings were presented as though the Areopagite, the friend and student of Paul, had written all of them. It was later determined that these writings were composed in the sixth century! Rudolf Steiner says that the most important information was passed on by word of mouth in all the esoteric schools at that time. It was also done this way in Paul's school. Pupils were prepared at the most intimate level before they were permitted to receive the loftiest truths, and this preparation, as well as their subsequent schooling, took place exclusively by word of mouth. The living spirit passed from teacher to student over long periods of time.[24]

I have the sense that the teachings were not written down until the sixth century because the closing of the School was foreseen; indeed, Justinian had signalled that the school would be closed. There is a famous painting by Raphael called *The School of Athens*. Rudolf Steiner referred to it once, saying: 'There is a longstanding dispute about who is actually portrayed there.'[25] The dispute continues today, even within the Anthroposophical Society. Are they Plato and Aristotle, or are they Paul and Peter? Arguments can be made for both. The older man points upward. It is Plato: You must hold to the world of ideas! The other, Aristotle, points downward: You must find the spirit in earthly work! It is an age-old contradiction. Hiram and Solomon—or Peter: We must have faith! Paul: No! We must know! Rudolf Steiner says that Raphael actually wanted to portray something else entirely. In these groups, around both focal points, he wanted to portray the nature of human knowledge. So if I think in a Christian or pre-Christian way, that is a gesture that directs me upwards. And then if I think in an Aristotelian or Pauline way, turning to the earth through knowledge, that is the other (downward) gesture. And everything else is transitional forms and distinctions. Here 'lives the contrast between what perceives and what speaks'.[26]

I am of the opinion for a number of reasons that this Christian-esoteric school was part of the great school of philosophers. They foresaw the closing of the school and now wrote down what had been taught orally for so many centuries. This is what we have in the work of Dionysius the Areopagite. Spiritual history says without hesitation, 'He is the founder of the whole of Western mysticism.'[27] Two of his four works stand out above the rest. The first is *The Heavenly Hierarchy*.[28] He was the first to describe the hierarchy of heaven—angel, archangel, archai, exusiai, dynamis, kyriotetes, thrones, cherubim, seraphim. When we read about this today, let us say in the context of the School for Spiritual Science, we should remember that it was Dionysius the Areopagite who created it. Human beings knew the hierarchies, but everything was mixed up and haphazard. As the second great thinker after Paul, Dionysius creates order and harmony in the realm of the hierarchies. And along with this, he lays the foundation for true insight into the being of the Trinity: first, second, third hierarchy; Father-forces, Son-forces, Spirit-forces. The second book is *Mystical Theology*; we would refer to this as the path of schooling. In both books, the vestiges of etheric astronomy are hidden, somewhat concentrated in the teachings about the hierarchies. The doctrine of humours is hidden in the path of schooling that views the human being as a moving, etheric being who must develop its spiritual schooling out of this etheric being. Above all, Dionysus creates something that should be counted among the great images we have of the turning-points. He is the one who establishes that the human being should, as Rudolf Steiner says, no longer be led by an outer guru, but rather by the Christ Who is experienced inwardly.

These writings are translated into Latin relatively late, by Duns Scotus Erigena in the ninth century, and they immediately begin a triumphal march through the entire Christian West; they become the most frequently read books after the Bible. All the great personalities referred to them—to the hierarchies, to the Trinity, to the path of schooling experienced in mysticism. There are also manuscripts decorated with wonderful images that deeply moved humanity at that time! We see a ladder. The ladder leads from earth up into heaven. We see how some people are climbing the ladder with difficulty, while others are falling off the ladder. One person has made it almost to the top of the ladder—and falls again! This moved people deeply. An infinite humility, the likes of which we can hardly imagine, permeated their inner life: 'Look! No matter how high we climb, in the end we will fall again.' In this way, deep inner experiences were at work at the time of the birth of the Western path of schooling, beginning with the mysticism of the Middle Ages.

The Risen One

Meanwhile, the good Mysteries of old continued; they had their straggling followers, and they had their effects up to the time of Compostela. We hear how, in the centuries after the Mystery of Golgotha, the Risen Christ Himself moved about in the Mysteries in order to reform them. What has come down to us as the sublime schools of wisdom, what then entered ever more into the thinking element of scholasticism, but also brought in the results of the Mysteries—these were the results of Mysteries that were reformed by the Christ Himself after the Mystery of Golgotha.

Lecture 3

Gnostic Impulses in Early Christian Art

Virginia Sease

We now have before us many powerful images of the development of humanity and the earth. We have reached the point where we see how, after the Mystery of Golgotha and on into our own epoch, people have sought at length to understand this Mystery. In fact, human beings will be able to achieve such an understanding only during the Venus period of development.

Even the Apostles of Christ were not at all able to understand this Mystery, these events immediately following His death. Understanding came later; only gradually did they achieve insight into the facts they experienced personally. In the centuries following the Mystery of Golgotha, the best minds of the time made frequent attempts at understanding this Mystery. Then, strangely, these efforts to gain wisdom with regard to the Christ-Jesus event suddenly broke off. It is spoken of as the breaking off of the Gnosis, of Gnostic wisdom. This breaking off can be a riddle.

The Wisdom of the Gnosis

About fifty years ago, the discovery of Nag Hammadi was unexpectedly given to humanity. This discovery of Nag Hammadi, with its many manuscripts, threw a new light on this whole period. An extensive body of literature about this Gnosis has arisen in the last half century. Many people have occupied themselves with this, and asked: Who were these early Christian Gnostics? Why did they write so much? What lay behind these writings? Wonderful translations of these writings have appeared in many languages. We see that they are not only full of wisdom but, in fact, are also great poetic works of art.

Rudolf Steiner concerned himself with the Gnostics and spoke of them often, in part because he wanted to avoid the possibility that anthroposophy might be understood as a newly invented Gnosis. That was one reason. He also highly valued the Gnostics as a bridge to understanding the Christ Event. Moreover, it was important to him that people encounter these great poetic works of art. He did not have the writings of Nag Hammadi. He had the *Pistis Sophia*; he had both *Books of Jeu*. But he also had something else—access to the Akashic Record. Rudolf Steiner knew that great works had been written; he knew that an abundance of wisdom existed there, and that it had been written down, noted, formed poetically by human beings.

In fact, he pointed to the Gnostics as 'religious and philosophical geniuses'. He did not often describe people as geniuses, but he did here. He said, '. . . in this period of transition, from which we begin our reckoning of time, there lived something like religious-philosophical geniuses. And we will encounter these religious-philosophical geniuses most clearly when we look at what came to expression in the Gnosis.'[1] For many years—even into the last years of his life—he referred again and again to the Gnostics and the Gnosis. In the Letter to the Members of January 1925, he speaks about 'Gnosis and anthroposophy' and stresses that dimensions opened up to the Gnostics as a result of their attempts at knowledge. He said that if people in the Mystery Gnosis did not understand something as a result of their own efforts, the gods helped them. The gods accompanied people who tried to achieve an understanding of the secrets of the Mystery of Golgotha, of the incarnation of Christ in a human body.[2]

But the kind of approach we find with the Gnostics cannot be our approach. We live in the age of the consciousness soul and we must find another way. Rudolf Steiner also pointed the way for those who want to pursue this path. But it is true that we can come closest to the original source for understanding these 'geniuses' of early Christian times if we immerse ourselves in the writings of the Gnostics. They are now available. This is important nowadays when many people have the feeling: History is finished; we only want to look ahead. Certainly that is also justified. But history is not finished. History comes in cycles of time, in rhythms, and if we do not acquire some sense of an understanding of the past, it will be impossible to explain the present or the future.

Lucifer's Incarnation

In order to understand the Gnosis at all, we must reach far back in time, back three thousand years before the Mystery of Golgotha. Lucifer entered into an earthly incarnation three thousand years before the Mystery of Golgotha. This is just as much a riddle for mankind as the riddle of the incarnation of the Christ-being, and just as much a riddle as the one surrounding the incarnation of Ahriman that will occur during the third millennium after the Mystery of Golgotha. Lucifer's incarnation took place in China. Rudolf Steiner describes how a child was born into an environment where rituals were performed, and how this child was brought quite early into connection with the temple. The child was accepted, and the priests felt inspired by his childish presence in a way they had never experienced before. At about the age of forty, this human being in whom Lucifer was incarnated began to understand things with his own intellect, to receive insights previously only possible through revelation. He was the first who could make use of his intellect, but only within the confines of the temple. It was the first time the intellect could be put to use within a human being himself. We might say that he had been able to set the organs of the intellect in motion. It began with a small seed, protected in the closest temple circle; and yet it signalled the moment that initiated humanity's power of judgement through the intellect.[3]

We see how long it was from the year 3000 BC until the beginning of the age of the intellectual soul in 747 BC. During this entire time, humanity continued to live under the old conditions; but intellect and the power of judgement had already appeared on the earth. With this luciferic culture came not only intellect and insight, but also everything experienced as beauty and as philosophy in the Greek culture; all this began to flourish. This extends beyond the time of the Mystery of Golgotha. The Gnosis was thoroughly fructified by this luciferic wisdom. Without luciferic wisdom, the Gnostics would have had no access to an understanding of the Mystery of Golgotha.

In the future, humanity will also have a task that is intimately connected to Lucifer. We have acquired many gifts, and continue to receive many gifts from this being, Lucifer. We have heard how we say for the sake of convenience: 'being of Lucifer'. But this being has many layers, for in the spiritual world there is always being within being. We have acquired much through the luciferic culture, through the being of Lucifer, and we have to make compensation for that. One day, mankind will compensate for this by being in a position to redeem Lucifer himself. This fact is actually related to the Gnosis, and to what has developed from it throughout the centuries; for it concerns the understanding, the knowledge of the Christ Mystery that every human being can and must acquire in the course of time. These steps of knowledge, taken by every individual human being, are steps that will redeem this high spiritual being, Lucifer, in the future.

Sophia and Achamod

The Gnostics developed very complicated, complex systems. They are also not consistent. It is in no way a closed system, yet some things are present throughout. When Rudolf Steiner spoke about these structures in a lecture, he said that this was naturally very complicated, but then so is the human being. We cannot expect world secrets to be simple when the membering of the human being himself would have to be viewed in the context of at least forty-nine relationships.[4] I will thus try to present a very simplified summary of some main elements that are absolutely essential.

The divine primal father, the foundation of the world, the primal spirit—this is the beginning of the whole thing. The divine primal father then unites himself with the silence. Now there are naturally long exegeses on the meaning of the silence. We will take it simply as silence. Cosmic beings arise from this union. These cosmic beings exist in a certain order consisting of thirty levels. The thirty levels are called aeons. On the thirtieth level—the lowest, yet a purely spiritual aeon nonetheless—is the Sophia, wisdom. As a result of her longing to rise again to the primal father and to the silence, this Sophia wisdom causes desire to be separated off from her. This desire is called Achamod.

Then comes a thirty-first aeon: our world. In our world, all creatures are designated as archons, with one exception—the thinking human being. The thinking human being does not belong to this category of archons; he stands slightly higher than the thirty-first level.

Achamod, the desire that was expelled, experiences a longing. He has a faint memory of the time when he was united with the Sophia. He has a longing for the primal condition. The primal father recognizes this and sends Christ and the Holy Spirit down to the earth for this reason. We find Christ and the Holy Spirit between the thirtieth aeon—that is, the level where the Sophia is—and the thirty-first aeon, where the human being is in this world. They radiate down and help everything that is on the thirty-first level.

The Demiurge

Throughout long periods of time, the Hebraic culture proceeded on the assumption that the creation of man occurred through the intervention of

Yahveh; this lived as the Hebraic tradition. This was a problem for the Gnostics because they all lived very strongly in the Greek Mystery tradition as well. As people of the first and second century after Christ, they were very familiar with the Greek system. This meant that they had to bring the Greek system together with the Hebraic, and find their way into the new Christian wisdom. As a result, they seized upon the idea of the Demiurgos, the most exalted being in the Greek tradition about the creator of the world. It was present, without material existence, in spheres of the loftiest spirituality. The worlds, the aeons, emerged from the creative power of the Demiurgos; this is where the systems intersect. And this reaches downwards to include a quite lowly, but still spiritual aeon, Yahveh. Yahveh then unites himself with matter, and from this union came the human being.

But now this system encountered the problem of Achamod. In this system, Achamod was not isolated as a desire or a quality in one human being or one folk group, but was present in all of humanity. Achamod, as a phenomenon of humanity, has a longing, a dim memory of his circumstances when everything was still united with the Demiurgos. A longing for something remembered is a theme in the Gnosis that we will also find elsewhere. The Demiurgos accommodates Achamod's longing—here we see how the systems mix with Christianity—and sends a very early, sacred, lofty aeon to the earth. This sacred, early, lofty aeon then unites itself with the human being, Jesus. From the standpoint of anthroposophy, we can much appreciate the fact that human beings almost two thousand years ago had come this far in their power of thinking, and were even able to put it in writing. This image of the world of the Gnosis echoed down into the Middle Ages. There are still echoes of this in the Waldenses, in the Cathars.

The Gnosis always tried to understand the riddle: How is it possible that a spirit, a god, unites himself with a human being? And, in a certain way, the Gnosis succeeded in understanding it because these mighty images of a hierarchical world stood before it. The Gnostics could see in their visions how the Christ-being descended step-by-step through the aeons. Rudolf Steiner stresses how truly tragic it was that the Gnosis was 'destroyed, root and branch', after a relatively short time. And he says that everything since then '... was small in comparison to the greatness of the Christ-imagination of the Gnostic times'.[5] When we hear and think about the idea that everything in the history of culture and religion from the third century to the twenty-first century was small in comparison to the Christ-imagination in Gnosis—that is a powerful idea indeed!

The Call

The Gnosis comes to expression primarily in poetic form; in fact, we see how an enormous creative force was present in this poetry. There are important themes that arise again and again. One major theme is what is referred to as 'the call'. It forms a central experience. The person feels himself addressed, and through this address from the spiritual world he has the feeling that something like a memory in him wants to respond. He is not a *tabula rasa*, but has qualities that can be reawakened as qualities of memory by the call.

The call is like a tone that sounds in the distance, and the person experiences his own soul as the string of a musical instrument brought into vibration through the call. I am mentioning this in particular, because we will soon concern ourselves with musical instruments. And that is a subject connected to this Gnostic feeling. The main point was that the human being should also respond when he experienced the call. Thus we read in Mandaiic sources (Mandaism is a sect that still exists today, although naturally in a completely different form): 'The messenger of all radiance spoke to me: O Soul, when I called you, you gave me no answer; now when you call, who should give you answer?'[6] There is almost a suggestion of Sufi mysticism in such words.

The Song of the Pearl

The so-called 'Song of the Pearl' is perhaps the most famous text in this literature. We find the 'Song of the Pearl' in the Acts of Thomas, as well as in the other Apocrypha. It was circulated far and wide through the oral tradition. This 'Song of the Pearl'—parts of it, fragments, images, and so forth—can be found in the most varied languages. It is quite complete in the Acts of Thomas where it enters the narrative as Thomas Didymus sits in prison and tells it to the other prisoners. Many sects of Gnostics were firmly convinced—it is an old tradition—that Thomas Didymus—whose name means the twin—was the twin brother of Jesus. Thus this song has additional meaning for the sects that believed in this tradition. The 'Song of the Pearl' is from about the second century AD, and begins in this way:

> When I was a small child at the court of my father, the king, and could not yet speak . . . my parents furnished me with the means to travel, and sent me forth from our home in the East. From the riches of the

> treasure stores, they put together a case that was large yet lightweight, so that I could carry it by myself. The top of the case was made from gold and plain silver . . .
>
> And they dressed me in garments set with gems and stitched with gold, that out of their love they had made, and a long gown of a golden colour that was suitable to my body's size. But they made an agreement with me, and wrote in my spirit that I should never forget them, and said, 'When you go down into Egypt and bring from there the one pearl that is with the devouring snake, you will once again don the gem-laden garment and the long garment over it, and with your brother, our second child, you will become the inheritors of our kingdom.'

The journey is very difficult; his guides leave the child in Egypt, and he comes upon the snake. The child tells the story:

> I knelt by its hole and watched for it to become drowsy and sleep in order to take away my pearl. I was alone, however, and foreign in my appearance . . .

He then put on different clothing, and the story continues:

> But I do not know why [the people] discovered that I was not from their country. However, they mixed cunning with deception against me, and I tasted of their nourishment. And I no longer knew that I was the son of a king . . . I forgot the pearl that my parents had sent me for, and from the heaviness of their food, I fell into a deep sleep. But when this befell me, my parents also perceived it, and grieved for me.

The king and queen write a letter to him, and send the letter to him in the form of an eagle. Then come some of the most famous words in all the Gnostic writings. The letter says:

> To our son in Egypt: Peace! Arise, free yourself from the intoxication of sleep and hear the words of this letter. Remember that you are the son of a king. You have come under a yoke of bondage. Remember your garment stitched with gold; remember the pearl for which you were sent to Egypt . . . that, with your brother, you may become the inheritor of our kingdom.[7]

He awoke then and remembered the pearl. He speaks and, through the word, he has gained power over the snake; he receives the pearl. The story goes on to tell how he returns home, how he is received, how the brother is there. With this brother, we recall—in the language of images—the two Adam-souls, the one who remains behind, the other who goes out into the world. Perhaps we even think of the two Jesus boys. There are many levels to the symbolism, but we will not address them here. The child brings the pearl back. The pearl is most often viewed as a symbol for the Christ Himself, or for the Christ-illuminated, individuated ego of the human being. The prince experiences the incarnation history of every human being. The Gnostics were so far advanced that they could formulate such images and bring them into stories and legends.

The Pistis Sophia

There are two writings that were especially important for Rudolf Steiner. One of these is the *Pistis Sophia.* The combination *Pistis Sophia* is noteworthy, for *Pistis* means 'faith' and *Sophia* means 'wisdom'. Thus it seems they are actually antithetical and, as a result, most researchers say this was simply because people at that time thought illogically. Rudolf Steiner gave an extensive explanation for this contradiction, placing it in the context of the entire evolution of humanity.[8] In earlier times, people had a strong experience of what occurred with inhalation and exhalation. With inhalation, people experienced that they were actually taking in the soul-spiritual element, which then became perception, observation. With exhalation, people were empowered to act. Thus: inhalation—exhalation; perception—deed, action.

For the Greeks, this process of breathing was more a moment of consciousness. They experienced it that way, then brought it together with the concept of the Sophia, so that with inhalation they could experience their whole head filled with perception, filled with Sophia forces, with powers of wisdom. This is simultaneously an inner experience of the head. The Greeks describe how the human being at that time actually experienced a powerful feeling of strength in connection with exhalation. That was the element of *Pistis*, of faith—not in the sense of doctrine, but of faith in the broader sense of *fides*, in the sense of faith that is strong enough to move mountains.

The theme of this *Pistis Sophia* gospel—a very long gospel—is the teaching Christ Jesus gave during eleven years after the resurrection to the men and women who were His disciples. He taught for eleven years, and His pupils perceived it supersensibly. The *Pistis Sophia* begins with a description that can lead us to an experience of several Gnostic elements, among them the light.

> For this light has come forth from the primal source of all light, from the final Mystery. This power of the light arose over Jesus and surrounded Him completely as He sat at a distance from His disciples, and He shone in the utmost measure, in a boundless light.[9]

It says in the *Pistis Sophia* that the Apostles are then no longer taught through images, but are brought directly to the secrets of the heavens. In particular, Mary Magdalene and John are addressed by Christ. There are many dialogues between Mary Magdalene and Christ, as well as between John and Christ. Since this whole gospel is closely bound up with the light, reference is made to a very high being, Melchizedek. We find Melchizedek mentioned often in the *Pistis Sophia*.

Normally we think of Melchizedek in connection with the Old Testament story in which Melchizedek came to Abraham with bread and wine. As a result of this visit from Melchizedek, Abraham experiences that the source from which Melchizedek speaks is the same source from which he draws his own inner life, his life in the Mysteries.

In the *Pistis Sophia* we find the sentence:

> And Melchizedek, the Paralemptor of Light, purifies all powers and bears their light to the treasure-house of Light.[10]

In the Esoteric School, Rudolf Steiner calls Melchizedek the Purifier of Light before Christ. That is an exalted, sublime task—Purifier of Light. We will see how this image of the Purifier of Light is also vital to the Manichaeans and the Cathars.

In the conversations between Mary Magdalene and Christ, the question of light comes to the fore again and again. We can quote here only a few sentences—which can also be experienced as linguistic works of art. When a work of art is given shape linguistically with a wonderful array of expressions, of innovative words, then it naturally works best in the original language. But if it is genuinely a work of art in one language, then it will also become an artful work in another language. Rudolf Steiner's many mantras and artistic works make this immediately apparent. They are lofty works of language that Rudolf Steiner created, and they remain works of art when they are translated into a foreign language—not to be compared with the original language, but works of art nevertheless. Thus we also hear a work of art here:

> ... then Mary Magdalene approached once more ... and spoke to Jesus, 'My Lord, what sort will those be who receive the Mystery of the Light in the midst of the final helper?'

The answer:

> Those who have received the Mystery of Light when they leave the body of the material of the archons, each will be in his place according to the Mystery that he received; those who received the higher Mysteries will remain in the higher place; but those who receive the lesser Mysteries will be in the lesser place. In a word, according to where each has received the Mysteries, there will be his place in the inheritance of the Light. Therefore, I once said to you, 'Where your heart is, there will be your treasure,' which means that according to where each has received the Mysteries, there he will be.[11]

The explanation now no longer occurs in an image as it does, for example, in the allegories or the parables in the Bible; rather the explanation is very logically built up in words of knowledge.

The Books of Jeu

This comes to expression quite poetically in the *Books of Jeu.* These are great poems, great hymns—even something like a topography of the heavenly world of Light and its beings. It is like a version of *Occult Science, An Outline.* This can sometimes be disconcerting; but we can also discover parts that are quite sublime, where we have a glimpse of a world to which we would otherwise have no access. Rudolf Steiner worked extensively with these poems, and had translated one of them himself. There is a short article by Thomas Maurer[12] about both of these poems—in the translation by Rudolf Steiner and another translation. Through this formulation in words, we can see how the effort to understand the main question about the relationship between the Christ-being and Jesus works into the deepest substance of the Gnosis teachings. I will quote from the translation of the poem by Rudolf Steiner, which is actually a prayer.

> Behold, O Father
> How this being on the earth,
> Aim and sacrifice of all evil,
> Wanders far from your breath.
> Behold, it flees before the bitter chaos,
> Unsure of how to find the way.
> Thus send me, O Father!
> Bearing the seal I descend,

Traversing the number of the aeons,
Interpreting every holy tiding,
Showing then the god's image.
And thus I give to you
The deeply hidden tiding
Of the holy path:
Now, for you, its name is 'Gnosis'.[13]

Rudolf Steiner says about another prayer that it is not merely a poem or prayer invented by a Gnostic; it was the prayer given by the Resurrected One to His pupils so they could put it into practice as a prayer.[14]

Actually, much of the Gnosis came down to posterity not through the Gnostics themselves, but through the opponents of the Gnosis. We think, for example, of Irenaeus, who was the Bishop of Lyons around 177, and how he wanted to destroy everything that was connected to these efforts. Irenaeus authored polemics in which he explained the systems and maligned them; as a result, they became more widely known in the world.

The *Pistis Sophia* and the two *Books of Jeu* were not available until later. The *Pistis Sophia* was found around 1785, and has since been in the British Museum. The two *Books of Jeu* became available a little later in the Bodleian at Oxford. The great discovery of the Nag Hammadi took place in the twentieth century and, through it, we have truly objective insights into this whole world.

Clement of Alexandria and Origen

There were great Church teachers who were Gnostics, for example, Clement of Alexandria (150–217). He had a thorough Greek education in philosophy and science, thus a Hellenistic, scientific education. But then he came to Christianity and immediately saw what was associated with it—namely, self-knowledge. Throughout that time, this note sounds loudly—self-knowledge. He brought to his Christian understanding everything he had acquired through Hellenistic philosophy about self-knowledge and the search for self-knowledge. He says, 'The greatest science is self-knowledge. Whoever knows himself knows God.'[15] He was the head of the catechetical school in Alexandria, and thus taught many people. Among them was Origen, his most gifted pupil.

Origen continued this tradition. An important point for Origen was his doctrine of pre-existence. One aspect of this stated that if the human being trained himself, he could go far back in time, could follow his own destiny through all the aeons. The other was an idea about redemption. In theological-philosophical terms this is called *apocatastasis*. The apocatastasis is the restoration of the world to come. It is the doctrine that, in time, everything will return to its primal refinement. This is a significant thought because it means that everything will be redeemed. For example, Origen stresses that God loves everything that exists and hates nothing. He taught this in keeping with Clement of Alexandria. The evolution of the world contains within it the question of redemption. Origen saw this: everything connected with the world will be redeemed. However, from another point of view, the question naturally arises: What if something is not related to the Earth's evolution; what if it is related, for example, to the forces of Sorat—what then?

The Image of Christ in the Gnosis

Mighty battles took place. Rudolf Steiner called Irenaeus the 'eradicator of the Gnosis'. Many of the writings by Irenaeus opposing the Gnosis were later taken as legitimate descriptions of Gnostic doctrine. The Gnosis ceased abruptly. Why? Not only as a result of the polemic, which was very strong, but because of the general development of humanity. We can look at the great cycles of time, the epochs, the ages. The culture of the intellectual soul begins in 747 BC; in AD 1413 it is superseded by the age of the consciousness soul. The year 333 lies halfway between 747 BC and AD 1413. After 1080 years (that is, in 333), the human ego enters fully into the intellectual-feeling soul. This indicates an enormous step. Before this time the human being had to have much more help with his relationship to the spiritual world. The Gnostics had already pushed this help aside, so to speak, and were becoming increasingly self-sufficient. They were truly pioneers. The ego will only fully enter into the consciousness soul at a time far in the future. According to this great evolutionary plan, that will take place in the year 2493.

With the discovery of Nag Hammadi a moment of awakening also came for humanity in the twentieth century. Millions of people have carefully read these writings—parts of which have been published—and again and again discussions have taken place about the light-nature of the Christ, the light-body of the Christ. Millions of people have perceived this with their intellect. Rudolf Steiner predicted that after 1930, more and more people would experience the Christ-being in the etheric realm.

1. Traditio legis: *The Returning Christ Delivers the Law to Peter. Mosaic, San Giovanni in Fonte, Naples*

2. The Priest-king Melchizedek of Salem Presents Bread and Wine to Abraham. Mosaic from c. *430. Santa Maria Maggiore, Rome*

It must remain an open question whether or not this happened in the way Rudolf Steiner imagined, whether many people experienced the Christ in the etheric as a manifestation of light. But it is certain that many people have formed images, at least in their thoughts, of Christ in a body of light in the spiritual world, images of Him after the resurrection as the teacher of the men and women who were his disciples. Thus, they have had images of Him in a body not unlike the phantom-body experienced by Paul.

We can see in Illustration 1 an image of the Christ-being delivering the law to Peter after the resurrection; he communicates to Peter what Peter is then to carry into the world as a disciple of Christ, 'Dominus legem dat.' This is part of a fifth-century mosaic from Naples, located in San Giovanni in Fonte.

Now we turn our attention to another mosaic (Illustration 2). It is of the priest-king Melchizedek, the 'Episcopus of Light', or the 'Paralemptor of Light'. He is bringing bread and wine to Abraham. We see the substances that will later appear in the Last Supper. Based on Gnostic wisdom, this is like an indication in artistic form that Melchizedek and Abraham will connect themselves with the Mystery of Golgotha. The mosaic is

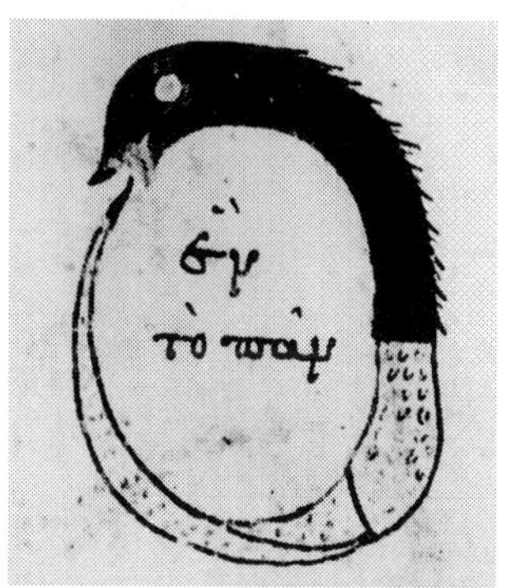

3. Uroboros (Tail-eater). MS graec. 299, Biblioteca Marciana, Venice

from around 430, and is located at Santa Maria Maggiore in Rome. The figure at the top is the Christ; He looks down at this event. Melchizedek is distinguished by the fact that he received the ether body of Shem as reinforcement for his mission, which is also for the future. Shem is the son of Noah, hence a powerful, etheric figure. This is like a promise, if we consider how replicas of the higher members of the Christ were and will be given to people who have specific tasks.

In the third image we see a snake (Illustration 3) called the *uroboros. Uroboros* means 'tail-eater', and the snake has its tail in its mouth. This illustration is from a third-century manuscript in the Biblioteca Marciana in Venice. It is virtually the oldest extant example about which it can be said that it is not just art, but life—Gnostic life. The snake played a very important role in many Gnostic sects, for example in the name of the Ophites and the Ophians. In Greek, *ophis* means snake; these sects named themselves after the snake. In one sect, the Perates—or Peratae—the snake was identified with the Logos itself. They developed the image of the Divine Son, the Logos, moving back and forth between the Father God and the material world. That was His task.

In another tradition, the snake is the direct image for Jesus Christ. In this tradition, human beings who know themselves and have freed themselves from the world are carried up and into the spiritual world by snakes that stand straight upright and act as a ladder for those who have freed themselves from the world through self-knowledge.

Lecture 4

The Establishment of the Grail Initiation in Northern Spain—Titurel and Parzival

Manfred Schmidt-Brabant

Motifs will be repeated here that have already appeared in my book *Star Paths.*[1] These motifs concern essential statements by Rudolf Steiner that cannot be disregarded in our considerations here.

At the end of the twelfth century and then in the thirteenth, the 'four great pillars' of Grail literature appear almost one after the other. Around 1180–1200 came Chréstien de Troyes' *Le Conte du Gral* [The Story of the Grail]. Robert de Boron's *L'Estoire del Saint Graal* appears at the same time—some scholars even say that it came first. Both books have been translated into English.[2] From 1203 to 1217, Wolfram von Eschenbach follows with his *Parzival* and the small fragment *Titurel.* And in 1270, as the last—and the most extensive—Albrecht von Scharfenberg appears with the so-called *Jüngeren Titurel* [Younger Titurel].

With these four basic works, the name of the Grail appears in Europe, and it endures even today in connection with the region we are considering here. A rich Grail literature is then added; Arthurian novels and much more appear in subsequent centuries. The question has been raised again and again and, in fact, has been answered positively: Were there forerunners of Chréstien de Troyes, Robert de Boron and Wolfram von Eschenbach? Wolfram certainly says there were writings, and he even goes so far as to accuse Chréstien de Troyes of not paying enough attention to them. There is no doubt that, no matter what it was called, there was Grail literature before these four works. Those familiar with the conditions of European archives know that it is not at all impossible that there are manuscripts yet to be discovered. In Spain, in the cathedral in Toledo, in France, there are whole vaults full of archives where virtually no one ventures—or has time to venture—because the government would rather buy tanks and planes than pay archivists. Even in the Vatican there is a room with hundreds and hundreds of enormous parchment-bound bundles that have remained unopened for centuries. Someone has actually calculated that it would take an entire team of archivists hundreds of years just to sort and catalogue them. It remains possible that accidental discoveries will be made, and that the famous manuscript of *Flegetanis* will surface, as well as others that are mentioned.

In any case, the concept of the Grail becomes exoteric at this time. Albrecht von Scharfenberg writes, 'The name "Grail" originates in the language of the angels.' Rudolf Steiner himself considers the description by Chréstien de Troyes to be the most accurate, but he also says that Wolfram von Eschenbach is the most initiated into the inner secrets of the Grail.

In a certain sense, this observation brings us to our own lives, because 'All pupils of Western esotericism are Parzivals.'[3] A way of initiation begins at that time that will continue through our time and well into the future. The basic experiences, the basic problems, the basic struggles of a Parzival take place today in the soul of each and every pupil of modern Western esotericism.

The Grail Vessel

When the Grail motif 'becomes exoteric', an esoteric stream is made visible. This stream had been prepared for an enormously long time. An event that reaches far back into the cosmic past presents itself to the consciousness of the West, an event that even contains the true meaning of Earth evolution. Sagas and legends point to this source. Rudolf Steiner tells this story repeatedly; I will cite it here in a condensed form but with all the essential elements. The saga tells that:

> . . . during Lucifer's fall from heaven to earth a gemstone fell from his crown. Out of this gemstone . . . the vessel was formed from which Christ Jesus and his disciples took the last supper; the same vessel in which was caught the blood of Christ as it flowed from the cross; the same vessel that was brought to the Western world by the angels and taken up by those who wanted to penetrate to a true understanding of the Christ principle. The stone that fell from the crown of Lucifer became the Holy Grail. What is the Holy Grail? . . . that gemstone is . . . nothing other than the full power of the human ego.[4]

It is not the ego—which originates from the elohim, from the exusiai—but the 'full power' of the ego, 'the soul power in the ego', as it is called in the Dionysian Mysteries.

The figure of one of the greatest initiates of mankind is closely connected with this legend—the figure of Titurel. Thus it is said—and this was related more than once by Rudolf Steiner—that angels had to bear the Grail in the spiritual world for a long time because humanity on the earth was not able to take it up until Titurel received it from the angels and prepared a place for it on the earth. This place was Munsalvaesche, the Mystery site of the Holy Grail.[5]

The First Two Grail Castles

Where was Munsalvaesche, the Mystery place of the Grail founded by Titurel? Where was the Grail castle? There is an extensive body of literature about this. We agree with Rudolf Steiner who stresses throughout all his works, from his early years through the last year of his life, that the Grail was in 'northern Spain'.[6] I will cite two passages that also draw our attention to specific aspects of this.

> It is no accident that it [the Grail] was to be found in Spain, where one had to go virtually miles away from what earthly reality offered, where one had to break through thorny hedges in order to penetrate to the spiritual temple that enclosed the Grail.[7]

What is described here is not meant in a merely external sense, but in a much more internal sense as well.

Rudolf Steiner draws attention to the fact that it was a very, very hidden place in Spain. The Grail was not to be found externally among the people. 'The invisible church, the supersensible church, which nevertheless can be found on the earth—it was this that concealed itself in the Mystery of the Grail.'[8]

Naturally, materialist fantasy—especially during the last centuries—always imagined the Grail castle to be like Neuschwanstein or similar castles. It was not at all like that! It was an earthly place, but those who did not seek the Grail passed it by. It was something that existed on the earth, but was invisible to those who did not open their eyes to it.

I have spoken about the fact that Rudolf Steiner once gave very precise indications about the location of the Grail castle to Ilona Schubert,[9] and that these directions confirm a great deal of research, including research carried out by non-anthroposophical scholars. He said—and this is already decisive—the first two Grail castles lay in the mountains called the Sierra de la Demanda. These are the mountains through which the pilgrims' path, the Camino, passes to the north; the pilgrimage site, Santo

Domingo de la Calzada, lies at the only entrance to this mountain range. These were the first two sites—for we will come to speak of the fact that the Grail changes location.

When did these first two Grail castles appear? Walter Johannes Stein reports that Rudolf Steiner was present during a Waldorf class lesson when *Parzival* was being discussed, and the children asked, 'When was this exactly?'—they were a bit uncertain. Rudolf Steiner then said several times that 'it was around the turn from the eighth to the ninth century'.[10] These Grail events begin around the year 800. In his book *World History in Light of the Holy Grail*, based on the descriptions of the star constellations, Walter Johannes Stein calculated that Parzival's visit to the Grail castle could have taken place around 823, and that the other events described took place before that. This was around the time the grave of James the Apostle was discovered in Compostela, and when the Camino opens itself to Europe.

Romans, Goths and Arabs in Spain

Spain had an indigenous population, the Iberians. Then the Romans arrived. Spain became a fully civilized part of the Roman Empire. Tarragona was acknowledged as a second Rome, just as beautiful as Rome itself. Had Rome not become the centre of Christianity, ruins would probably still be scattered about there as they are in Tarragona today. Roads, bridges, great aqueducts—for instance, in Segovia—are there to admire; in Melita there is a granite bridge that measures eight hundred metres in length, with cars driving across it today! It was a magnificent architecture, culture and civilization. But then the Roman Empire gradually collapses, the folk migrations begin, and the Goths arrive. The Visigoths conquer Spain and southern France, and sometime after 419 they create the Visigoth Empire, the Tolosian Empire, named after Toulouse, the capital city of Aquitaine.

Then comes the great invasion of the Arabs. In 711, General el-Tariq crosses at Gibraltar, which therefore bears his name. The Arabic army sweeps through all of Spain in a mighty triumphal campaign, smashes the Gothic Empire, is in the process of conquering all of Europe—until 732, when it is thrown back by Charles Martel at Tours and Poitier. Charles Martel was the seneschal—a particular title in the Middle Ages; a kind of chancellor, the imperial administrator—of the Merovingian king. The Merovingian kings were already in decline. The rise of the Carolingians begins with this battle; his grandson becomes Charlemagne, who will then play an extremely meaningful role in our Mysteries.

The Arabs are beaten back; Europe remains Christian. But Spain becomes Moorish—except for a thin northern strip of land, namely, those wonderful mountains which adorn northern Spain across the Europa Peaks up to the Galician highlands. The Arabs shy away from them. They were at home on their horses, accustomed to riding across the plain, the *meseta*. Thus this little region remained Christian. Very small Christian states were formed and the so-called *reconquista*, the re-conquest, also spreads from here. But it took the Christians eight hundred years to finish this re-conquest. Not until 1492, when the Alhambra in Granada—the wonderful architectural creation—is conquered, does the last Arabian kingdom fall. In 1492—thus at the same time—America is discovered. In 1492, all the Jews have to leave Spain, and the Inquisition begins.

The Moorish Culture

The famous Moorish culture develops in Spain during these eight hundred years, a brilliant civilization that outshone Europe by far. The *reconquista* advances slowly. But there were not yet religious wars; conflicts were actually cultural, primarily dynastic ones. Everything was still thought of in feudal terms, one person wanting the land of another. The famous El Cid fought on both sides! Even the Arabs they fought against were completely different from those we might imagine today. The caliphs were tall, red-headed, with enormous beards. Why? They had assimilated the Goths, so the North was naturally obligated to pay tribute. For example, the Arabs said: We will leave you in peace, but every year you must send us one hundred virgins. These Gothic virgins were highly prized and were married to the nobility, so that many a caliph had a blonde or strawberry blonde mother—and now wanted a wife just like his mother.

It is quite sad that this eight hundred years of history remains unknown in Europe. What is actually known about this history? With her famous book *Allahs Sonne über dem Abendland* [Allah's sun over Europe], Sigrid Hunke shed some light on the situation, but still not enough. The Arabic civilization reached its peak, its culmination, in Spain. Sigrid Hunke writes about Cordoba, 'There were 113,000 homes, six hundred mosques, three hundred public baths, fifty hospitals.' In Europe, no one knew how to treat an injured leg, except by amputation. At the same time in Cordoba, there was an advanced surgery; wounds were treated with penicillin-like medications; there were 'eighty public schools, seventeen universities with a high degree of scholarship.'[11] Charlemagne never learned to write or read properly; in Cordoba there were multi-lingual scholars versed in mathematics, astronomy, and so forth, 'twenty large libraries with hundreds of thousands of books, eighty thousand shops, paved streets with street lamps'. In Strasburg, as late as the beginning of the nineteenth century, the town council decided that 'There shall be no street lights because our dear God made the night dark for good reason.'[12]

Thus we see a brilliant, radiant culture in the plains, in the heroic battles, in the heroic songs of the *reconquista*. But underneath this, says Rudolf Steiner, we see a spiritual marriage of Gothic Christianity and Moorish wisdom. Slowly the Gothic Mysteries, the Mysteries of the Visigoths, take shape.

A fantastic culture blossomed in Spain; but it represented the Gondishapur impulse which was supposed to settle on the earth, to make the earth a paradise—and paradises were to be found in Spain! Charlemagne's imperial palaces were glorified farm houses, while in Spain there were palaces that covered hundreds of acres, with gardens, fountains, woods, and so forth. There are still some remnants of them in the south for us to admire. It was a brilliant, seductive civilization, dedicated to leading people solely to the sensuous.

Seekers after the Grail

We can understand from this that seekers after the Grail had to penetrate through the thorny hedges of abstraction, the thorny hedges of all that was connected to an external, seductive civilization. Of course, there were also the thorny hedges of the Sierra de la Demanda; we can still get a feeling for this today if we set out from Calzada towards Escarei, a nearby town located in this basin. The Sierra de la Demanda creates an enormous crescent, pointing downwards. It is virtually impossible to enter it. There are very high mountains; the only entrance into this basin where the first Grail castle was situated is gained from above.

It was necessary to penetrate external hedges. But, according to Rudolf Steiner, there were also the thorny hedges 'of abstraction ... and ... of utterly materialistic writings'.[13] This was actually the great conflict—a deepened, inward Christianity against a tremendously impressive outward culture of the intellect. Until a certain point in time (which we will come to momentarily), it was a battle of consciousness and culture; and at the same time, it was a quest for the Mysteries. It was a quest by people who knew from the ninth century onwards that the old etheric astronomy had come to an end along with the esotericism of a true medicine of the humours, an esoteric medicine. Rudolf Steiner says that they sought these things again as the 'Mysteries of the Bread and the Blood' of the Grail.[14] And now the important nuance that is usually overlooked: the Grail chalice is not only the vessel that caught the blood, but it is also the chalice in which Christ shared the bread with His disciples at the Last Supper. According to Rudolf Steiner, the bread is the Christianized image of the etheric astronomy; the blood of Christ is the image, the imagination, for the Christianized medicine of humours in the old Mysteries.[15] Let us remember that Melchizedek brings bread and wine—a cultic offering.

What we think of as Spain begins only in the fifteenth century with the regency of the two Catholic monarchs Isabella of Castile and Ferdinand of Aragon. They were married in 1479, and instituted the Inquisition immediately thereafter (1481). Only now does religious dogmatism begin. Until then, an eight-hundred-year culture of extraordinary tolerance existed.

Titurel and Melchizedek

An inner, spiritual process ran parallel to this. Here stands the figure of Titurel, from whom two elements emerge. He prepares a place for the Grail. He creates an earthly entrance to the true, spiritual Grail event, the invisible church. Once again we come to an old principle. What had Hiram done? He had built a temple that was quite modest, one that could not be said to mirror all the mysteries of the universe. Hiram had built a temple that allowed people to use its forms to penetrate to the true, spiritual Temple of Solomon. Titurel also founds something in the physical that creates an entrance to spiritual events. When the Grail was held aloft by the angels, it was certainly no physical object; but physical objects and places could create the entrance to it. And the second element is that Titurel founds the Grail initiation, the principle of the initiation of Parzival in the human being; it begins at that time and lasts into the present, into the future. Rudolf Steiner says that Titurel was one of the highest initiates, long secluded in the spiritual world during the Mystery of Golgotha. After completing an earlier enormous task, he returns.[16] A number of us agree that we have here a reflection of the great

Melchizedek—the one who brought the chalice and the bread to Abraham. Now, as Titurel, he prepares the Grail, and with it he prepares the bread and the blood for mankind.

Melchizedek is described distinctively in both the Old and New Testament. It is known that he is called 'a priest of the highest God'; he is a priest of Jehovah, a god known in the Mysteries, but not the highest god. It is said of him in the Epistle of Paul to the Hebrews: 'Without father, without mother, without descent, having neither beginning of days, nor end of life; but made like unto the Son of God; abideth a priest continually.'[17] And then it says that Christ is 'a priest for ever, after the order of Melchizedek'.[18] We know that Melchizedek is addressed again and again in the *Pistis Sophia* as the 'Light Purifier' before Christ; and when we read 'like unto the Son of God',[19] we then understand that the Gnosis says, 'He was a manifestation of the Holy Spirit.'[20]

Rudolf Steiner deals with Melchizedek frequently, and shows that familiar images are related to him; if we can speak of incarnations in regard to such beings, Melchizedek was Manu, the great Sun initiate of Atlantis, the teacher of Zarathustra.[21] As mentioned earlier, we cannot speak here of an incarnation in the way we usually hear it discussed in lectures about karma. It is as if such beings squeeze into a physical corporeality, but innumerable parts of their existence never appear in the physical world. Manu was the one in the Sun Temple who guarded the plans for the evolution of the Earth. He was the leader of the great White Lodge. And we meet him once more in the figure of Noah who led mankind out of watery Atlantis into the solid realm of the post-Atlantean epoch. He was the one who drew the plans of the physical body as we carry it with us today. Noah's ark is an image of the proportions for our modern corporeality, and therefore our foundation for developing an ego and individuality.

Now Titurel appears again, inaugurating the Grail event. He calls on two spiritual beings who work from the divine into the earthly; they are called Flore and Blancheflor in esotericism, the rose and the lily. Rudolf Steiner characterizes them as two beings who—we might say, by assisting Titurel—take part in the Grail Mystery and accompany the Mystery. Flore and Blancheflor inspire that personality whose place in the whole event is so difficult to see clearly. They draw to them and inspire the one we call Charlemagne in physical existence. Rudolf Steiner says he is familiar with all the criticisms of Charlemagne; but he says we should set criticism aside! A completely different perspective is needed to do justice to such a personality. 'Charlemagne ... was the reincarnation of a high,

Indian adept . . . he was an instrument'[22] to serve the even greater Titurel. Rudolf Steiner says this when he speaks of the Grail Mysteries but he does not say why Charlemagne is necessary in the Grail Mysteries. He was needed to open up and protect the entry to the Grail Mysteries in Europe.

Klingsor and Iblis

In this discussion, we cannot avoid an occasional glance at the dark side of the history of the Mysteries. We see the effect of Klingsor's opposition to the Grail. Rudolf Steiner says that Klingsor's name is connected with 'everything that . . . [works] into the realm of the Grail as misery and hardship'—even today![23] Klingsor was a great, but dark, initiate. Klingsor is a level of initiation achieved by black magicians who connect themselves more and more deeply with evil during the course of repeated incarnations. It is a degree of initiation in which such a black magician becomes capable of entering into an evil, cosmic marriage, the marriage to the evil black goddess, Iblis. She is a feminine, evil side of Lucifer. Rudolf Steiner says that, 'Among all the bad unions that have come to pass in Earth evolution . . . the worst of these unions . . . is the one between Klingsor and Iblis.'[24] Here we stand before the question: How can initiates turn evil? There is a commonly held, naïve idea that when someone becomes clairvoyant and looks into the spiritual world, he sees everything exactly as it is—God the Father, Christ, Rudolf Steiner, the greats of humanity! However, in the spiritual world we see what we have prepared ourselves to see. It is a question of judgement.

We can actually understand this very well out of ordinary life. Just think about how people focused on Adolf Hitler, or how they could not really judge Rudolf Steiner. The formation of the capacity of judgement, even for an initiate, is prepared throughout long incarnations. The ability to recognize our divine-spiritual nature in the spiritual world requires preparation, requires self-knowledge, requires schooling. But above all it requires becoming attentive to something lodged within human beings since the first activity of Sorat in the far distant past, something that can become ever stronger in them if it goes unobserved. Rudolf Steiner says that this begins to show itself very clearly in our time as the love of evil, the fact that people love to do evil. It is not a matter of erring and thinking that they are doing good; they are clear about the fact they are doing evil, and love doing it.

We now meet something similar in the opposition to the Grail. This opposition also has its castles—Kalot Bobot in Sicily, Klingsor's realm, as well as Terra de Labur in Calabria. The mighty blow against the Grail Mysteries begins from there. It is the attack on the sexuality of the human being. Wolfram expressed it in this way:

Once the king rode all alone,
To seek adventure far and wide,
Enjoy love's pleasure on his ride,
He went to find his fill of love.

It is quite unambiguous. The young king Amfortas is seeking an adventure of love. And now he is pierced by the spear of a heathen, behind whom we see the power of Klingsor. The account of where he was wounded is quite unmistakable:

With a lance well soaked in poison,
He was wounded in the fight,
And never healed from his plight.
In his testicles your uncle felt
The deep wound that he was dealt.
It was a heathen who fought him so,
And gave the wound that laid him low.[25]

In editions for school children, it is always said that he was wounded 'in the loins'. But Wolfram makes the situation very clear.

Of course, Rudolf Steiner uses the word *sexuality* differently than we are accustomed to today as a result of the sexual revolution, and so on. He means something deeper, and we can see it immediately when he says that sexuality is one side of the coin, nationalism the other. And vice versa, chauvinistic nationalism is only the other side of sexuality.[26] What is meant here is dependence on the blood, what the Apocalypse calls 'fornication with matter'.

There is a vast difference between someone saying: I am a Spaniard— or an Italian, or a German, and someone saying: I, as a German or as a Spaniard. If a person says, 'Sexuality is everything', then he fornicates with matter. However, if he allows it to be spiritually refined by the love between human being and human being, then sexuality is placed where it belongs; then it is a divine gift.

The fact is that the union between Klingsor and Iblis not only took place at that time, but these spiritual beings are still with us; they were the starting-point for something that is at work even today. It is important to understand how Rudolf Steiner portrays this.

At the time of the old Mysteries we lived extensively in the sentient soul. The intellectual-feeling soul does not begin until around 700 BC, as the great Mystery centres are closing. We lived with sense perception when we lived in the great Mysteries in Egypt, Babylonia and Assyria at that time. Indeed, *sentient soul* means the immediate experience of the senses, the immediate experience of feeling, the immediate experience of the will. Everything we experienced at that time—the processional avenues, the temples, the statues of the gods, the rituals—all deeply impressed itself on the sentient soul, forming it.

And then came the move inwards, the intellectual-feeling soul. Outer imagining becomes thinking; the School of Athens opens; people also begin to experience the conscience inwardly. The sentient soul can no longer be nourished in the same way that it was in the Mysteries. And Rudolf Steiner says that this results in the creation of dead fibres in the sentient soul, constrictions in what was experienced at that time. These constrictions can no longer be enlivened and nourished—not until these constricted places, these dead parts, can be loosened again by a new life in the Mysteries.[27] We see here the meaning of Goetheanism, the re-enlivening of sensory-moral perception: What is red, blue, white? What are forms? But for now, these dead, constricted places, these dead parts, exist in every modern person, and the work of Klingsor and Iblis is directed at them even today.

This began with the wound of Amfortas, and passes through every human being. Rudolf Steiner says rather apodictically that every modern person is a 'wounded Amfortas', but every person who seeks the spirit is also a 'Parzival'.[28] He even describes in detail how Goethe, with all his greatness, suffered under this; how even he was a wounded Amfortas who suffered the arrows of Klingsor and Iblis.

What we see here is the poison thorn of Sorat. Since Gondishapur, mankind has not only been dealt a blow down into the body, but it also has this thorn in the body; and it is really Klingsor-Iblis who uses it. The annihilation of the ego now comes from the counter-demon of love. Here we understand the bleeding head on the silver salver, the severed ego. The initiates certainly knew who John the Baptist was. Adam's head is severed from us, for all egos are still connected. Only at the end of Earth evolution will each person be a self-contained ego. The ego still has its separateness through the body, but it is united above with all the other egos—egos, not souls! In the stream of time, they are all connected to Adam, the first human ego. The severed, bloody head of the first Adam, of the first ego-human being, is an image of what the Sorat powers want—the annihilation of the ego in humanity.

The Historical Parzival

Into these events enters the historical Parzival. He really existed; there actually was an original, historical-physical Parzival. Four of his incarnations are known. I will deal with the first and the last; Virginia Sease will look at the other two. Parzival appears as the 'Youth of Sais',[29] about whom it is reported that he lifted the veil of Isis (which was forbidden), whereupon he fell dead to the ground. Rudolf Steiner says this was utterly characteristic of those old Mysteries. The person was called. The initiates went about through mankind, looking into the aura to see who had the capacity; they gathered these people together, and the person learned what he was supposed to learn. He was not permitted to question.[30] Questioning was most strictly forbidden in the old Mysteries; a person had to wait until the initiators determined his readiness, until the gods revealed themselves to him. The Youth of Sais was the first to breach this rule; he is remembered by mankind for saying, 'I want to know. Who is Isis?' This is the image; he removes the veil, and there it was written, 'I am the past, the present, the future. I am the all. No mortal may lift my veil.' He lifts the veil and dies.

He returns as the Youth of Nain and as Manes, and then he becomes the historical Parzival. And now everything is turned completely upside down. In the old Mysteries, questioning was forbidden. In the new Mysteries, the pupil must ask! Everything depends on his asking.

Parzival's first visit to the Grail castle is almost accidental; there he sees the wounded Amfortas—and remains silent. We may excuse him for this; after all, he had received all sorts of prior instructions from Gurnemanz about how a knight conducts himself. A knight holds his tongue; he simply does not ask. But Parzival's negligence is all the worse! He should have broken with convention and posed the question to the king who was obviously suffering!

The initiates—because they were initiates surrounding the Grail Mystery—are greatly dismayed! They knew who was there in Parzival. And he fails. The one who is actually to become king of the Grail one day, on whom all hope for the future rests—and he fails. He had been so well prepared. His mother, Herzeloyde, is also a historical figure; she actually existed. In her lived Julian the Apostate who had sought the Mysteries, who had been murdered for his Mystery quest, who had opposed the Church of Constantine. He becomes the mother of Parzival and, it is said, bestows upon him an entirely spiritual education, indifferent to the outer world. And then she sends Parzival out, Rudolf Steiner says, 'in order to seek the esoteric paths for Christianity and to point the way'.[31] This is the old impulse of Julian the Apostate, which was to open the Mystery paths for Christianity.

Parzival fails; Wolfram describes it quite beautifully. The next morning he is unceremoniously thrown out of the Grail castle; he wanders around. And then comes the meeting with Trevrizent. These are all brothers and sisters. Amfortas is Parzival's uncle, and the brother of Amfortas is Trevrizent. Trevrizent has become a hermit on account of Amfortas' serious wound—in other words, because of the difficult destiny of the Mysteries. One of his sisters is Herzeloyde, and we will meet yet another. According to Rudolf Steiner's research, Trevrizent was actually at the hermitage in Arlesheim. After wandering about for a long while, Parzival arrives at this hermitage. They quickly recognize one another, and Trevrizent admonishes Parzival for roaming about this way on Good Friday. Then Trevrizent's long initiation discourses follow. Trevrizent says that Adam was born of the virgin mother earth; he says other things as well. Trevrizent tells Parzival the whole history, then sends him again to the Grail castle. Now Parzival knows what is happening. He sets out on the path that Rudolf Steiner calls 'the nature initiation of Parzival'.[32] It is quite wonderful if one knows Europe a bit and can say, for example: Here is where Parzival rides away from Arlesheim through the Burgundian Gate. His route can be followed through France, possibly even over the Ronceval Pass, until he arrives at the Sierra de la Demanda. Rudolf Steiner even describes it briefly. Past mountains, through forests, past lakes, through thickets, week by week Parzival rides. He goes through the world of nature and the elements. This nature initiation can be described very precisely. It always leads first through the world of the senses, through the world of the temperaments; then through the world of the elements; through the elements to the planets, the planetary forces in nature; then to the experience of the Pillars of Hercules which are also called Jachin and Boaz; and through the Pillars of Hercules to the ocean of the fixed stars—which is what the pilgrims also experienced when they actually arrived at Finisterre.

During this nature initiation, Parzival has encounters with spirit beings, encounters with elemental beings, but also with nature demons of all sorts. What takes place on this path must take place on every initiation path: the catharsis of the soul, the purification of the soul from all ties to the earthly, an opening up, a preparation of the soul for higher initiation. And thus, Rudolf Steiner relates, Parzival appears for the second time before Titurel, now as a 'cathar'.[33] What is meant here by cathar is not the Cathar stream, which also called itself this for good reason. Parzival appears before Titurel as the purified one, as one who has undergone catharsis.

The Grail Initiation

Only a few elements of this Grail initiation will be described here. Rudolf Steiner gives more detailed descriptions. It must be noted that what we will discuss here are only the first steps of Grail initiation. These steps are not yet fully complete; high levels of Grail initiation are yet to be realized in the future of humanity.

The first step after the catharsis begins with an imagination arising through intensive concentration and meditation—the image of a lily-like tree, a lily tree, white and pure. And Parzival hears the helping voice of Blancheflor, the lily, who says, 'This is you! You are now a cathar, one who is pure, one who is white!' Then she makes him aware that 'there is, nevertheless, an unpleasant odour about this tree'. He discovers that this odour is all the bad things a person removes from himself, but it is now in the outer world. He is prompted to create a second imagination, and before him arises the black cross with the red roses. Now he hears the voice of Flore, and she says to him, 'This is what you will become, because you must take into yourself and purify all the bad things that you have removed from yourself. You cannot carry your refuse into the world; you have become a pure one. Now use the purifying powers of your soul to ennoble what you have removed, just as the lower drives ennoble themselves in the rose.' Deep meditative experiences follow in connection with nature; enormous loneliness is mentioned, devotion to the deity, a deep, inner experience of light. With that, the first level of Grail initiation ends. Outwardly, everything becomes dark. Parzival experiences himself inwardly as light. Then it is said that in this light the head opens itself in the shape of a chalice, like a chalice, in order to receive the divine light from on high. He experiences himself as the Grail chalice. Into this experience—it is interesting that Rudolf Steiner says it this way—sound the words that we know as Rosicrucian words, words that begin with the phrase, 'Ex deo nascimur', followed by 'In Christo morimur', 'Per spiritum sanctum reviviscimus'. Parzival has passed through the first stage of the Grail initiation. These are imaginations that may have appeared differently to each person.

The Work of the Grail

We first know the Grail through another image, namely, that it heals and nourishes all human beings as it is carried in, and anyone who has seen it cannot die for a week following. Who carries it in? The only being the Grail allows to carry it—no one else may carry it. This being is Repanse de Schoye, the sister of the king. In her, we again find the soul of the Queen of Sheba. Chrétien says that the Grail shines.[34] On the other hand, Wolfram von Eschenbach says that the virgin, Repanse de Schoye, shines.[35]

Why does the Grail heal and nourish? Because the restored phantom works in it through the blood. This restored phantom nourishes and heals the human being. If a person genuinely unites himself with the Christ, he penetrates himself with the restored phantom, and it nourishes him, heals him, carries him; it is life. This is brought to expression in the image of the Grail being carried in to nourish the people.

But why is Amfortas not healed by the Grail? Amfortas, in unbearable pain, is kept alive because he sees the Grail again and again. But the Grail cannot heal him. Here we have that peculiar mystery—the Grail cannot heal him without some intervention, because the wound is the counter-Grail itself. Rudolf Steiner once said:

> The reproductive forces of humanity transform themselves. In itself, the reproductive force is the most holy thing we have because it is immediately divine. The more divine the thing we drag in the mire, the greater the sin. Our reproductive organs will become our heart and the larynx. As the word became flesh in Christ, so must the flesh become the word 'in the future'. That is the Mystery of the Holy Grail, the holy lance of love, the fructifying light of the sun, which will once again unite with Eve.[36]

Rudolf Steiner speaks again and again of the 'holy lance of love', through which a fructification by the light of the sun will take place in the future. Yet here the poisoned spear of the counter-Grail is at work.

But then the healing does take place. The Grail can now have its effect because the love of another person—Parzival's love—is added to it.

Rudolf Steiner often gave compassion as the first definition of true love, its first characteristic, so to speak. There is that wonderful saying of his about the other love—that the love between man and woman is the nectar and the ambrosia of the gods; they are nourished by it. Parzival arrives, and now this impulse flames up in him, 'Uncle, what ails thee?'[37] He is filled with compassion, and in that moment the Grail can work. Amfortas is restored to health.

The Replica of the Ego of the Christ

It is not easy to feel our way into the depths of these Mysteries. Nor is it easy to look at that other Mystery in which it is said that the bodily members of the Christ were preserved following His life so that they could be replicated at the appropriate time in human history: the ether body, which many—like the author of the *Heliand*—received; and the replicas of the astral body of Christ in Francis of Assisi and Elisabeth von Thüringen. But the replica of the ego was held in reserve for a long time.

> And thus the secret had to be found, the secret of how this ego could be preserved in complete silence, in profound Mystery, until the appropriate moment in human and Earth evolution. For this purpose, a brotherhood of initiates was formed to preserve this secret, the brotherhood of the Holy Grail.[38]

They protected the chalice containing the blood of the Redeemer until humanity was so developed through the evolution of Grail initiation that it could take from the Grail chalice a replica of the ego of the Christ.

The Knights of the Grail

The knighthood of the Grail, the Grail Knights and the Templeisen—also called the Knights of the Swan—were created because a Mystery had begun its work. Such a knight was always a two-sided figure—a living side and a dead one. Certain select members of the Grail community united themselves after death with a living Grail Knight, so that the Grail Knight was always a two-sided figure—a living person and the deceased one who rode with him. This knighthood was established after Amfortas' misfortune, right at the beginning of the whole development of the Grail, because the dead are no longer susceptible to the temptations of sexuality.

Someone who is dead cannot be wounded by the attacks of Klingsor-Iblis. This gave rise to the knighthood of the Grail in which the one who is alive is led and protected by the one who is dead.

These knights protected the Grail from those who were unworthy, and from the avarice of black magicians. Here we stumble upon an enormous secret; Wolfram deals with it when he writes about the heathen with his poisoned spear:

> The heathen trusted in his strength,
> Hoped to make the Grail his.
> Out he rode, prepared to fight,
> To win and claim the Grail's might.[39]

Even the opponents of the Grail wanted the power of the Grail.

Today, this theme of evil desiring the Grail in order to possess its power is still widespread. There was a film that premièred in America in 1989. Millions of people saw it—*Indiana Jones and the Last Crusade*. What is its theme? The evil Nazis are after the Grail in order to rule the world through it. And a noble archaeologist—naturally, he's an American—stops them. We see how the evil people and the good people go after the Grail; they find it in a mountain cave where it has been guarded for centuries by an ancient Templar who cannot die because the Grail nourishes him and keeps him alive. The Grail then falls into a rocky crevice, evading the grasp of human beings. Interestingly, some of the people involved in the film were close to anthroposophy, had their children in a Waldorf school, and so forth. One of the great Grail themes: Knights of the Grail, Templars, protect the Grail from the grasp of those who are evil.

The Third Grail Castle

The Grail impulse begins to move about. The first two Grail castles lay in the Sierra de la Demanda. The first was deep in the interior where there are some rather peculiar ruins. In the ninth or tenth century, the second Grail castle was already somewhat more accessible, probably in San Millan de Suso, that quaint architectural monument that still touches the heart today. Then, according to Rudolf Steiner, the Grail leaves for San Juan de la Peña. Its Grail chalice is still preserved, although admittedly, it is just a stone cup. If you look at the illustration, you see that the whole pretentious mounting was added much later; only the onyx cup was the Grail vessel in San Juan de la Peña. The Grail goes to Montségur where the castle was specially built to protect the Grail (1204); but Montségur is destroyed in 1244 as a result of the catastrophe of the Cathars.

Naturally a material object does not move about on its own. What moves about is the possibility of access to the Grail itself. Only initiates are capable of uniting a place or a material object with the spirit so that people can reach the Grail by means of the material object or through the place. We say a Grail castle, but it can be a very simple building, for it is only in a supersensible, invisible Grail church that the shrine of the Christ Ego is preserved. It is beyond space, and entry to it is found when a place or material object has opened this entrance.

It has often been said that there are additional Grail sites—Glastonbury in England, for example, where the mysterious Avalon is supposed to be. Dion Fortune, the well-known English esotericist, writes, 'There are three paths: the path of history; the path of the saga; but then there is the secret, craggy path of the soul, the mystical path to the inner Avalon, the mystical Avalon.'[40] And then we might also mention the region of the Upper Rhine, Malsch, the Odilienberg, the Dornach hill. The Grail impulse radiates into the world and finally comes back to Jerusalem, to Mount Moriah, the old sanctuary of Melchizedek who was, after all, the King of Salem. The Grail is at work there in the initiation of the Templars.

4. The 'Holy Grail' in the cathedral at Valencia

Prester John

But then it is said—and Rudolf Steiner also takes this up—that the Grail disappears; it withdraws again, and goes east to the priest-king John, a legendary figure of the Middle Ages, in the eleventh and twelfth centuries. Rudolf Steiner says that this priest-king John—as he is described—is not to be understood in the physical sense; a spiritual place is meant.[41] Actually, there are wonderful miniatures, drawings in manuscripts, where Prester John is seen sitting on his throne. Albrecht von Scharfenberg writes about how the aged Titurel—together with Parzival—brings the Grail to Prester John because it must be withdrawn from European humanity for a time. Rudolf Steiner says that it had once again to leave what is physical and enter into the spiritual.[42] We see that there are seven steps leading to the priest-king John. The seven steps are the overcoming of the seven deadly sins: greed, sloth, envy, anger, gluttony, lust and pride. This means: Overcome what exists in you as any kind of greed, any kind of sloth, any kind of envy, and so forth. When you overcome these, then you climb the steps to the place of the Grail.

In the lecture cycle *Christ and the Spiritual World, The Quest for the Holy Grail,* Rudolf Steiner summarizes this in another image; he interprets it differently:

> At the time of the Crusades, people still revered the realm of Prester John, the successor of Parzival. And if we consider how people sought this realm, we would have to conclude that the location of John cannot really be found on the earth, even though they expressed all this in earthly, geographical terms.
>
> Might this be a presentiment within the European saga that set out to continue the Parzival saga—a presentiment of the fact that, unbeknownst to us, the Christ has also worked beneath the surface in the Orient since that time? A presentiment that what takes place at the level of consciousness in the Orient as religious strife might perhaps give way to the influence and revelations of the true Christ impulse, in the same way that, in keeping with the Parzival revelation, this began to happen in the West? Might it be that the sunlight of the Grail is called to shine upon all the gods of the earth, as is symbolically indicated by the virgin carrying in the chalice that bears the secrets of the Grail within, by the radiance of the Grail outshining all other lights? ... Let us make ourselves capable of understanding Him [the Christ], so that we do not misunderstand what He might say to us when it is time for other faiths of the earth to be permeated by His impulses![43]

Lecture 5

Light and Dark—Cathars and Troubadours in the Stream of the Manichaean Impulses

Virginia Sease

We now want to take up the theme of light and dark, the Cathars and the troubadours, in the Manichaean stream. Manichaeism is not merely an element of the Gnosis. There are points of agreement between the Gnosis and Manichaeism, but the Gnosis actually sprang from much different sources, from other folk contexts. Manichaeism can be traced to one person, Manes or Mani—not to be confused with Manu. We are referring here to Manes or Mani, the individuality who had an incarnation in the Youth of Sais. The Youth of Sais was forbidden to question; but he did so by lifting the veil, and died. This same individuality re-emerges in the Youth at Nain (Luke 7:11–17), who was awakened from the dead by Christ. We hear nothing further of him in the Gospel. We know that he became a disciple of Christ, and thus remained connected with the Christ.

Various forms of initiation can be found in the Gospels. The first of these is the initiation of Lazarus-John. This form of initiation brings with it the immediate possibility of seeing into the spiritual world, and of having experiences there. Another form of initiation, the kind experienced by the Youth at Nain when he was awakened from the dead, rests quietly in the soul and the spirit of the one affected, and does not come to light until the next incarnation. In the same incarnation, during the period of rest following the awakening, the Youth of Nain gathered the enormous powers that were brought to him through the initiation. His next incarnation begins when he returns as Mani in AD 216—thus he was in the spiritual world for only a short time.

Mani had the enormous task—then and far into the future—of 'penetrating Christianity with the teachings of reincarnation and karma'.[1] He was already setting about this task in his third-century incarnation. We heard earlier about his subsequent incarnation as Parzival. This is an individuality that accompanies mankind.

The Cologne Mani Codex

We have been in a position since the end of the 1960s to know much more than we did about this individuality, Mani. At the end of the 60s a tiny book measuring 1.378 inches × 1.776 inches was found in a papyrus collection at the University of Cologne (Germany). Named the Mani Codex,[2] it is the smallest book to come down to us from antiquity. It is small enough to fit into a matchbox. On each parchment page, written in a wonderful script, are twenty-three lines. The writing is small and quite elegant—and had to be read without magnification. Of course, there were no magnifying glasses at the time, only glasses filled with water which were far from ideal.

This Mani Codex revealed a great deal about Mani, his work and his biography. We will look at two historical sources in relation to his incarnation as Mani. Rudolf Steiner once hinted at how Mani's life in the third century had developed. He connected it to a well-known tradition that had come down through many centuries; of course, it was also possible for Rudolf Steiner to confirm his research in the Akashic Record. Both of these sources exist and their images complement one another. In esoteric research it is always important to bring all the existing sources together, even if they contradict one another. Then we must simply put up with the need to find our way through the inconsistencies surrounding the subject.

Rudolf Steiner explains[3] how a merchant living in the Near East wrote four large manuscripts. This merchant was very learned. When he died, he left these texts to his widow, a Persian. When she died, she passed them on to a slave whose freedom she had bought, and whom she herself had educated. This slave was Mani. This tradition goes on to explain that Mani, who was known in his own time as a great teacher, found in these four great manuscripts the wisdom he possessed and taught.

In the Cologne Mani Codex we read manuscripts thought with certainty to have been written by Mani or to date from the time he lived. The biography presented in it is somewhat different from the one by Rudolf Steiner, but with a little effort the two pictures can be brought together. It is said that when Mani was four years old, his father joined a popular Judaeo-Christian sect, the Elchasaites, that followed the doctrine of baptism. Shortly thereafter, he brought his son into this sect. Mani lived there, took up all of the teachings, connected himself with these teachings, with the customs, with the way of life. It tells how, after this, he experienced two special moments in his childhood and youth. What seemed to be his twin appeared to him twice—when he was approximately twelve years old, and again at twenty-four. However, it is not a physical twin, but what he says was a 'beautifully wrought and powerful reflection of my form'.[4] This is how it is described in the Mani Codex. This twin or reflection is often translated in the manuscripts as 'fellow companion', and is frequently identified with the Paraclete of the Gospel of John. Each time this reflection—or twin—appeared, Mani was in danger and it rescued him.

Mani described himself as the Paraclete, the Comforter. However, he also clearly defined this as meaning he was not the sole incarnation of the Paraclete, or the Holy Spirit, but rather a vessel in which the Paraclete could find shelter. This is an important image, because later in this path of schooling with the Cathars we will see that it was their goal in life to be a shelter, a vessel for the Comforter, whom the Christ had promised to humanity.

At the age of twenty-four Mani leaves this sect and becomes a teacher himself. He travels extensively to India, Persia, in Babylonia, and throughout this whole region of the world. Because he made so many trips, we find that over the centuries the most diverse groups cite Mani as their source, even though their customs, practices, the content of their beliefs, and their languages differ considerably.

In time, the priests became upset about Mani's presence and his teaching. This culminated in a great religious trial; he was imprisoned and after twenty-six days he died. During these twenty-six days, he passed along great teachings to the disciples who were permitted to come to him. He was sixty years old at the time of his death. We discover all of this through the Mani Codex. It is truly a miracle how again and again throughout the twentieth century we have come upon sources that open up the past for us; this has also been the case in connection with the Gnosis. We ask ourselves: What kind of spiritual secrets lie behind the fact that such a discovery suddenly reveals something at a certain moment in the history of humanity?

Mani's Teaching about Evil

The teachings of Mani are often characterized by what differentiates them from Christianity, especially in regard to the concept of evil. The Manichaeans say that evil is just as eternal as good—evil and good are equally old—while Christianity, of course, states that spirits that were originally good fell away from God. A vast difference is apparent in these views. Like other teachers of humanity, Mani created a great legend that was then widely disseminated. This legend is actually known in great detail and, of course, in many variations.

Rudolf Steiner noted that all spiritual streams connected with initiation relate their secrets exoterically through legends. But the legend of Mani is a great, cosmic legend. It is in a category unto itself. Rudolf Steiner gave a beautiful summary of it:

> Once upon a time, 'the spirits of darkness wanted to storm against ... the realm of light. In fact, they reached the border of the light realm, and were about to conquer the light realm. However, they were unable to have any effect against the light realm. Now they ... were to be punished by the light realm. But there was nothing in any way evil in the realm of light, only what was good. Thus the demons of darkness would have to have been punished by something good. What took place? The following. The spirits of the realm of light took a portion of their own realm and mixed it into the material realm of darkness. Because a portion of the realm of light was mixed with the realm of darkness, something like a yeast, a ferment, arose that set the realm of darkness into a chaotic whirl, from which it received a new element—death. Thus the realm of darkness continually consumes itself, and carries in itself the seed of its own destruction ... It was the primal human being who was sent by the realm of light to mix with the realm of darkness and, through death, to overcome what should not exist in the realm of darkness; the human being was to overcome it in himself.[5]

Thus, this is the mission of death. Death serves to overcome darkness.

Here, of course, we must think of Part II, Act V of Goethe's *Faust.* The little devils are sent on a mission by Mephistopheles to prevent the escape of Faust's soul! They are there and stand guard. What happens? The angels come with roses, the little devils are dazed, and Mephisto begins to fall in love with the angels! The way Goethe does this is really quite humorous but, in fact, it serves to highlight this legend in dramatic form.

Light According to Mani

The role of light was important to Mani. Because he had himself experienced an initiation through the Christ, he also had access to the light that was virtually unique, with the exception of John the

Evangelist's. Mani describes in his writings how the living spirit formed the sun and moon from light. It is rather like Mani's version of *Occult Science, An Outline*. The third messenger from the third epoch of the world—this is a language of imagery, but here we also think of the pre-earthly sacrifices of Christ—takes his place in the ship of the sun. The ship of the sun is a vessel for the Christ. And Jesus, who is called 'the Splendour', Jesus the Splendour, takes his place in the ship of the moon. A deep symbolism lies behind this image, which became a particularly fundamental image for the Cathars. Mani's calling reads as follows in the Codex:

> In my youth I was protected by the strength of the light-angels and the strong powers which had received from Jesus the Splendour the task of sheltering me.[6]

Melchizedek works through him or, more aptly put, with him. This is mentioned in the Codex; from the spiritual world, Melchizedek, as the 'Light Purifier' before Christ, works with Mani on his earthly task.

Mani always designates himself as the 'Apostle of Jesus Christ'. He wrote seven major works. This Mani, who had an enormous life force, always had the task of bringing reincarnation and karma into connection with Christianity. Of course, we immediately remember that Rudolf Steiner also had this as a task, and that he regretted being prevented from taking it up until late in his life because he had other tasks at the start of his career. The great helpers of humanity provide mutual support for one another in their work for humanity.

Mani intends to undergo an incarnation in the twenty-first century, at a time when a condition will be met that will allow him to unite that incarnation with his ageless task. The condition requires that it become possible for him to receive a proper form of education. If that is not possible, he will be unable to fulfil his task. It is sincerely hoped that the Waldorf schools can continue to fulfil their tasks properly in the decades ahead.[7]

Augustine as an Opponent of Mani

Mani's teachings had a widespread popularity. But they were also subject to enormous attack, particularly by one personality—Augustine. At first, Augustine was very interested in what came through Mani; but then he turned away from this stream, and became an opponent of Manichaeism, the teaching of Mani. He conducted a conversation about this which has been handed down in written form as the *Contra Faustum*. However, it is thought that Faustus was not a real person, and that the work was merely written in this format.

We must recognize that Augustine's position cannot be evaluated only ecclesiastically, but must be viewed cosmically. For Augustine had received into his ether body a replica of the ether body of Christ Jesus from the Christ-being Himself. We see here the emergence of a new principle. We already mentioned how a replica of the ether body of Shem appeared with Melchizedek; but that had occurred within the relationship of the blood. At this turning-point that is the Mystery of Golgotha these replicas of the etheric body and the astral body are present, and—for our time, and far into the future—the I, the I-nature is present as well. Augustine was not the only one to receive a replica of the ether body of Christ Jesus; there were several people between the fourth and tenth centuries who possessed full or partial replicas of the etheric body of Christ Jesus. As a result of this, and the fact that the ether body is the memory body, Augustine also possessed the possibility of bringing to life great memories in himself. He felt as though he himself had taken part in the Mystery of Golgotha, as though he himself had been there. Naturally, what took place then in the astral body and in the I-nature were mistakes, confusions, and so forth—but what took place in regard to the ether body is something quite extraordinary.

Augustine was strongly influenced by three factors. He was influenced by the words of Paul—Rudolf Steiner calls Augustine the 'best interpreter of the Epistles of Paul'.[8] Like other Church Fathers at the time, he was under the aegis of the Apostles who were in the spiritual world. The Church Fathers worked under the aegis of the Apostles who let treasures of wisdom stream down. And, finally, Augustine had this replica of the ether body.

It is quite moving, for example, to experience a quotation from Augustine in which he connects himself with the Christ-being. 'To me, it was as though I perceived Your voice from on high, saying: I am sustenance for the strong; grow, and you will partake of Me. You will not transform Me into you, like the sustenance of your flesh, but instead you will be transformed into Me ... then You called from afar, "I am the I am." '[9] Augustine is in the position of hearing the call of Christ: 'I am the I am.' We could say that he penetrated into this ether body, and then the great insights came to him. This was the same Augustine who fought strongly against Manichaeism; that was his task.

Old and Young Souls

Both streams—the Augustinian and the Manichaean—work into the Middle Ages. We see that this touched human souls very strongly in a variety of ways, especially those souls with a long history behind them. When the sun separated from the earth and the danger arose that everything human would become mummified, the division into planets took place. They were lifted away because they were unable to endure the forces of the moon. Souls who were mature enough went with the sun, with the Sun-intelligence, Michael, and with the Christ-being. Other souls went to other planets with their own intelligences, Mars with Samael, and so forth. When the moon was expelled, the souls returned from the various planets. But they did not all return to the earth simultaneously. Many of them stayed away much longer, while others returned immediately or very soon afterwards. When the souls returned, they were able to experience their centres of teaching, the Mysteries—Sun Mysteries, Mars Mysteries, and so forth—so that they could somehow find their way on the earth.

According to Rudolf Steiner, the souls can be grouped into the so-called old souls—these are the souls who returned earlier to the earth—and the young souls who returned later. This is the case not only for those on the sun, but for all the planetary sojourns. Many returned earlier, many later. By the time of the Mystery of Golgotha, these souls who once were sun souls had many incarnations behind them. The old souls are described as Christianity-weary, the young souls as longing for Christianity. We should not interpret Christianity-weary to mean that these souls would say: We have now had at least one incarnation after the Mystery of Golgotha; now we have had enough of Christianity. No, quite the contrary! They are weary as a result of Christianity; they are weary because they have always taken great initiative for Christianity; they have suffered for Christianity. Among these souls who suffered in the conflicts are those souls we later find as heretical souls.[10]

The old souls have diverse life paths; their lives often go in completely different directions. We also discover heretical souls who have nothing to do with the stream we can call the Michaelic stream. The old souls have actually had enough of strife, of dogmas; they have suffered under the question: How might Christianity gain a foothold on the earth?

The Cathars in Southern France

One particular group was called the Cathars by their opponents—from *katharos*, which means pure, perfect. There is another derivation connected with the root *heretic.* But the people who were friendly with them, who actually received their gifts, called them *bons hommes, bonnes femmes*; they were 'the good people'.

The Cathars appear suddenly in the south of France during the twelfth century. They can be traced back to the Bogomils from Bulgaria who came over from the east through Italy and made their way into southern France. The Bogomils received their name from a Bulgarian priest named Bogomile who lived during the middle of the tenth century. He started a sect that was quite influential, but it cannot be said that the Cathars are merely another group of Bogomils. There are vast differences between them. The Bogomils were themselves strongly influenced by the Paulician sect, and were also admirers of Paul. The Paulicians put their faith in the Epistles of Paul. There were numerous Bogomil texts written in Old Church Slavic, and their texts were widely disseminated during the Middle Ages.

The Bogomils exhibit major Gnostic characteristics. The human soul is descended from the good god. But this human soul is always in danger of being claimed by the evil god, and for this reason the Word, the Logos, came to the earth. This is something quite essential; they refer to the Logos as being 'in the manifestation-body of Christ'. The Bogomils could not come to terms with the incarnation of the Logos in the corporeal body of Jesus. They call it a manifestation-body, and this concept is passed on, in part, to the Cathars. However, among the Cathars themselves there are various interpretations of this. The Bogomils wanted no hierarchical structure, no sacraments, no cult of saints, no relics, no icons, because these were all merely Satan's creations. They have only the Lord's Prayer and another form of the act of confession.

At the end of the eleventh century, during the twelfth century, and on into the thirteenth century, these groups—whether the Bogomils, the Waldenses, named for Peter Waldes, the Cathars, the Albigensians from Albi in France, or the Paulicians—all have in common that they live in a Manichaean mood. Good and evil are two principles of creation; evil can be overcome only in so far as the light mixes with it, and in so far as death is redemption. We can say that this was a counter-Church.

Among the people who connected deeply with anthroposophy during the twentieth century is a man who lived to be one hundred years old and who died in 1978. Déodat Roché of France is known today as the leading researcher of the Cathars. His famous book on the Cathars, previously available only in French, was published a few years ago in German.[11] Déodat Roché was a highly-respected lawyer who lived in Argues, a small town south of Carcassonne. Because he grew up in this land of the Cathars—it is only a day trip to Montségur, to Peyrepertuse, to Quéribus, and so forth—he had a very early connection to this history. Before Déodat Roché, little was known about the Cathars. In 1922, he had a conversation with Rudolf Steiner that lasted more than an hour. He never spoke about the content of the conversation, not to anyone at all! We can imagine that vast perspectives were discussed there—perhaps in relationship with the Cathars, perhaps not—for it is striking that Rudolf Steiner mentions the Cathars only rarely. He speaks about heretics, but he had this particular group very much in mind.

Déodat Roché held certain ideas about the Cathars based on his extensive research. Many things were accessible to him because of his profession. About the connections between the Gnostics, the Manichaeans and the Cathars, he wrote:

> In examining the connections among the Gnostics, the Manichaeans and the Cathars, we should not forget that all the old Mysteries ... flowed into Christianity through the instruction of Mani ... [We] must ... see that it was the archangel Michael who, after revealing himself in India as Indra, and in Persia as Mithra, was the leader of the Manichaean 'elect' and of the Catharic 'Christians'. It was Michael whose light, like a flashing sword, dispelled the dragon's darkness.[12]

At that time, the general situation in southern France—in Languedoc—was such that many streams came together there. We hear from Bernard of Clairvaux that around 1140 he suddenly received a report stating: There is a small sect in southern France, not far from Toulouse, with no founder, but with an enormous following, and they want nothing to do with the Church. Bernard of Clairvaux had the matter investigated, and it can be said with certainty that, from that moment on, life became increasingly more dangerous and turbulent for the Cathars and other so-called heretics who actually wanted something other than what they found in the Church. Even the nobility was part of this group. In fact, the nobility had a strong, anti-clerical inclination, in part because of the power and the greed of the Church at that time. Besides, the nobility of this region around Toulouse, Carcassonne and Foix were for the most part of West Gothic descent, a fact that left its stamp on this whole region in southern France—and which should not be underestimated. They disagreed with what was happening in the Church, but they did not put up a fight. For in their view, good cannot fight against evil; good can only become better so that—one might say—it infiltrates evil.

The Rituals of the Cathars

The Cathars organized themselves into groups called listeners, the *Auditores*. These were people who simply found the teachings interesting but carried no responsibilities. Then there were the faithful, the *Credentes*, who were the supporters. Beyond these were the people who had taken up the teachings as a personal path of schooling. They were the Perfect Ones, also known as the *Perfecti*, the *Parfaits*.

Over time, the Cathars developed various rituals. There were four levels. The first level, the so-called *Melioramentum*, was later the subject of slanderous attacks. It was merely a way for people to show reverence towards someone so highly developed that the Paraclete could live in him. At this level, the feelings of reverence were so strong in the participants that they bowed three times when they came upon such a person, called a *Perfectus*, a perfect one.

Then there was the *Apparellhamentum*. Once a month, the faithful gathered with the others for a public confession of sins before the community; they could participate if and when they wished. Absolution was given in the name of the community, based on the idea that only the community can carry the sins of the individual. This *Apparellhamentum* enraged the Church because it encroached on the confession. It was not a sin to marry and have children as long as a vow of chastity had not been taken; however, this vow was required if the highest level of the Cathars was to be achieved. This vow was always made in agreement with the spouse. The Cathars fully understood the necessity of rebirth, and thus they could not claim marriage should be forbidden. The path had to be prepared for souls to find their way again into another earthly incarnation.

The imparting of the *Paternoster* was a name given to the celebration of investiture. This happened in the middle of the novitiate when the man or woman was empowered to pray the Our Father for himself or herself. This praying of the Lord's Prayer is often called the *Traditio*.

Then came the *Consolamentum* which was like a spiritual baptism, a word ritual. The eldest took the Gospel and laid it on the head of the novice, and the other *Perfecti*, the 'Perfect Ones' who were present, laid their right hands on his shoulder. Then the eldest embraced the novice and gave him the kiss of peace. A woman was not embraced or kissed—that would have been contrary to the vow of chastity—but the Gospel was laid upon her shoulder. The ritual represented the understanding that the Paraclete, the Comforter, could begin to work in this person.

They did not lead a life apart; they lived fully within the community and practised various professions. They were also tutors for the nobility, and were generally welcomed by noble families, especially by the Counts of Foix. A member of this family, Esclarmonde de Foix, was even a Perfect One who was deeply associated with the destiny of Montségur. A small poem says:

Comme Esclarmonde,
L'astre de Montségur,
Muse Brémonde,
Tu éclaires la nuit![13]

Like Esclarmonde,
The star of Montségur,
Muse of Brémonde,
You illuminate the night.

The Extermination of the Cathars

The Cathars lived as weavers, herbalists, lay jurists; they were highly respected. Nevertheless, Pope Innocent III instigated the eradication of these people. He commissioned Simon de Montfort as military commander. This eradication might be thought of as an omen of the beast from the depths; it was very brutal with thousands upon thousands of Cathars murdered, most burned at the stake.

The remarkable thing was that the Cathars were not afraid, at least not outwardly, and they were probably quite steadfast inwardly. Only the *Perfecti*, the Perfect Ones, were burned at the stake. When these acts were carried out with some fairness, the believers could recant if they wished—but the persecutors were rarely fair. Still, when it came down to it, many went to the stake. They did not experience less pain from the fire than anyone else, but they said to themselves: The elements of light that live buried within me by the darkness of my corporeal nature will be liberated through this death by fire. On a pillar of light they find their way back on high. The pupils of Mani thought about it in this way: 'For even though they knew about asceticism as a means of releasing light from the human being while damaging the remaining light as little as possible, what mattered was raising up the freed light out of the sublunary world, and bringing it still further into the heights. To this end, the third messenger [Jesus after the resurrection] invokes the "Pillar of Glory", on which the elements of light can rise.'[14] Thus they went singing to the stake.

Although some of the Cathars lived in court circles, it is often said that they were opposed to art because they did not build churches, did not create sculptures, and because they themselves wore plain grey clothing even though they were skilful weavers. They were not opposed to art; however, art was not their task. For them, art was connected to the transformation of earthly substance. The Cathars wanted to free themselves from earthly substance because it was permeated by darkness. They felt more strongly and directly affected by language. Few of their writings remain; for the most part, their documents were burned, destroyed. However, two dogmatic treatises and two books of rituals survive, among them a translation of the New Testament in the Occitanic language of Languedoc—a wonderful language, according to the people who can read it—and the *Liber de duobis principiis* [Book of the two principles].[15]

The Troubadours in Southern France

Added to language were the elements of music and song. Many of the Cathars were quite musical. Troubadours were always welcome at courts sympathetic to the Cathars—not only those troubadours who brought news of the world and sang about adventure, but those who were more philosophically and religiously inclined. There were troubadours in this stream who were sympathetic to the Cathars—although they were not Perfect Ones, for that would have been contrary to the troubadour's calling. In the land of the Cathars, in Puivert, a little south of Carcassonne, there is a great castle in a wonderful landscape where they held what amounted to singing contests, competitions, tournaments, and so forth.

Here we think in particular of the famous troubadour Peire Vidal. He lived from about 1160 to 1205; he was born in Toulouse, and is believed to have died during a Crusade—in any case in Salonica. Toulouse suffered especially under the assault of the papacy led by Simon de Montfort. The battle cry of the papacy was, 'Kill them all! God will recognize his children.' Whole cities were laid waste, every citizen murdered. Peire Vidal took up various themes that we find in Manichaeism. He developed a particular style called *Trobar Clus*, the dark style, the hidden style. He lived a somewhat unworldly life, and listened to what he experienced as a calling. He then attempted to reproduce this in his songs. Approximately forty poems and thirteen songs by him have come down to us.

At the end of this period comes Peire Kardenal (1195–1275). He had a very interesting life. Having escaped from Toulouse, he worked as secretary to Count Raymond VI of Toulouse and fled along with the Cathars. His songs are often critical of the times. Three of his works remain. I cite the following lines by Peire Kardenal as a small example of how religious and philosophical these troubadour songs could be. The last two lines unite belief with knowledge.

Das Kreuz zu nehmen sei bereit.
O pflücke dir die süße Frucht
Und bleib' getreu an Seiner Seit'!
Denn Christus ist des Wissens Frucht.[16]

Prepare yourself the cross to take.
O pluck you now the sweetened fruit
And faithful be for His own sake!
Since Christ Himself is knowing's fruit.

William IX of Aquitaine is regarded as the first troubadour. He was a great collector of songs, but he was also quite creative in his own right. He lived from 1071 to 1126, and is credited with being the first troubadour known by name.

Mystical Experiences of the Troubadours

Of course, like the *Minnesänger*, the troubadours were concerned with *minne*, the adoration of the beloved woman which rises to quite mystical spheres. Ideally, the singer, the troubadour, who celebrated this woman in song, could fill this ideal image of the woman so completely with his own striving for the Sophia that the image was able to stand alone, whereupon he experienced it as his counterpart. He experienced it as the woman, the beloved, the Sophia of his own soul. He clothed it in poetry, accompanied it with music, but quite often these were enormous mystical experiences.

Many troubadours in southern France experienced the strong contrasts between light and dark, withering and blooming, joy and suffering, and this streams through their songs. Of course, many superficial comparisons can be drawn between the songs of the troubadours and the songs of the German *Minnesänger*, but their different qualities become quite striking when the comparisons are more closely drawn.

Among the troubadours were a few women, referred to as *trobairitz*. For example, there was Beatrice, Countess of Dia, a noblewoman who wrote many poems set to music by troubadours, and who set some to music herself.

In fact, the troubadour culture was extraordinarily interesting. Many troubadours wandered from countryside to countryside, from castle to castle; many stayed in one place. But we never hear that they required an interpreter. Another kind of understanding existed at that time, not only through the language, but also through the music itself.

After-death Experiences of the Cathars

There is a difference between the Cathars and the troubadours in the world after death, even though their lives were often spent side-by-side. The Cathars frequently suffered a painful death at the stake. They entered the spiritual world and saw that their efforts were actually focused on experiencing Christianity in a more inward way. Among the few remarks Rudolf Steiner made about the Cathars, there is quite an impressive statement during the medical course for young doctors. In that course, he describes how the souls of the Cathars who had sought to become more inward in that incarnation now had a different kind of access to the secrets in the spiritual world, as well as to the people there. In 1924, he makes the following statement about people born at the turn of that century, hence the young doctors: 'We can say with a clear conscience that all those people who sit here are reborn heretical souls.—Now, you must not take this as a compliment.—They are heretical souls who experienced a strong urge between death and a new birth to creep into all the places in the human being and, in so doing, subconsciously made an enormous riddle of the human being.'[17] Of course, they then become doctors so they can solve the riddle. With the help of musical experiences, however, troubadours were able to find other paths into the spiritual world. They are still seeking the Sophia, the 'Beloved' of every human being.[18]

Lecture 6

The Camino to Santiago de Compostela and the Original Form of the European Mysteries

Manfred Schmidt-Brabant

A great pilgrimage path must be viewed in connection with the country and the continent through which it passes. Here in Spain, we stand upon an ancient piece of the earth. According to old maps drawn according to clairvoyant insights—and to which Rudolf Steiner also referred—this place already existed in the Lemurian time. Curiously enough, a small strip of land in North America—the present-day California—also existed in the Lemurian period. People familiar with both Spain and California are always struck by the similarity of their landscapes; and it is not by chance that California was settled by Spaniards, so that we find there names like Los Angeles, San Francisco, Santa Barbara, and so forth.

We know that a harbour like Càdiz was already a busy trading port at the end of the Atlantean period. Much later, around 1200 BC, the Old Testament refers to Càdiz as one of the most important trade and distribution centres. In Spain, there are after-effects of two great Mystery realms: the Jupiter Mysteries in northern Spain and the Venus Mysteries in the south. Both of them worked their way into the spiritual history of pre-Christian Spain and, especially, Christian Spain.

Spain looked quite different at that time. In Roman times, it was said that a squirrel could hop from Biscay to Gibraltar without touching the ground. Mighty forests covered the countryside through which the Romans built their first roads. Ancient, sacred Atlantean spirituality lived in these forests. Rudolf Steiner speaks again and again about this spirituality in which people in Lemuria and on into Atlantis felt the landscape as part of the constitution of their own being. They did not say: Here I am with my body, and nature is out there. Instead they experienced body and nature as one. Rudolf Steiner makes note of the fact that remnants of this are preserved in Australia, for example—which was part of the old Lemurian continent—by its indigenous inhabitants, the Aborigines. He called them the very last Lemurians. We know that they sense a source of water a hundred kilometres away, or that they sense far distant food as if it belongs to their body. This same experience is found with North American Indians. The song of an Indian chief, astonished by the fact that white men wanted to buy the land, says: How can someone buy the land? It is our brother! The wind cannot be bought either; it, too, is our brother! Nor the water, for it is our sister! In this way, up through the nineteenth century, this Atlantean attitude lived on in Native Americans in North America. Nature is brother and sister. Such an attitude also resounds in the Camino and works through it into the situation in Europe.

The Grave of James

In Christian times, word spread throughout Europe, followed by waves of emotion: The grave of James has been discovered, along with the bones of the Apostle. This was some time between 812 and 830. It is astonishing how this report immediately inspired pilgrimages. We can document that pilgrims arrive as early as 844—Norman pilgrims, pilgrims from Frisia. Recently, Islamic source materials have been discovered in which we read that pilgrims immediately streamed in from Nubia and the Coptic (Red) Sea.

Which James was this then? People at that time felt that it was James, the brother of our Lord, our brother and the Lord's brother. Today, biblical criticism says that this is wrong! There were three individuals called James: James the Elder, James the Younger, and James, the brother of our Lord. Modern biblical criticism states that only James the Elder can be connected with Spain, a view already noted in the *Legenda Aurea* in the thirteenth century. Even Emil Bock struggles intensively with this question, but has a number of serious problems with it. He says that this kind of quibbling interpretation of the life of Jesus—who was related? who was the brother?—is actually only 150 years old, and emerged from Protestant-Evangelical biblical criticism. Even when this more recent approach is used, the Gospels are by no means clear. We come across 'the most difficult ... personal-biographical conundrums'.[1]

Now let us consider the ninth century. There was no learned knowledge of the Bible! There were few manuscripts of the Bible or manuscripts of the New Testament in the monasteries; and not all the monks could read. People heard the stories and did not differentiate between 'the Elder, the Younger, the brother'; what remained with them was 'James, the brother of our Lord'. And so these feelings poured forth that 'the bones of the brother of Jesus had been found!' The persistence of this image was confirmed for me by a renowned historian who writes even today that the grave of James, the brother of our Lord, is in Compostela.[2] This impulse works that strongly in European history! At the time, something else was added that is not in the New Testament, but is instead part of the tradition of early Christian legends. James, the brother of our Lord, looked so much like Him that pilgrims went to Jerusalem to experience the image of our Lord in James.[3]

Peter of Compostela

In one of the karma lectures, Rudolf Steiner prepares his remarks about Compostela very carefully and precisely. To begin with, he relates how remnants of the Mysteries were active for a long time after the Mystery of Golgotha, and how the Mystery path slowly retreats, beginning in the fourth and fifth centuries. Eventually, the path transforms into 'lofty centres of knowledge'[4] that existed until the eighth century, and it is cultivated as a teaching into the fourteenth century. Having laid this groundwork, he comes to speak directly of Petrus of Compostela, or Peter of Compostela, apparently the last straggler who still 'cultivated . . . a living Mystery-related Christianity'.[5] Those around him cultivated it with him. Thus we have the impression from this whole context that a school of living, Mystery-related Christianity still existed here.

Now comes the question: Which Petrus was this? There are a number of them. The best known is Bishop Petrus of Compostela. He was bishop between 985 and 1002. Then there is a bishop in the next century who is soon removed by the Pope because the great conflicts between Rome and Compostela are already beginning. And then there was a third, Magister Petrus of Compostela, some time around the year 1154, thus another century later. A text is attributable to him, *De consolatione rationis* [On the consolation of reason]; this text clearly dates from the twelfth century. Rudolf Steiner does not say that the Petrus of Compostela who taught a Mystery-related Christianity authored a text, but speaks instead of the teachings of Petrus of Compostela. He also does this with Dionysius the Areopagite who always taught by word of mouth. When the Church choked off everything connected to the Mysteries, and when Compostela came to an end, Magister Petrus, perhaps one of the last of this school, wrote down all of these teachings.

Rudolf Steiner describes in moving terms what lived in Petrus of

Compostela. This Petrus spoke of the goddess Natura as the 'Helper of Christ'.[6] She first leads the pupil, the soul, into the elements, from the elements into the planetary world, and from the planetary world into the starry world. Then seven goddesses from the starry world appear to the soul of the pupil, blessing and inspiring it. Natura leads the soul to seven goddesses: Grammar, Dialectic, Rhetoric, Arithmetic, Geometry, Astronomy and Music—in this ascending sequence. Grammar (the lowest), Dialectic and Rhetoric—the trivium; then the quadrivium, consisting of Arithmetic, Geometry, Astronomy and the highest level a person could develop at that time, Music.

Of course, that Grammar was not at all what we think of today as the grammar painstakingly learned in school. Grammar was the inner sense of the speech of mankind, the first step of spirituality through which the human being reveals himself. Dialectic was not argumentation, but was instead the teaching of the secrets whereby things that are contradictory nevertheless belong together. The seven liberal arts were taught as the path to the Christ-being.

Rudolf Steiner notes that in Spain, France and Italy there were many such esoteric schools where a Mystery-related Christianity still lived. Even though the great ancient Mysteries that shaped cultures had come to an end, initiation never ceased! Always and forever, right up to the present time, there has been initiation of pupils by teachers.

Being a Pilgrim as a Way of Life

Now we will look at the background that helps us to understand what happened when a person became a pilgrim at that time. Today, we think abstractly that a person would undertake this to receive absolution or a blessing, to save his soul by making a pilgrimage to holy relics. This is not the case. Being a pilgrim was a way of life. A person became a pilgrim in the same way that he became a monk by entering a monastery. It was a complete separation from home and family, from everything; the likelihood of returning was perhaps one in two. Of every two pilgrims who went to Compostela, one returned! It is a known fact that hundreds of thousands of dead lie along these pilgrimage paths from Europe to Compostela.

The way of life at that time was strongly permeated by a completely different relationship to nature. Into the thirteenth century, people experienced nature as a part of their own being. When a person moved through nature, he was moving through his own soul. Thus, those people who travelled the pilgrimage path felt less intensely, but nevertheless deeply, what Parzival had experienced as he went the path of nature initiation. Outwardly, there were certainly the dangers of death, the strains of a passage from central or northern Germany to Compostela that took perhaps a year and a half. But people were not afraid of this mortal danger, because anyone who died on the pilgrim path was saved. People thought: What good does my body do me if my soul is lost? That was still strong in their consciousness. A completely different relationship to the spiritual world existed than we can imagine today. Thus, external mortal danger was not the frightening thing on a pilgrimage. Much more important was the fact that many sorts of inner trials took place. A mortal danger for the soul was present when the pilgrim met these various trials and temptations along the way—because in leaving home, he had separated himself from its supporting forces. When a person lived in such a small medieval city or village community, its social life supported and carried him. Desires, drives, passions were suppressed by the regular church life, the festivals, the socializing. On the road, he tore himself loose from all of this; he was free as a bird. Now all the previously repressed desires, drives and passions rose up in him, and he had to struggle against them. We see this struggle depicted in the capitals of hundreds of columns found in places from Vézelay to Compostela. In these capitals, clairvoyant artists captured what the souls were undergoing. Art historians speak of demons or other kinds of figures they cannot explain.

Mary Magdalene

This path was characterized by a peculiar polarity. The path started in Sainte Madeleine at Vézelay, where there was an abbey, already old in the ninth century when the pilgrimage path actually began. There, according to people in the ninth century, lay the bones of Mary Magdalene. Here we come across the great secret of Mary Magdalene. She actually plays the main role in the *Pistis Sophia*. Christ gives preference to her before all the Apostles, and says of her, 'thou art she whose heart is more directed to the kingdom of heaven than all thy brothers [the Apostles]'. He calls her 'the blessed beyond all women', the 'beauty in her speech', 'thou (all blessed) Pleroma [fullness] who will be glorified among all generations'; he calls her 'thou blessed one who wilt inherit the whole kingdom of light', 'the all-blessed one', the 'Light-Purity', and so forth. This goes so far that the

Apostles complain that He continually gives preference to Mary Magdalene over them.

We have already taken note of the fact that historical personalities are also bearers of great cosmic principles. Mary Magdalene was a historical personality at the time of Christ Jesus described in the Gospels. We must never forget that the Gospels are initiation writings and not journalism. Rudolf Steiner relates that Mary Magdalene was not just an earthly personality, but also the bearer of the sentient soul of humanity. He notes that the esoteric school of Dionysius the Areopagite taught that Mary Magdalene is the sentient soul of Christ Jesus.[7] Even though this was not presented through the conceptual words we use today, it lived deeply in the imaginations of that time.

When the Camino began, there were two leaders of esoteric Christianity, Mary Magdalene and James. Both Mary Magdalene and James were considered figures who lead people along the right path. Mary Magdalene, the sentient soul, made a connection between people on the pilgrimage path and the world. James, the intellectual soul, led people within. We go from Mary Magdalene to James; we go with Mary Magdalene into the interior of the soul, into the brother of our Lord.

There are legends that say Mary Magdalene went to France after the death of Christ. This would not be so odd—that area was also part of the Roman Empire, and there was considerable traffic back and forth. Today, she still plays a role in esotericism and in occultism that is difficult to grasp. In past decades, she has been placed in a rather peculiar light because the rabbinical scholars in Jerusalem say it is utterly impossible for Jesus to have been unmarried. They say that would have been such a breach of all Jewish law that He would have been expelled. Furthermore, they say He was married to Mary Magdalene. And that has led to a flood of scorn and derision. Salcia Landmann writes: The whole of Christianity is based on what? On the testimony of a whore who allegedly saw the Resurrected One, and everyone repeats her testimony![8]—The hatred is still there. We must examine these things, otherwise we will not understand what is rumbling below the surface of the present.

The situation was completely different at that time. We have to take into account that many knowledgeable individuals from esoteric schools travelled the Camino; they were fully aware that human beings accompanied Mary Magdalene through the world of elements into the interior, to James, the brother of our Lord. These paths were not accidental; they were ancient star paths, star routes. What we mean by this is the following. Although the earth rotates, every place on the earth corresponds to a part of the firmament of the fixed stars. It is as though the phantom of the physical earth contains the reflection of the starry heavens, so that routes, areas, places correspond to particular places in the heavens. In the *Chymical Wedding*, Christian Rosenkreutz climbs into a large globe—Rudolf Steiner even speaks of this in his commentary—and from inside this globe, he looks through the earth and sees an array of tiny lights; he sees how the starry heavens really live there in the earth. Thus we can understand that the path to Compostela was the path of an ancient star knowledge.

Star Routes

Two years ago a book appeared, *Sternstraßen der Vorzeit* [Star routes of antiquity] by Heinz Kaminsky, founder of the observatory in Bochum and director of the Institute for Future Research. In it, he observes, 'It can be demonstrated that, at least 4000 years before Christ, all inter-regional cultic centres in Megalithic times were joined in a network.' 'There are three great star routes. The first leads through northern Spain, from Cape Finisterre through Compostela; the second runs through Britanny; and the third went through the south of England.'[9] He continues, 'It is certain that long before the later Christian pilgrimages to the grave of the Apostle James, the spiritual leaders and wise men of the Megalithic peoples of Middle and West Europe travelled to this important cultic location in the north-west of the Iberian peninsula, known today as Santiago de Compostela.'[10] He shows how Vézelay lies on another north-south star route; Chartres, Troyes, the Odilienberg, and also Glastonbury in southern England—which we mentioned earlier—all lie on one of the great routes. He depicts it as more of a network, and does not actually think that they rest on a straight line. As I have already pointed out, we must understand these star routes organically, in a broader and narrower sense, but definitely from this point of view.

There are hundreds of statues of pilgrims in Europe, every one with a staff in his hand. Heinz Kaminsky had these staffs measured, then compared the length of the staff with the height of the pilgrim. He consistently arrived at the same ratios. He says, 'It is nevertheless a mystery that these pilgrim staffs'—later deviations aside—'were clearly conceptualized in olden times as having a particular relationship to the length of the body.'[11] This is understandable because these pilgrim staffs—and this includes the walking-sticks of itinerant journeyman in the last century—were not only for support or for fending off wild animals; they brought the person into a relationship with the conditions of the etheric geography.

For many reasons, the star route of northern Spain was the most important of the three routes. Those who travelled along the star route as far as Cape Finisterre had the experience: Here is the end of the earth! He arrived at the same situation that the modern pupil faces when standing at the abyss: Here is the end of the sensory world, the abyss! And if I am able to comprehend it, the spiritual world approaches me from the other side. That is the typical experience at Cape Finisterre. The experience is completely different on the second star route that reaches the sea at the great stone alignments in Carnac. Standing there, we have the impression: Something comes to meet me here; prehistoric times rise up here; what speaks from old Atlantis enters into Europe here. And the northernmost star route was always experienced in this way: How are the spiritual and the physical in balance? Thus completely different mysteries are to be found there. Along the route to Compostela, however, the experience was the path the person took, step by step, from the sensory world up to the threshold of the spiritual world.

The Path of Nature Initiation

If this were not true, it would make no sense to say those who failed to reach the ocean failed to make the pilgrimage. Compostela was a final, decisive juncture on an inner spiritual path that was simultaneously a path of nature initiation.

Rudolf Steiner describes the steps.[12] The first two steps involve the person removing himself from the familiar surroundings of his home. He goes through the senses, through the temperaments. If someone lived in a small Bavarian or north German village, his senses were bound up with his surroundings; he lived in them. In the broadest sense of the word, his senses lived in the social milieu. Now he tears himself way. Now he has only the route, and he must experience the reality of the senses, the temperaments. Then comes the next step. Starting from Vézelay, he passes through the elements—air, earth, fire, water, in that order, at least as they were experienced. The entire passage through the Burgundian hill country to the foothills of the Pyrenees is the path through a world in which the sylphs are the dominant factor, and air Mysteries of all sorts play a role. Then the path ascends sharply—it is a steep passage that rises a thousand metres from bottom to top. Here the pilgrim encounters the world of the earth, the gnomes. Even today, anyone who opens his eyes just a bit can have the experience of being in the mountains, passing through ravines, and being addressed (so to speak) from out of the rock. Once on the other side, the path descends towards Pamplona, towards Eunate, and the oven of the *meseta* plains open up, scorching hot, without any water! The world of the salamanders emerges. Once past León, after this has been endured, the refreshing humidity of the Galician highlands begins. The undines come there from the ocean; the experience of freshness, of water, is clearly to be had there.

Rudolf Steiner says that the planetary experience emerges in these elements because the planets are mirrored in air, earth, fire and water. Jupiter and Venus are mirrored in the air, Saturn and Mercury in the earth; the sun and Mars live in the fire beings, and the moon lives in water. At that time, all of this was a completely living experience. Then came the moment when the pupil was led through the inner experience of planetary processes to the 'Pillars of Hercules'.[13] Gibraltar is also called the Pillars of Hercules, but we do not need to go to Gibraltar in order to experience the Pillars of Hercules. These are the two pillars called Jachin and Boaz in Freemasonry; the pillar of strength and the pillar of wisdom, the pillar of the red blood and the pillar of the blue-red blood. The person was led to the limits of physical nature. He experiences what constitutes his physical nature; but he also experiences how his true human existence is formed by uniting these two pillars—blood pillars, pillars of the forces that constitute the world. Through beauty, piety and love, the human being unites the pillar of wisdom and the pillar of strength, also of magic. We will again find these three—wisdom, beauty and strength—in connection with the Templars, except then it is beauty that leads from a cosmos of wisdom to a cosmos of love. Strength was always understood to mean the new and future relationship of human beings to one another. And after someone had stood at the Pillars of Hercules, the ocean of the fixed stars emerged before them.

This was actually the substance of the Camino. What nature wants to say to the individual was experienced through Mary Magdalene; and James, who appeared inwardly, asked: How must you react to this experience, inwardly and outwardly in your soul? Rudolf Steiner says that the guide along this path was the 'goddess Natura';[14] this gigantic female figure is still present today. The young people around Rudolf Steiner were often rather impudent. A small group of them walked around Dornach with him, and one of them asked, 'Doctor, why do you always carry an umbrella with you? As a clairvoyant, surely you know whether it's going to rain!' This young person was quite surprised by his own temerity—the story is handed down by the person who asked the question—but Rudolf Steiner turned, laughing kindly, and said, 'I have explained to you that Natura is a goddess, hence a woman; and you never know with a woman what mood she'll be in next!' A humorous answer, but one that also goes to the very heart of the matter.

This etheric path—because that is its true nature—was always experienced as Mary Magdalene; the prayerful attitude—which arises inwardly—of self-discipline, of self-control, of piety was experienced as James. All this was interwoven with the souls of the dead which worked ever more intensely, interwoven with the dead whose nature—ether body, astral body—remained interconnected with the Camino.

This whole route also resounded and echoed with songs and music. Even the prayers of the people lingered there at that time. That was certainly what the clairvoyant artists saw. They looked into the Akashic Record of this Camino and created it in stone or on canvas.

Compostela and Innocent III

If we want to understand the real spirituality of this route, we must consider its earliest phase, not the later symptoms of decadence that evoke a completely false image. The early period in the ninth and tenth centuries, from 840 on, is the era of the hidden Mystery, when the first pilgrims are documented and when a very small church stood in Compostela on the site of ancient ruins left by the Romans. During a second phase (from 1000 to 1200), the Mystery reveals itself quite clearly to those who want to see it. The *Codex Calixtinus* dates from 1139; the two great tympanums are created in the same century—Vézelay around 1135, and the Pórtico de la Gloria in 1188. The second of these already leads into the third phase, 1200–1400. Grail literature appears as an outcome of the Mystery. It is no longer the Mystery itself. That has gone elsewhere. This literature creates a way to approach it for anyone whose heart is open. Around 1400 at the latest, all this begins to fall into utter decadence. The whole thing becomes a carnival sideshow.

We must be aware that a Mystery battle is taking place behind the scenes, one that is very important for that time. The teachers in the Mysteries at Compostela were thoroughly aware of their position; like Peter, they called themselves 'bishops of the Apostolic See' and 'prelates of the whole world'. They were justifiably conscious that the centre of mystical Christianity was here. In Compostela, the so-called Mozarabic ritual was cultivated, a Christian cult full of spirituality that arose in Moorish Spain. Interference from the Roman Church begins in the eleventh century. Everything spiritual is repressed, and there is a renewal of the battle between the official Church of Constantine and mystical Christianity. The Mozarabic ritual is forbidden and the Roman ritual is imposed; a bishop is excommunicated because he continues to call himself 'bishop of the Apostolic See'.

The following comments are not intended to offend anyone's sensibilities. We all know that the Catholic Church is a world unto itself. Francis of Assisi, Thomas Aquinas, Albertus Magnus all belong to this world. Many Popes belong as well, including the terrible Innocent III (1198–1216), who had the innocent Cathars so brutally persecuted. Like Justinian, he is a man full of hatred towards everything spiritual. The eradication of everything reminiscent of the great Mysteries at Compostela is essentially traceable to him.

It is characteristic of Innocent III that he set out very specific tasks for the Catholic Church. We could ask, just as Rudolf Steiner did, 'What, in fact, is the task taken on by the papacy after the great epoch I just discussed—the tenth, eleventh and twelfth centuries? What has been the mission of the papacy since that time? The mission of the papacy in the Catholic Church is essentially to prevent Europe from recognizing the reality of the Christ. It is a matter of more or less consciously founding a Church which had as its task a complete misunderstanding of the true Christian impulse, preventing the true impulse of Christianity from becoming known among the people.' Allow me to repeat: even after this period, the Church still had many true saints, true knowers of Christ, but it also pursued this mission of the organized Church. 'Europeans have accepted a Christianity that is no Christianity, and one of the significant results of this is the absolute impossibility of speaking today about the Christian Mysteries. There is nothing that can be done about this; lengthy preparations will be required to make it possible to speak of these Mysteries again.'[15]

We will be able to experience the true history of the Mysteries only if we have the courage, again and again, to approach inwardly the abysses that open up in this history and to face them fearlessly. This does not mean that what we say about the Christ today is false; but it is still not what is most essential. Even today, a tremendous number of images and representations live in all of us, for we are the children of this age and children of the education we have received. These images and representations in no way signify the Christ, but we take them for the Christ. Naturally, anyone who characterizes the destruction of the Mystery impulses as the work of the organized Church is attacked today.

The Church was able to destroy all of the esoteric secrets that lived externally, but it could not prevent clairvoyant artists from preserving in the portals, tympanums and capitals a vast amount of material from the esoteric secrets. After all, the imaginations of people had impressed themselves into the ether. But from the thirteenth and fourteenth centuries on, nature's slate was full, and the ability of even the clairvoyant artist was stilled.

Charlemagne

Why did Rudolf Steiner mention Charlemagne in connection with the Grail Mysteries but not describe his task? The history of Charlemagne is described in the *Pseudo-Turpin Chronicle.* It has been established philologically that Archbishop Turpin, Charlemagne's contemporary, is not the author of this work. It was written late; hence it is referred to as 'Pseudo-Turpin'. We read in it how James appeared to Charlemagne in a clairvoyant vision, how he showed him the star route, and said:

> The star route you saw in heaven means you will go to Galicia at the head of a vast army and, after you, all peoples will make pilgrimages there until the end of time. I will help you and, as compensation for your efforts, I will secure Paradise for you from God, and your name will remain in human memory as long as the world exists.[16]

Then there is a wonderful depiction of how Charlemagne conquers the Moors, how he comes to Compostela, how he goes to the ocean and thrusts his spear into the ocean, into the Leviathan, into the abyss, above which lies only the starry world of the spirit.

These are images that people at that time naturally understood much better than we do today. Rudolf Steiner frequently mentions the way of experiencing then that cannot be communicated today because the spiritual world was much more real than the physical world for people at that time. Today we can say exoterically: the Camino would not have existed without Charlemagne. The fact that the power of Charlemagne held back Islam is not only a military question but a spiritual one as well. Rudolf Steiner put it this way: '... we must be conscious that a man like Charlemagne was significant simply because of his personality, simply because he appeared exoterically in Europe.'[17]

Rudolf Steiner says the same thing about Bernard of Clairvaux who worked simply through his etheric aura. Behind the church in Vézelay, there is a high slope on top of which Bernard of Clairvaux stood to preach the Crusade. Hundreds of people were inspired by him. Standing atop the slope today, we realize only the few people standing nearby could have understood anything that was said. The slope drops down into the valley below, and no matter how loudly he might have shouted, the sermon would have been completely impossible to hear at a distance. The effect was not dependent on the physical words. He worked so strongly through his etheric aura that even those who stood furthest away were still affected by it.[18] This happened four hundred years after Charlemagne. We must imagine that people perceived through Charlemagne something of the spirit beings connected to the ruling houses. Today this is no longer the situation. During the time of the Merovingian dynasty, significant spirit beings—not only angels but archangelic beings—were connected with such dynasties for hundreds and hundreds of years. Then they separated themselves off. The spirit departed, leaving the last Merovingians like helpless children. Afterwards, the Carolingians arise with Charles Martel, and once again powerful spirit beings connect themselves with them. They radiate through an individual personality, creating the charisma of such an emperor, and people saw this. In an introductory chapter of his second book about the Testament of Adam, Andrew Welburn gives an extraordinarily clear description of how people saw the radiant aura of a ruler from afar.[19]

Charlemagne worked in such a way that people saw him still active in the spiritual world after his death. Rudolf Steiner relates that Charlemagne rides with his twelve paladins through the spiritual world, and there, in the real spiritual world, he continues the deeds of Christ. He is a likeness of Christ with the Twelve Apostles.[20] As such, he becomes the protector of the Camino and the Grail Mysteries that are bound up with the Camino.

The Seventh Step of Initiation

It is a great enigma that the Grail Mysteries are founded deep in the stillness of the wilderness, while at the same time this pilgrimage route is opened up into Europe and a flood of people begin to travel it. Those who had been prepared receive directions. It is not yet determined that this took place in Compostela; it could also have been on the route to

Finisterre. However, I assume that those who had made themselves Cathars in the Mystery School at Compostela, who had gone through this nature initiation, received an indication of how to find the Grail when they returned.

It is strange how people speak the truth, and then turn against it. In 1951, a book by the renowned Swedish art historian, Ringbom, appeared with the title *Gralstempel und Paradies* [The Grail Temple and Paradise]. In this book, he cites Albrecht von Scharfenberg, who clearly says, 'Those who have been in Galicia know San Salvador and Salvaterre.' Ringbom continues, 'In earlier times it was considered an established fact that the province of Galicia in Spain is meant here and, generally speaking, the Grail saga is usually connected with Spain.'[21] In 1951, he still does not know about the Camino and Compostela, otherwise he would have mentioned them; he writes only about the province of Galicia. Then, however, he goes on to assert: 'It is not Galicia, but Cilicia in Turkey; that's where the Grail is!'[22] He belongs to that large group of people who do not want to see what stands clearly before their eyes.

Those who had been prepared learned in Compostela where they could find the Grail, particularly during these first two centuries. Like a portable measuring tool, the staff made it possible for pilgrims to have a connection with the activity of the etheric geography. We find this staff again in the so-called Abacus of the Grand Master of the Templars who carried a staff of office upon which were inscribed secret measurements.

The sea, the ocean, belongs inevitably to the pilgrimage path. The oyster shell in which the pearl is created is just another symbol for the Grail. We have heard it mentioned in the 'Song of the Pearl', and it is found throughout medieval iconography—the pearl is the Logos, or the ego that has received the Logos. Those who wore the shell on their hats expressed consciously or unconsciously: I want to become a bearer of the Logos. And just as the oyster labours in pain to bring forth the pearl when a grain of sand is inserted into it and it encases the grain with nacre—this may or may not be biologically and zoologically completely correct—so too does the human being create the Logos in himself through stress and pain and self-denial.

When all this had been completed, those who were sent even further on the way knew: Now comes the seventh step. We have gone through the senses, through the temperaments, through the elements, through the planets; we have stood inwardly at the pillar of the blood—both the red and the blue-red; we have perceived the heaven of the fixed stars, the ocean of the spiritual world. That is six steps. Now we arrive at the seventh step: We want to take up the Christ into our own ego while, at the same time, the Cosmic Christ emerges from the cosmos that we have experienced and enters into the inmost part of the human being.

Manes and Klingsor

It was a fact that the route of nature initiation first travelled by Parzival had left its traces. When a great initiate moves through nature, he not only has nature experiences with the elemental beings, the nature daimons, with planets, and so forth; he also leaves an impression on nature itself.

After the incarnation of Manes, a great spiritual conference takes place in which Manes participates. In connection with this, Rudolf Steiner calls him '... a sublime emissary of the Christ'.[23] In preparation for the consciousness soul, this sublime messenger of the Christ-being enters into the Parzival incarnation. He is the great Sun initiate. When he passes through nature, the beings of nature receive his imprint. The result is something people can still experience today. When travelling through the Pyrenees, people are strangely moved. Why? Rudolf Steiner says there are Grail elemental beings everywhere in this area.[24] They descend from the slopes of the Pyrenees, and they can be found in the mountains of Spain. Parzival, and those who came after him, impressed upon nature the character of the Grail, the mood of the Grail.

This was the inner question addressed to the pilgrims: You are travelling to Compostela. What will you wish for? Are you prepared to perceive the Christ-permeated elemental beings in the nature that surrounds you? Do you allow them to speak to you? Do you attune your soul inwardly through prayer and piety, through overcoming the drives and passions that arise in you, so that these Grail elemental beings are able to speak to you?

The routes, especially the one from Vézelay to Compostela (but the others as well), are visible, spiritual, Christian arteries in the Mystery landscape of Europe. Today, much of this may be obscured, especially if we travel by car. But I know that there are still stretches of silence on the Camino where suddenly a whisper of this is perceptible; and I know that others experience it, too. Many people have experiences they cannot explain without some knowledge of the spiritual background. They have experienced elements of a nature initiation. Naturally, this will become more and more obscured in the future.

When we touch upon this theme, we must also refer to another one.

Klingsor has left his traces behind, too. All occultists know for a fact that one of the greatest of his plagues has spread from his centre of activity into our own time. The Mafia and organized crime originated in Sicily. Today it is spreading throughout the whole world. Criminal behaviour can mean that someone acts out of passion or greed. However, abstract intellectuality used to organize the instinctual nature of the human being—that is the effect of Klingsor in the world. He, too, has built roads through Europe—but they are roads of evil.

The Mystery Countenance of Europe

Among the many riddles connected with Compostela is the fact that James is the patron saint of alchemists. A well-known professor of chemistry who also writes about alchemy says, 'Even today, in our own time, alchemists make pilgrimages to Compostela to receive inspiration for their laboratory work.'[25] Basilius Valentinus, the great alchemist, went to Compostela to fulfil a vow. He returns with so much alchemical knowledge that it was, as he writes, 'to the fame and credit'[26] of his monastery. It is known that alchemists called their work either the 'Milky Way' or the 'Path to Compostela'.

The substance of the Mysteries took shape out of the cosmos at the same time as the earth, when the first human configurations came into existence. In Lemuria, the whole earth was a Mystery site. Lemuria was a Mystery continent. Gods and human beings were interwoven, and the human being was so connected with nature that he moved mountains, he formed nature with his will. The human being was a powerful nature magician. Then, in Atlantis, this contracts. The great planetary regions are formed—a region of the Mars Mysteries, of the Venus Mysteries or of the Jupiter Mysteries, as in Spain. All of northern Spain was the realm of the Jupiter Mysteries; all of southern Spain was the realm of the Venus Mysteries. Only gradually then was there further condensation so that distinct Mystery places are formed—limited areas like the Odilienberg—encompassing a few square kilometres.

This means that the earth, quite apart from all its geological processes, develops a perceptible Mystery form. The hierarchies cause the earth to have a physiognomy, a Mystery countenance. This Mystery countenance—and we want to speak only of Europe now—is divided into the west, the middle, and the east. Each of these regions suggests something human. Thus, in Western Europe—and, above all, in Spain—we have a connection with the region of the human head. In the direction of England, this transforms into what human hands are; and then towards France, into what the human larynx is. Then we arrive in Central Europe. We have the heart Mysteries in Central Europe; the Mysteries of the breath in the direction of Italy; and in the direction of Scandinavia, around the region of the Baltic Sea, we have the Mysteries of the etheric backbone. In the East, it passes over more into the realm of the metabolism. This becomes less clear from Russia down to Greece. At the Christmas meeting of 1923, Rudolf Steiner describes how Europe is really separated from Asia spiritually by a mighty wall that goes from the Urals to the Black Sea; he says this wall holds back everything connected with old, decadent pleroma experiences still found in Asia, everything connected with partially black or grey shamanism. It is a wall that makes it possible to create a European culture in Europe based on thinking, on the Mysteries. And so he says, 'The whole of European culture is a gift of the European Mysteries.'[27] These three star routes radiate into this configuration of Europe—into the head organization, into the middle, into the metabolic organization. The most important of these star routes is the one to Compostela, a route that leads to Finisterre in one direction, and through northern Spain to the Pyrenees in the other.

The Centre of Inspiration at the Extern Stones

Rudolf Steiner describes a mighty centre of inspiration within this organism of the Mysteries that dates back to primeval times. It is in the spiritual world above the region of Detmold and Paderborn, at a place where the Extern Stones can be found below. From that place radiated what 'the Nordic archangel of the region received as its mission', 'the mission of the most sublime spirits'. This was long 'before the Celtic folk spirit, as the Celtic archangelic being, had constructed a new centre in the Grail castle'. Then the dissolution of the great, old centre of inspiration from the primeval past takes place, 'the centre which later surrendered its principal activity to the centre of the Holy Grail'.[28] The population in northern Spain came from the Baltic Sea, from the region of the Baltic Mysteries. The Suebi moved during the folk migrations to the area of Compostela; the Goths moved from the south of Sweden to northern Spain. They brought with them in their blood, in their traditions, in their etheric bodies, what had lived among the people in these Baltic Mysteries; they brought what had come from this great centre of inspiration, as well as what had come from that powerful hierarchical being that Rudolf Steiner calls the 'Sea Dragon'. Out of the North Sea, this 'Sea Dragon' forms the Baltic Sea into three gulfs—the Baltic, the Finnish and the Bothnian gulfs. It is this being that inspired Europe, and made people who were connected with it fully clairvoyant.[29] All this was brought by way of hidden paths. I always had the impression that something is being carried out there by the gods, that the focus of experience shifts from the centre of the heart into the head, a shift that will take place a little later in the whole of humanity.

Through this we can come to a real understanding of Rudolf Steiner's statement that a ray had emanated from Peter of Compostela towards Chartres in order to bring about the next great development in Chartres. Compostela had to lose the battle with the organized Church. It was the last remnant of the great world of the Mysteries; it had given souls great gifts in the process. But now the path to inwardness had to be travelled, the path to the inner teachings of the School of Chartres, of the Dominicans. Compostela had given people the deep inner experience of individuality; a person is only a human being when on the path. Many who have approached anthroposophy were perhaps inwardly wakened—without knowing it—when they heard, 'Anthroposophy is a path of knowledge that seeks to lead the spiritual in the human being to the spiritual in the universe.'[30] In the same way, the Camino, the route, once led the human being from an inner personal existence to the great ocean, to the world of the fixed stars, to the spiritual in the universe.

This was the inward gift that Compostela gave to those in the first centuries who could still travel the right path. Today, the people who experienced this, and can re-enliven it in themselves, know that there are different ways to understand the statement: 'I am only human when I am on the path.' There is a Being, however, Who says, 'I am the way, the truth, and the life.'[31]

Lecture 7

The Mystery of the Music of the Spheres, and the Twenty-four Elders of the Apocalypse

Virginia Sease

We now want to turn our attention to the Mystery of the music of the spheres, and to the twenty-four elders of the Apocalypse.

It was understood into the Middle Ages that the spheres of the heavens are not merely silent and empty; instead, it was clear to people at that time that the cosmos consists of sounds, that it is filled with sound. People held the view that the so-called natural cosmos reaches upwards from beneath the earth, through the earth and into the cosmos; and certain numerical relationships were thought to prevail there. These numerical relationships are identical to the harmonies of the spheres, and they are crucial in deciding the variation of tones in the harmony of the spheres. The harmony of the spheres is determined by the numerical relationships, and the laws governing the motion of the stars determine these numerical relationships.

Interestingly, we find a difference between Plato and Aristotle on this point. For more than a thousand years most people have continued from where Plato left off. But Aristotle rejected this acoustics, and said that it was actually impossible for the variation of the tones to be connected to the laws of stellar motion. He distanced himself from this notion. Plato and the Platonic way of thinking persisted during the Middle Ages; we find it in the very subjects we want to consider here.

The Sounding Cosmos

Rudolf Steiner speaks in an interesting way about the 'arithmetic of tone':

> Uniform space would be without sound; a space organized arithmetically is a sounding space. An example of this exists in the way we are able to look into the Akashic Record. If we can elevate ourselves to perception of the inner arithmetic that remains from the tone in space,

> we can again, at any time, hear a sound that a person has spoken. For example, we can hear what Caesar said at the crossing of the Rubicon. The inner arithmetic of the tone remains present in the Akashic Record.[1]

Around AD 500, the philosopher, poet and writer Boethius lived in Ravenna at the court of Theodoric, king of the Ostrogoths. Boethius divided the world into levels of music. He described the *Musica* mundane—the harmony of the spheres, the harmony of the cosmos—as completely filled with sound. Then he described a second level, the *Musica humana*, which was everything expressed as music, as tone, in connection with the life of the soul as related to the bodily nature of the human being. Finally, he described a third level, the *Musica instrumentalis*, which was made up of musical instruments, the human voice, but also of teachings about music and applied music itself. All of this was included in the *Musica instrumentalis*. This idea of several levels left its mark throughout many centuries. For example, we find it around 1100 in Hugo of Saint Victor, a learned scholar in Paris who picks up the idea again.

The musicologist Reinhold Hammerstein found a substantial difference between the way music was perceived in the pre-Christian era and the way it was perceived in Christian times. He notes that the Old Testament says the cosmos is arranged numerically and permeated with sound. That is the fact of the matter. But then there is more: the Creator of the whole cosmos hears for Himself the angels' praise; He experiences a cosmos that offers praise. What was described at that time is a cosmic liturgy, the singing hierarchies. Then, as time passed, these singing hierarchies even began to be depicted in art.

The spheres had cosmic sound, which was at the apex of the natural cosmos; then there were the liturgical beings, the angels, the supernatural cosmos in all its parts. We find an echo of this organizational concept in the eminent Gnostic Origen, who wrote, 'We praise the Father and His only begotten Son in the same manner as do the sun, the moon and the stars, and all the heavenly hosts.'[2] This is a totality; heaven and human beings are united in this song of praise.

Nine Liturgies

As Christianity spread, various liturgies quickly developed, religious services, different conceptions of the Last Supper, and so forth. Most often, nine principal liturgies are identified. Four of them are Eastern: the Syrian, the Egyptian, the Persian and the Byzantine rites. The latter also encompasses the Armenian rite.

In the West, we find five main liturgies. The Hispanic-Galician rite was mainly Latin mixed with Spanish and Galician elements. It was widely disseminated in Spain, France, northern Italy, England, Scotland and Ireland during the early Christian centuries. In Spain, there was the Mozarabic liturgy, a Christian liturgy celebrated where there were Arabs, Moors. The Mozarabic liturgy was actually the national liturgy of Spain. Then it was forbidden under the Roman oppression beginning at the end of the eleventh century. In the sixteenth century, a priest of the Church, Cardinal Ximines, had enough insight to write down the liturgy and create a college of priests in Toledo that cultivated this liturgy for centuries. This Mozarabic liturgy can be heard in the mass at Toledo and Salamanca, although with evident Roman modifications.

The Galician-Gothic liturgy was the national liturgy of France until the beginning of the ninth century. Then it was repressed by Charlemagne and replaced by the liturgy of Rome. There was also the Ambrosian or Milanese liturgy by Ambrosius of Milan (Italy), which was also connected through its language with certain folk elements. And finally, there was the Roman liturgy, not to be confused with the one that came into existence through the papal liturgy. In Rome and its environs, the Roman liturgy was conducted in Greek.

Along with the great liturgical upheavals over the course of centuries, there arose an interpretation called the 'Heavenly Liturgy'. Today this has become a technical term. The 'Heavenly Liturgy' is based on the Revelation of John. It is the praise offered by the four apocalyptic beasts together with the twenty-four elders; angels might also be included. For the most part, it is shaped around the Christ, around the Lamb of God. The oldest commentaries are based on the Revelation of John itself. John writes:

> And round about the throne were four and twenty seats: and upon the seats I saw four and twenty elders sitting, clothed in white raiment; and they had on their heads crowns of gold.[3]
> ... four and twenty elders fell down before the Lamb, having every one of them harps, and golden vials full of odours [frankincense] ... and they sung a new song ...[4]

The oldest surviving commentary on the Apocalypse was written around 300 by Bishop Victorinus of Pettau (d. 304), and summarized by St

Jerome in the Middle Ages. The bishop's interpretation is quite wonderful:

> The new song.—A public testimony of faith is offered. The Son of God is new; His passion and death at the hands of men are new; His resurrection on the third day is new; His ascension in a body is new; His forgiveness of human sins is new; His seal on the human being with the Holy Spirit is new ... And the harp, made from strings stretched across wood, signifies the flesh of Christ, bound to the wood of the Passion ...[5]

The Heavenly Liturgy in the Visual Arts

The oldest extant representation of the 'Heavenly Liturgy' in the visual arts is from the fifth century. It is a mosaic on the triumphal arch of the Basilica of San Paolo fuori le mure [St Paul outside the walls] in Rome. Here, the twenty-four elders hold their crowns but have no instruments (Illustration 5). Further representations of this theme appear in miniature paintings, in illuminated manuscripts, and particularly in manuscripts of the Apocalypse.

Then the manuscript illuminators begin to draw stringed instruments. The instruments are part of the offering brought by the twenty-four

5. Majesty. Triumphal arch, mosaic, mid-fifth century (heavily restored). St Paul outside the walls, Rome

elders; in most cases they are not being played. There were also frescoes with this theme, but unfortunately they were either painted over, as were most of the early frescoes, or they faded with time. There is an example of this in Saint Martin de Fenollar in southern France. Then the theme was taken up in stained glass windows, in the church of Saint-Denis in Paris for example. A very late example of this theme is found in the Duke de Berry's *Book of Hours* from the beginning of the fifteenth century.

The oldest extant example of a portal with the twenty-four elders is the tympanum of St Pierre in Moissac, France (Illustrations 6 and 7). Moissac is located north of Toulouse. The tympanum in Moissac was completed in 1115, while the two oldest tympanums in Spain—San Juan in Portomarin and Santo Domingo in Soria—date from the middle of the twelfth century. The abbey of Moissac goes back to the beginning of the sixth century, to the time of Clovis, and it has a long history. Moissac lay along the pilgrimage route to Compostela; the pilgrims visited this church.

The twenty-four elders in the Moissac tympanum hold a stringed instrument called a rebec. There is controversy as to whether this

6. Tympanum. Benedictine Abbey and Cloister of St Pierre, Moissac

7. Tympanum (detail). Benedictine Abbey and Cloister of St Pierre, Moissac

instrument is of Arabic origin; there is strong evidence for an Arabic origin. At the cathedral we can see a wonderful example: King David holds a rebec, a stringed instrument with two or three strings tuned in fifths. In the tympanum, we can see the Christ figure in the middle, surrounded by apocalyptic figures—above on the right is the eagle; below it, the bull; on the left side is the lion, and above is the human being in the form of an angel.

This Christ figure itself is unique as a work of art because it has three arms. Its left arm is on the book. It has two right arms, one raised in a gesture of blessing, the other on its heart. Naturally, there are many explanations of this. It is said most often that the Christ with the three arms is symbolic of the Trinity: Christ Himself, the Son, has His hand over His heart; the blessing hand is the Holy Spirit; and the hand on the book is the Father God. It can also mean that the hand on the heart is pointing—like all of revelation—towards the future, towards the Day of Judgment, when the Christ will judge every human being, when He will pass judgment on every person, but when every judgment will be handed down based on his Heart's understanding.

On either side is an angel, one with a closed prayer strap, called a phylactery, to represent the Old Testament; and another, whose strap is unrolled, representing the New Testament.

What interests us in particular are the twenty-four elders. They hold stringed instruments, and each of the elders looks in rapture at the Christ above—a quite wonderful gesture.

We find the theme of the twenty-four elders at Compostela and Chartres, and elsewhere as well. In Chartres, they hold a stringed instrument and a censer. This motif in Chartres is on the west portal, which is also the case in Moissac and Compostela.

The Pórtico de la Gloria in Compostela

After 1188, pilgrims encountered the Pórtico de la Gloria in Compostela, and were filled with hope. We know that Peter is traditionally described as faith, John as love, and James as hope. And pilgrims were greeted in Compostela by James, by hope. At that moment, they were given something like a backward glance, but also a kind of premonition. This is what is noteworthy about these figures of the twenty-four elders—we can say that they were described by the author of the Apocalypse many centuries ago, and from this point of view they come from the past; yet they also have a bearing on the future.

The creation of the Pórtico de la Gloria in Compostela is actually quite a miracle. A Master Mateo transformed this west façade in an unbelievable way. He removed two entry porticos so that a load was removed from the central pillar of the crypt. At the same time, by removing these two porticos, he created a space, an opening in the narthex, thus in the inner vestibule of the church. The doors were added later; these figures are protected by them. He worked on this Pórtico with its sculptures for 20 years. On 1 April 1188 it was completed when he placed the lintels and the tympanum. It was the Friday of the fourth week in Lent. There is an inscription under the lintels:

> *Ecclesiae: Beati: Jacobi: sunt collocata: Per: Magistrum: Matheum: qui: a: fundamentis: ipsum: portalium: gessit: magisterium.*

The twenty-four elders with their vast array of instruments are arranged like a crown in the uppermost rounded arch; and in the middle, directly under the two central figures, sits the Christ figure on his throne (Illustration 8). Surrounding the Christ, we see the four Evangelists in human

8. Pórtico de la Gloria, Cathedral at Santiago de Compostela

form. What is extraordinary is that each holds his attribute in his lap—John has the eagle; Mark has the lion; Luke, the bull; and Matthew has the appearance of an angel. Here we see a profound dimension—Master Mateo understood that one day in the future all the constellations would be humanized in a particular way. These attributes were derived from imaginations which people saw as great imaginations, the imaginations of the constellations of Leo, Taurus, and so on. And that is what Master Mateo humanized; the Evangelists hold these attributes.

Under the Christ figure stands James as the welcomer (Illustration 9). He holds a text, 'Misit me Dominus'. The James on the Pórtico de la Gloria has a staff in the form of the Tao, which, of course, is also symbolically meaningful. He sits with a lion on either side. People were familiar with this symbolism, which was handed down to them through

9. James. Pórtico de la Gloria (detail), Cathedral at Santiago de Compostela

the oral tradition. Lions are an allusion to royalty going back to the time of Solomon.

The theme of the twenty-four elders was widespread in Spain as well as in France, partially in manuscripts, but also in the sculpture of the twelfth and thirteenth centuries. Then this came to an abrupt end. There is a depiction from the fourteenth century in Sásamon, not far from Burgos; figures can also be seen there, but I cannot say with certainty that these are the elders. They hold instruments, but their number is not limited to twenty-four. Other figures are also mixed in. There is a figure that plays a double flute, an impossibility in this theme because of an inherent tradition with which Master Mateo was quite familiar. In this tradition, woodwind and percussion instruments actually belonged to a lower hierarchy because they were also played in the Dionysian rituals. They were only used for secular, not sacred, purposes. Since the hierarchies were very important in the Middle Ages, we find the twenty-four elders carrying stringed instruments. Plato speaks of how the strings of the soul must be strung so that the individual can come to the spiritual on his own in the right way.

Master Mateo was an extraordinarily great master, and he fits Rudolf Steiner's description of human beings who worked during the Raphael Age. They brought great achievements, they received great inspirations, and it is often the case that they remained relatively unknown. This is characteristic of the Raphael-Mercury Age.

The Twenty-four Elders

A tradition accompanies the twenty-four elders that says: twelve are figures of the night, twelve are for the day; or, twelve and twelve are regulators of time. We can look at it in this way. However, Rudolf Steiner offers another interpretation that summarizes their historical meaning and brings us further with respect to the future. He describes how each great period has seven stages. Saturn had seven epochs and it was there that a group of beings experienced their existence as humans, naturally in a completely different way than we experience our humanity on the earth. But these beings had an experience of their own ego-nature, which is the decisive factor in experiencing what it means to be human.

In the case of Saturn, we see how this experience is divided symbolically into seven stages, and how in the middle stage—the fourth stage—the beings of the archai can be seen or imagined. They experienced their humanity there. It is the same with the Sun period, which is also divided into seven stages. In their own way, the archangels have an experience of their humanity at the mid-point. On the Moon, there are again seven steps, and at the mid-point the angels experience their humanity. Before the current earth period, twenty-one beings have had their own experience of their ego-nature.

Then three other beings went through their human stage ahead of the present-day human being on the earth. At the time of the Munich Conference, as well as frequently in the Esoteric School, Rudolf Steiner speaks about the Masters of Wisdom and the Harmony of Feelings: 'These sublime beings have already travelled the path which the remainder of humanity must still go. They work now as the great "teachers" ...'[6] These are the three earlier stages connected with the Earth.

The fourth being is the human being as we know him. It is now our time. And for this reason it is so significant that James is there when we approach this Pórtico. James is the brother of mankind, the representative of the best human qualities.

These twenty-four beings look back at their stage of humanity, at their own developmental stages, and have an understanding of the developing human being as a result. There exists an early and somewhat mysterious description related to the twenty-four elders. It is apparent that this description has been deeply significant in esotericism over the centuries.

Mary Magdalene poses many questions in the *Pistis Sophia.* She asks, 'My Lord and my Redeemer, what type are the twenty-four invisibles—what sort, or rather what quality do they have, or what quality does their light have?' She receives a very long answer, which includes the following sentences: 'Now Mary, in this world there is no type, neither light, nor form comparable to the twenty-four invisibles; soon I will lead you and your brethren and the apostolic disciples to all the places of the heights, and thus lead you to the three realms of the first Mystery ... and you will see all their forms in truth without simile.'[7] This is a description of an elevated level of initiation that was promised here by Christ.

The twenty-four elders are at the very top of the Pórtico de la Gloria in Compostela, and look downwards. In Chartres, as well as in Moissac, we see just the opposite: the heads look upwards. However the imagination is quite appropriate here because the twenty-four elders looked down, so to speak, when the Christ united Himself with the Jesus-being. Beneath the figure of the Christ is the figure of James; this imagination is also appropriate if we remember how the Christ-being not only conveyed essential teachings to the disciples during His life, but continued to do so inspirationally throughout eleven years following the Mystery of Golgotha.

The Instruments of the Elders

In the Pórtico de la Gloria there are twenty-four elders depicted, each holding a stringed instrument. These instruments form a very important tradition in the construction of instruments. They are studied frequently and attempts are made to reproduce them.

We cannot be certain about how these instruments sounded; we can only imagine that inwardly. But the precision with which these instruments are crafted in the stone sculptures is astonishing. Some of their parts are only millimetres long, tiny and perfectly made. They are somewhat smaller than the actual instruments probably were; the figures holding them are also smaller. They are made from stone to which stucco was applied, and then they were painted. But since the doors were added much later, the colour has almost entirely disappeared. There is a church in Orense where a reputed student of Master Mateo painted the portico and the colours are more readily visible. The elders have similar instruments there. For a number of reasons, it is now almost certain that this work was done by a pupil of Master Mateo—and not the master himself. What is striking about the presentation of the twenty-four elders in Orense is the fact that they surround Mary rather than the Christ. Naturally this also had a deep meaning at that time, although today it seems puzzling.

José López Calo, the well-known researcher in this field,[8] lives in Compostela and has conducted the most extensive investigations of the twenty-four elders. He is of the opinion that Master Mateo did not create these instruments based on his own fantasy but had modelled them after actual instruments, that they were available to him at the time and he then made these very precise copies of them. However this opinion is not universally held. He is also of the opinion that some of these instruments were brought to Galicia, but that many—though not all—originated there. It is certainly true of the larger instruments that they were made there rather than carried there. It would be impossible to transport a harp through the *meseta*! There are also disagreements about just how many Arabic influences are present. They are probably limited to the instrument described as a rebec. After the sculptures were covered with stucco, and paint had been applied, the whole had a dazzling appearance. There were no doors on the west, and the sun would shine in on these figures later in the day. Seeing that would certainly have been an impressive experience.

Twenty years before the Pórtico was finished, a description of the pilgrims appeared in the seventeenth chapter of the first book of the *Codex Calixtinus*. Naturally the pilgrims played their instruments, and we read about zithers, lyres, percussion instruments, wooden flutes, trumpets, harps, violins, and a large number of other instruments that helped them to stay awake at night. There is a saying from this period that can be applied to the way these sculptures were created, 'No trabajan para nosostros, sino para mayor gloria de Dios'—'We work not for ourselves, but for the greater glory of God.' This was the feeling throughout the whole of the Middle Ages. We see what is Gothic, what is Romanesque, the capitals high above, hardly visible even with binoculars. At that time, people could not actually see them even though they had much better eyesight than ours today. However, the spiritual world could see them, and that was what mattered.

The Pórtico de la Gloria
The Twenty-four Elders with their Instruments

Figure of the Elder	Instrument	Figure of the Elder	Instrument
12	Organistrum—a kind of hurdy-gurdy for two players	13	See figure 12
11	Figure-of-eight fiddle—3 strings	14	Figure-of-eight fiddle—3 strings
10	Zither	15	Figure-of-eight fiddle—3 strings
9	Lute	16	Figure-of-eight fiddle—3 strings
8	Harp	17	Zither
7	Oval fiddle—3 strings	18	Psaltery
6	Oval fiddle—5 strings	19	Harp
5	Psaltery	20	Lute
4	Gourd (Calabash)(?)	21	Gourd (?)
3	Oval fiddle—? strings	22	Oval fiddle—3 strings
2	Oval fiddle—5 strings	23	Oval fiddle—5 strings
1	Oval fiddle—3 strings	24	Oval fiddle—5 strings

We can now turn our attention to the instruments. The first figure on the left side (Illustration 10) has an oval fiddle with three strings, and the figure next to it has one with five strings. This oval-form fiddle was also played with a bow, but the bow is not depicted here. The oval-form fiddle is one of the very first forms in European music. Then we have the third figure which holds an oval-shaped stringed instrument, but it is impossible to see how many strings the instrument has. The fourth figure is quite noteworthy. It has no instrument, but holds something in its hand. What it holds is strongly contested. López Calo believes that it is a kind of gourd (Sp. *calabaza*) that might have also been used as a musical instrument—not in the Dionysian way, but more for the rhythm. Other people say, no, it is a censer because the twenty-four elders hold censers. If that is the case, then it is somehow upside down.

With the fifth figure, we see a psaltery; we will see this instrument again with the eighteenth figure. The psaltery is a very old instrument also mentioned in the Psalms. We notice how the hand rests upon it. And here we arrive at another point of controversy. It is said that the elders did not play the instruments, but only held them in order to tune them in preparation for the Last Judgment. However, it certainly appears as though some of the instruments are being played.

With the next figure there is again an oval-form fiddle with five strings, but we observe a variation in the peg-box. We will also see other variations. The one depicted here is in the shape of a diamond. It is these variations in the peg-boxes that make the whole thing so realistic when we look at them.

Then we again have an oval-form fiddle with three strings; this is the seventh figure. And the peg-box here is more almond-shaped.

With the eighth figure, as well as the nineteenth, we see a very nicely formed harp; these harps are beautifully decorated. The size of the two harps is somewhat different. However, they are typical harps of the Middle Ages, small and sturdy.

The ninth figure holds a lute which was plucked. This figure, like the twentieth, is depicted as having a plectrum with which to pluck the instrument.

Now we come to the tenth figure. It holds its instrument on its lap as does the seventeenth figure. It is a zither. These zithers are similar to the psaltery; they are represented here in a rather simple form. The musicians hold them horizontally on their laps; both hands rest gently there. It looks as though they are playing with their fingertips, but in fact they are playing with a plectrum—which means they are plucking the zither. And figure ten actually has two small plectra, a fact confirmed from above by someone who climbed a ladder to investigate the matter. The figure holds the plectrum like a pencil. With this figure, the head is positioned as though listening. It listens to the music, perhaps to the new song, to the call.

The eleventh figure has a figure-of-eight fiddle with three strings, which was a favourite type of fiddle. There are four figure-of-eight fiddles among these sculptures; the figure eight is one of the most common forms for medieval stringed instruments. The sound boxes were simply assembled from two rather well-formed circles joined together. Here this is done very nicely. Of course, we do not have any idea how they looked when they were painted. Like the figures, the instruments were also painted with a variety of colours. The neck of these figure-of-eight fiddles is rather short and fat; and it is quite interesting to compare the shape of these fiddles with the circulation of the blood in the heart, and to ask

10. *Figures 1 and 2*

11. *Figures 3 and 4*

12. *Figures 5 and 6*

13. *Figures 7 and 8*

14. *Figure 9*

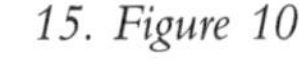

15. *Figure 10*

16. *Figure 11*

17. *Figures 12 and 13*

whether much of this might not have been handed down out of esoteric wisdom.

Now we come to the twelfth and thirteenth figures, and to the most famous instrument of the whole collection—an organistrum. It is said that the word is probably a compound of the words *organum* and *instrumentum*, but that is only a theory. It is the most impressive instrument, not only because of its size, but also because of the ornamentation, the decoration, and because of the way it was played. It had to be played by two musicians. It is a stringed instrument with a wheel, and when this wheel was turned the strings were strummed. The wheel rubbed against the strings.

In this depiction there are three strings and a very large neck. On this large neck there is a row of eleven keys, and the intonation resulted when these keys were pressed inwards. The keys are placed vertically below the strings. This is truly the most complicated instrument in the whole Pórtico, and it was frequently reproduced. It can be seen not only in Compostela, but in other places as well—for example, in Orense. It was probably an instrument for transposing music; with it, the pitch of a composition could be changed or regulated, especially in the relationships of the fourths and the fifths. This was a slow process; it was not played quickly. All three strings sounded together, and their sound changed simultaneously every time a key was pressed. In all likelihood, it was fairly clumsy and suitable only for slow melodies.

With the fourteenth figure, we again see a figure-of-eight fiddle with three strings. The hand gesture as it points to the organistrum is so wonderful. It is interesting that the two middle figures unite both halves of the Pórtico, not merely through the instrument, but also because of how they look at one another, as though they were sharing a secret with one another.

With the fifteenth figure, there is again a figure-of-eight fiddle with three strings, and the right hand holds something like a gourd or spiral-shaped object. Many musicologists claim that this gourdlike object was used to strum the strings; however, it would have been a little awkward to create a tone in that way.

With the sixteenth figure, there is also a figure-of-eight fiddle that has three strings. We arrive now at the seventeenth and the eighteenth figures. Along with a zither, the seventeenth figure actually seems to hold its gourd-shaped object like a plectrum on the strings. Then, with the eighteenth figure, we see the psaltery; the harp appears again with the nineteenth elder, and the twentieth has a lute. The twenty-first elder holds no stringed instrument in his hand, only this gourdlike object—

18. Figure 14

19. Figure 15

20. Figure 16

21. Figures 17 and 18

22. *Figures 19 and 20*

23. *Figures 21 and 22*

24. *Figures 23 and 24*

actually, it may not resemble a gourd. The twenty-second has an oval-form fiddle with three strings. He tunes his instrument.

The twenty-third and twenty-fourth elders have oval-form fiddles with five strings. Each holds the fiddle differently; one holds it close to himself, while the other lets it rest on his knee.

It is significant in the course of human history that such depictions of the elders suddenly stopped. They stopped when the era in which the Platonists were active came to an end, approximately when the teachers at Chartres were returning to the spiritual world. There were a few later references, but on the whole these depictions disappeared at the end of the first quarter of the thirteenth century.

The School of Chartres was the home of the great 'Platonic teachers', as Rudolf Steiner called them. We think of Fulbertus, Bernardus Silvestris, John Salisbury and Alanus ab Insulis with their large student followings. It is likely that these students made the journey to Compostela where they could perhaps experience the kind of education certainly connected with Master Mateo. A master as great as Mateo had his pupils, too. He was a master of musical instruments, and not only of their construction; he would have to have been a master in order to bring this collection of many forms into a single form. As we study these figures and ponder the whole Pórtico more fully, we see a deep wisdom behind every gesture of the hand, every position of the head.

The Continuing Effect of the Pilgrimage to Compostela

The question today is: Where does all this go from here? There are currently the twenty-one elders of the past, the three who are added in the course of Earth evolution, then the fourth stage, present-day humanity. But three realms—the animals, the plants and the minerals—must still go through the level of humanity in their own way by somehow experiencing the ego. The masters somehow knew this intuitively. We think of the countless capitals (for example in the Romanesque) where we see plant forms—out of the fullness of entwined plant forms, a human head suddenly emerges. It is a puzzling thing.

Many thousands of people have travelled the route to Compostela in the course of the centuries. They have seen various depictions of this very theme; they have also heard descriptions of the music of the spheres, experienced this music for themselves, and they carry the memories of this when they make such a journey or pilgrimage today. The great question in our time may be expressed this way: Will the people in whom these past experiences arise also be able to establish a connection with the esotericism of our time? For example, will they be able to make the leap from antiquity to the future; will they take note of the moment when they experience what they are meant to experience in this incarnation? Will they also connect themselves with spirituality through the possibility brought by the consciousness soul? Will they now be able to connect consciously with the Christ-being? For example, will they be awake when they have the opportunity to come to the Goetheanum where they can experience something modern and future-oriented?

Several years ago, a leading esoteric researcher in France, Pierre A. Riffard,[9] wrote a book in which he describes the twelve most significant buildings, monuments of humanity. Included on his list is the first Goetheanum. He names the twelve most significant human beings, philosophers and helpers of humanity; among them is Rudolf Steiner. And included on his list of the twelve most significant books of Western esotericism is *Occult Science, An Outline*. Thus, it is clear there exist people who are also very attentive. Yet the question remains, 'Can this attentiveness spread to all those souls who are seeking to find something?'

Lecture 8

The Esotericism of Music and the Songs of the Camino Pilgrims

Virginia Sease

Looking back at the phenomenon of pilgrimages to Compostela, we see how the pilgrims were outfitted for their journey. They have their hat, their walking-stick, the rosary of course, a backpack; and they were also equipped with their own music. It is possible that they had brought along small instruments; above all, they had the songs of their homeland with them and sang them aloud whether they travelled alone or in groups. The importance of this cannot be underestimated when we imagine how it was for someone to travel alone or with a few others. They sang. We think of the old Spanish saying, *andando y cantando*, walking and singing. It was, in fact, a musical pilgrimage. In earlier times, people had a very refined sense for the importance of singing; they saw it not only as human, but also as heavenly. This is expressed, for example, in a text by Basilius: 'The psalm drives the demons away and draws the help of the angels close. It is the work of the angels, the heavenly consecration, the spiritual incense ...'[1] Of course, we are speaking of singing when we talk about the psalms. At that time, there was a word for the human being who sings—*psallierende*. Bernard of Clairvaux mentions this: 'For the angels of heaven take care to join with the *psallierende*.'[2] Thus the human being was never alone so long as he sang.

The Music of Spain before 1074

Until about AD 1000, pilgrims undertaking the pilgrimage could experience the elements of early Christianity in Spain; then these original elements were forbidden and driven out by the Roman Church. In particular, the pilgrims could experience the music handed down through various traditions. For example, in Seville at that time there was already a large centre of learning where much of this came together. In the sixth century, San Isidor of Seville collected many songs. He also wrote the only surviving history of the Visigoths. Although we do not always want our focus here to be on personalities, we must remember nevertheless that history is carried by people. People did these things. When we experience this inwardly, if only a bit, then history begins to come alive in another way.

In AD 417, two hundred years before San Isidor of Seville, Severo de Menorca wrote in a letter: 'We march into the church with hymns, singing as is our custom, and also singing psalms ... we celebrate the Mysteries, and then we leave the church.'[3]—'Nosotros marchamos a la iglesia, come de costumbre, con himnos, candando y salmodiando ... Y celebrados los misterios, salimos de la iglesia.' We can imagine how humble the church building was in AD 417.

Many of these traditions were later eradicated, but early pilgrims experienced them; the Hispanic, Visigoth tradition was always connected with much that was pagan. They had songs for the seasons, and songs for death (the *plantos*). They had the cultus of the sun at St John's, the cultus of the moon, especially the Celts; these rituals then merged with the Hispanic tradition. They danced outdoors the whole night through; they also used shells as rattles; they played tambourines, and various instruments. They celebrated various cults for fertility, especially animal fertility and the fertility of horses most of all; they celebrated the cultus of war, the sword dance, as well as the cultus of health which was closely connected with the Mysteries of water. Early iconography depicts this.

The Christian liturgy separated very slowly from the Judaic ritual, especially in Spain. The Jews were driven from Spain in 1492; before that a large Judaic culture had existed there. Paul wrote to the Romans that he intended to visit the Jews in Spain, although we have no evidence he did so. Only gradually did the separation of the Christian liturgy from the Judaic ritual take place, and that meant a gradual separation in regard to music. The Judaic elements retained in the liturgy were, for example, the singing of psalms and reading from the Bible; these fundamental elements were kept.

We also read in the work of musicologist Ismael Fernández de la Cuesta about how Christian music was first protected in the bosom of Judaism.[4] In Spain, this music developed slowly out of Judaism, and we occasionally hear an echo of this early music in its sounds. The music was not noted down, however—there was no need to do so because it was all known by heart.

From AD 711, there were Arabs in Spain. After only a few years, Cordoba became an important city, and after 719 it was the seat of the emirate. Soon there was a rivalry between Baghdad and Damascus over the culture and the court in Cordoba with its many musicians, singers and other artists. In Sigrid Hunke's book, *Allahs Sonne über dem Abendland* [Allah's sun over Europe],[5] a charming story is told about a singer, Sirjan of Baghdad, who was the favourite singer of Harun al Rashid. Sirjan left the Baghdad court to seek adventure and was joyously greeted in Cordoba. He proceeded to set the tone for the cultural life of the court in Cordoba for many years.

There were many Arabs at the Spanish courts; Arabs, Jews and Christians lived together peacefully, especially in regard to culture, music, song and instrumental music. As the pilgrims wandered into Spain, they could find these elements. Even the Spaniards of the courts undertook the pilgrimage to Compostela; they brought along the Arabic and Jewish songs, and sang them with one another. A kind of pentatonic originating in the Arabic world was very influential throughout all of Europe. This tuning in fifths with a sequence of pure fifths lived on and exercised a strong influence into the late Middle Ages.

Naturally the pilgrims also came to know the Mozarabic liturgy and the Mozarabic songs. In so far as we can determine, these songs were kept very much in a minor key. We can well imagine this; Christians who practised their religion in areas occupied by the Arabs were themselves in the mood of a minor key.

The Intrusion of Gregory VII

At the end of the eleventh century in Spain, a profoundly meaningful event took place both exoterically and esoterically—the introduction and cultivation of Gregorian chants in all of the churches. Gregory VII had been the monk Hildebrand. When he became Pope, one of his first deeds was the suppression and the eventual elimination of Hispanic song. All the elements that had converged there—Visigoth, Judaic, Celtic, Arabic—were levelled out and prohibited. This took place at a significant turning-point in history; soon after this time, a system was invented in which music could be preserved in readable notation. Unfortunately it was too late for the earlier Hispanic musical tradition. In 1074, Gregory addressed his papal bull to the Kings of Castille, Léon, and Aragón, demanding that these old Hispanic rituals be abandoned. The new Roman ritual—which became known as *la lex romana*—was to be used.

In the karma lectures, Rudolf Steiner describes the next incarnation of

Pope Gregory VII as Ernst Haeckel, and he describes Haeckel's strong support for the blossoming of materialism. Rudolf Steiner was deeply knowledgeable about the works of Haeckel. We must recognize the strange way modern people have entered into their present incarnations out of the past. Thus the Ernst Haeckel who so angrily fought the Church was the reincarnated monk Hildebrand; this same Haeckel had worked in his previous incarnation as Gregory, the great Pope.[6] Another description states, 'And the successor of Irenaeus in our time once again fights against everything that comes from a true knowledge of the spiritual world. Who is the precursor and who is the successor? Irenaeus, the Bishop of Lyons, who fought against the Gnostics; and the Irenaeus of our time, the bishop of materialism from Jena, is Ernst Haeckel—the successor of Irenaeus.'[7] Thus there is a line of development: Irenaeus (who died around 190) suppresses the Gnosis through his written refutations; Pope Gregory VII suppresses early music, suppresses the Hispanic ritual; Ernst Haeckel promotes the materialistic world view.

The radical upheaval that resulted from the intrusion of Pope Gregory VII brought about fundamental changes. People were not familiar with the Roman ritual; they did not know its music. Thus began extraordinary efforts at transcription, especially in the monasteries along the Camino—Santa Maria de Ripoll, Santo Domingo de la Calzada, San Juan de la Peña, San Millán de la Cogolla—all of them significant places connected with the Grail tradition. These monasteries had large scriptoria, and priests were brought to Spain in order to eradicate the indigenous elements.

Pilgrim Songs of Later Centuries

What could not be eliminated, however, were the songs sung from one person to another, the songs of the pilgrim's route. In spite of the laws, poetry lived on. The pilgrims entered the churches, experienced the mass and the singing, and in their free time they told one another the stories of their own lives. These songs can be viewed as a gift from this period, along with the architecture and the Romanesque sculptural art. They are a confirmation of the spirituality of the time, a genuine cultural inheritance. It is unique in human history that the thousands of miles in this area were suffused with singing. There is nothing like it in all of world history. This singing lasted for centuries and, naturally, it lives on in the ether realm; this is the source of the feeling we can have in those quiet places unreachable by highways, in its more remote locations. Many elements of this can also be heard even today in folk songs.

The most popular song from this period is called *Canto de Ultreja*, or *Dum Paterfamilias* (from its opening words). This song has had a special destiny. It has been sung for more than a thousand years without major changes. Frequently pilgrims from throughout the world and the most varied religions—even non-Christians—sing this song several times a day in the cathedral at Compostela. The melody has a slight Germanic element.

There are Gothic words in the refrain. The translation of the beginning says, 'When the Almighty Father, the King of the Universe, divided the provinces among the Apostles, he gave the Spanish lands to James. Light that illuminates the world, the first among the Apostles, martyr of Jerusalem, James is holy through the most noble martyrdom.'[8] Then the Gothic words follow, 'Herru Sanctiagu, Grot Santiagu'—'Lord St James, Great St James.'

Rudolf Steiner states, 'The musical element is connected with everything that has to do with development, with the future; the sculptural-architectonic element is connected to everything that has to do with the past.'[9] It is moving to think that not only sculpture and architecture have been preserved for centuries, but that this one song has also endured through the generations.

Polyphony in the Pilgrims' Songs

We have already heard of the *Codex Calixtinus*, also called the *Liber Sancti Jacobi*; it is often called a pilgrim's handbook. It was written around 1120 and was ascribed to Pope Calixtus, perhaps in order to give it credibility. This codex contains proof that many songs recorded in it had their origin in Compostela. Not all the songs were imported, although some were. This is significant for a number of reasons. For one thing, it means that a large music school was housed here, one where instruments were not only built and copied, but where music was also composed. When Peter of Compostela speaks of the seven benefactresses—among whom Music is most lofty—we experience the significance of the fact that this is where many songs were once written.

This is also significant from a second point of view. It has been shown that these songs were sung by the people, and not only in church. This is connected to something else, namely, that polyphonic songs are also found here, songs made up of many voices, thus in a contrapuntal style where the voices are woven in among one another. The oldest song to come down to us is a song from the *Codex Calixtinus*. In Latin it is called *Congaudeant catholici*, and it consists of three voices in a polyphonic style of a fugue. It begins, 'All of Christianity rejoices, the dwellers in heaven are jubilant on this day.' It is noteworthy that this song is virtually never mentioned in histories of music written outside Spain. Some scholars claim that this sort of polyphony is even more advanced than the polyphony of the two great masters of Notre Dame, Leoninus and Perotinus.[10]

A third significant aspect is that people had the ability to sing such a song—in order to do so, the individual had to be in a position to hold his own part. This ability belongs to the development of the consciousness soul culture. The individual must possess a consciousness of his own ego in order to carry his own part. For this reason Rudolf Steiner advised that music in the Waldorf school should begin with songs in a pentatonic, in a mood of fifths. At approximately the age of nine years—when the ego of the child is somewhat more apparent and has connected a bit more with the metabolic system—one can sing songs which are canons. And songs with several voices should be introduced only later, with the twelfth year when the skeletal system is a bit more solid. At this point in history we are dealing with people in the approximate position of the twelve-year-old child, because in this kind of singing there arises something like a presentiment of the consciousness soul culture. Interwoven voices must really have sounded like the harmony of the spheres to the pilgrims hearing polyphony for the first time when they arrived.

Even songs from France resounded there; for example, a *Kyrie* by Fulbertus, a Platonist of Chartres and a bishop in Paris. A *Kyrie* is always intended for the human being's path after death; it is an intercession on behalf of the soul of the deceased so that the spiritual world—the Father, the Son and the Holy Spirit—will have mercy on the soul.

Songs of Mary

Of course, the pilgrims had mystical experiences during their journeys. They saw visions, heard voices and calls; but today all that is usually interpreted psychologically by describing such things as hallucinations. In part, it is possible that some of them were. The pilgrims had prayed a great deal and fasted, either intentionally or by force of circumstance; and they also meditated a lot. These mystical experiences were often connected with the figure of the Virgin Mary. The complex veneration of Mary that emerged over the centuries in connection with the Camino dates back to those experiences.

We have inherited a unique treasure trove of songs about Mary. This is the collection known as *Las Cantigas de Santa Maria*. Around 1250, King Alfons the Wise of Castille (Alfons X el Sabio) collected songs and also composed many songs himself. Today Alfons el Sabio (1221–84) is thought of as a quite remarkable person. He wrote a legal code and a history of Spain; without him we would know little of Spanish history. He also wrote a history of the world, and translated many Arabic texts—scientific writings, artistic texts and medical documents. To translate something, a person must be familiar with the material. Much of Aristotle's work that had been rescued by the Arabic culture was translated by Alfons into what was then a modern language, either Latin or the vernacular. Christians, Jews and Arabs lived harmoniously together at his court, which was quite musical.

If we look at these songs and read their lyrics, we find that they often are concerned with a purification of the soul. It is not merely a veneration of Mary; it goes much deeper than that. Veneration leads a person to the possibility of purifying his own soul. Many of these songs are quite mystical in concept, and many simply tell legends and stories about Mary. These *Cantigas* are numbered. Number 103 tells of a monk on the way to Compostela who had prayed to Mary to show him what it is like for a person to be in paradise. Of course, people always lived with thoughts about death; they knew that the route was dangerous. And this song tells that Mary allowed him to listen to the singing of a bird for three hundred years. As a result, he was able to enjoy the song of the bird for three hundred years, thus well past death.

There are three volumes containing these 420 songs and their texts, as well as wonderful miniatures of the musical instruments of the time. There is a reprint of them at Compostela. *Cantiga* 253 describes how the Camino was also a pilgrimage route of penance for people who had committed sins. This song contains the punishment for the pilgrim—he had to carry a heavy iron staff until he had received forgiveness at one of the stations along the way; then he could lay aside the pilgrim's staff there and take up another made of wood.

Of course, there are many songs about the feasts of Mary. At the time, the soprano, alto and mezzo parts were sung by young boys. Women did not sing in church. *Cantiga* 413 concerns the festival of Mary's virginity. The feast was experienced in a joyful mood; in this song the rhythm has an iambic character.

Cantiga 414 is set in a more trochaic mood. In this song, the Trinity is portrayed in Mary through her qualities; Mary is part of the Trinity. This closely approaches the Gnostic view of the Sophia. Mary is the earthly reflection of the Sophia-being and a part of the Trinity connected with the Holy Spirit. Very early on, the Church suppressed the Gnostic insights concerning the Sophia, or combined them with the veneration of Mary. Nevertheless the Gnostic insights about the Sophia lived on in the oral tradition. In the long text of this song, these qualities are introduced into an analogy with the Trinity.

The Experience of Music after Death

If we consider the music of the Camino in the light of karma, we recall how everything experienced with the limbs as an expression of the will during life will be transformed after death and will appear in the next life as a predisposition for thinking and consciousness. This is a significant thought because, during the Middle Ages, thousands and thousands of people had experiences through music and their travels and then brought these experiences with them into the spiritual world after death.

We now stand at the beginning of the twenty-first century and many of these souls are preparing a meaningful next incarnation—especially the souls we refer to as more Platonically oriented, who have waited a long time for another incarnation, but the Aristotelians as well. We must recall that the after-death experiences of people are, to a significant extent, connected with the religious and musical experiences of earthly life. We remember that people in the early centuries knew that when a person dies the soul is accompanied in a twofold way—through the loving thoughts of the people who remain behind, and through music. There is perhaps an echo of this still alive today in many souls. Thus there were the great musical accompaniments in the requiems sung after death. In particular, people of high standing commissioned their own requiems long before their deaths. We know this was the case in Mozart's biography; he had written his own requiem; there is something very mysterious about Mozart's requiem. People once knew that music could accompany them after they had set aside their physical body. Of course, the manner of the death influences the conditions of the soul—whether death occurred at the stake, through an accident, because of illness or in battle. This has been known throughout the centuries.

After death, the human being comes first into the moon sphere. He sees in this sphere everything that was imperfect about himself and he perceives how he puts together an Akashic image through his imperfections. He also sees where he has contributed certain accomplishments. This can be a time of enormous surprise for the person. The time he thought he had failed can be the very moment when he actually achieved something; and the time he was perhaps a bit proud in his earthly consciousness, thinking he had achieved something in a good and positive sense, precisely the opposite is the case. In the moon sphere, he also experiences his unfulfilled intentions, sees them objectively before him. He sees what he actually wanted to do and what he did not accomplish. This can become a seed for a next life, or he can push it aside as an intention that was actually irrelevant.

When the human being enters the Mercury sphere after kamaloka—that is, right after kamaloka—he experiences himself either as a hermit, lonely and isolated, or together with other beings. These experiences of one or the other kind are connected with the moral constitution he cultivated for himself on the earth. At this point, we begin to understand the importance of art. Every genuine art that calls upon creative forces strengthens the moral constitution. Great secrets lie behind this aspect, and it is for this reason that Rudolf Steiner spoke over and over of the art of pedagogy, the art of healing, and of art itself.

What the individual then experiences in the Venus sphere is related to how he was connected with his own religion. Was he pious in his religious activity—naturally, this is not necessarily connected with religious denominations—or did his life have an atheistic orientation? Of course, someone can have an atheistic attitude and yet attend church every Sunday, or the temple every Friday, or the mosque. If he was not pious, he is isolated in the Venus sphere. Here we see that every true religion is also comprised of an artistic element, especially music and singing; and in so far as a person took part in this element during life, it is something that is brought over into the Venus sphere. It is, so to speak, a fructification of his soul through music, and we cannot undervalue that. This is not something we can view as trivial in any musical tradition—whether Christian, Jewish, Islamic or Buddhist music. Even if some type of music may not speak to us, it is still important during life after death for the souls of those who had participated in it.

Then the person enters the sun sphere where the relationship he had to the Mystery of Golgotha plays a decisive role. Although we look at this from a Christian perspective, it is also necessary for us to see and have a feeling for the effect of the Christ-being in all other religions. Or we must at least know with certainty that the Christ-being does not confine Himself to one religion, but is found equally in elements of other religions. It is a matter of karma whether someone approaches the Christ-being through Christianity or through other world religions. The important thing is that 'Christian' means more than what is connected with denominations or confessions. If we are raised in a Christian religion, how can we sense where elements of the Christ might be present in other religions? Of course, we can approach this through poetry and literature, and find a great deal; but it is to be found especially through music. Wherever we sense in music even the subtlest suggestion of transformation of form, we know something Christian is coming to expression.

The Region of the Music of the Spheres

Next, the astral body is laid aside after the sun sphere[11] and, as a result, the musical experiences that are an echo of earthly life are finally laid aside. The human being then enters the actual region of the music of the spheres. He is in spirit land and is led by Lucifer through Mars, Jupiter and Saturn.[12] Therefore, in the sun sphere, it is utterly critical for the human being to recognize the Christ-being, regardless of the religion that the individual practised on earth; otherwise he in danger of incorrectly judging the actual identity of the Lucifer-being. In the Mars region, the person strongly experiences the harmonies of the spheres. They sound towards him, always assuming different forms. In the Mars realm, the harmonies of the spheres have a strongly orchestral character; they sound towards him like a mighty orchestra.

In the Jupiter realm, this harmony of the spheres changes again, and has a songlike character. The human being experiences it like a resounding song. This song becomes more and more meaningful for the human being. It does not just resound like song, but it also has a content that leads to an experience of the Cosmic Word. In the Jupiter realm, it is essential that the human being finally free himself from his earlier religion so that there are no threads that could bind him beyond the Jupiter realm. This is significant if we look at the elements of fundamentalism in every religion today. It is possible that the people who live strongly in fundamentalism will not have an easy time in the Jupiter realm. In the Jupiter realm, it is necessary for the human being to be in a position to free himself from his prior religion so that he can experience the whole cosmic sound of the Cosmic Word.

Then in the Saturn realm the music of the spheres as Cosmic Word becomes a genuine experience for the human being. It is also experienced in the sense that the Cosmic Word works creatively, that it can be heard not only with spiritual ears but can be perceived as a creative principle as well. 'The music of the spheres receives content when we proceed into the sphere of Jupiter; and in the Saturn sphere it becomes fully content, the expression of the Cosmic Word from which all things are created. And that is what is meant in the Gospel of John, "In the beginning was the Word ..." '[13]

The consciousness of the human being is dimmed after the Saturn sphere; he leaves the spirit land and enters into the world of the stars. He has his experiences there. And when he returns in his next incarnation, he experiences the Cosmic Word during his journey back through the various spheres. The experiences that he had during his ascent after death will be utterly essential for the formation of his soul in the next incarnation; they are also connected with the way he experienced music in earthly life.

The Experience of Music in the Twenty-first Century

Today we see that precisely these musical experiences are in great danger. They are being extinguished; influences from the most varied quarters are making it impossible for people to have these musical experiences. The human being is attacked today by what passes for music. In the course of his whole life, a person may not have one genuine experience of music. This is symptomatic of the ongoing work by the forces of Klingsor.

Rudolf Steiner describes Klingsor's influence at the singers contest on the Wartburg. There, Klingsor stood beside Heinrich von Ofterdingen and used a demonic being to inspire him in his competition against Wolfram von Eschenbach, the poet of *Parzival*. Klingsor and his powers are not forced to yield until Wolfram sings of Christ. 'Klingsor is driven a bit into a corner by Wolfram von Eschenbach. For when Wolfram von Eschenbach notices that there is a spiritual element at work, he sings of the Last Supper, of the transubstantiation, of the presence of the Christ in the communion—and the demonic spirit must yield; he cannot bear it.'[14] These forces used by Klingsor are the very forces that work against the human being through music, through song; they rage on in an ever more intensive way today.

On the other hand, we experience how music will eventually become the vessel that allows us to experience the Christ-being—and this will become ever stronger, starting in our time. At Torquay in 1924, Rudolf Steiner explains that humanity could come to an experience of the Christ-being through music: 'The Christ impulse can be found in what is musical . . . And thus we can reach the point one day—and this is entirely dependent on human beings—that the Christ impulse will also appear in its true form before the backdrop of the musical element itself.'[15]

When we look back upon the long musical tradition of Central Europe, we can only be filled with gratitude.[16] Yet today we must take quite seriously the fact that everywhere in the world there is a mighty campaign against precisely this European tradition. What does it mean that forces are at work that want to exterminate this culture of the middle, and want to venerate other cultures instead? That remains an open question.

Lecture 9

The World Mission of the Templars as Emissaries of the Holy Grail

Manfred Schmidt-Brabant

The description of the Templars as the true emissaries of the Holy Grail originates with Rudolf Steiner. He spoke frequently about the three steps: Grail—Templar—Rosicrucian. It is in just such a context that he connects the Grail to the Templars and says they are 'the true emissaries of the Holy Grail'.[1]

Three hundred years after the founding of the Grail Mysteries, approximately three hundred years after the opening of the Camino, the Crusades began. In 1096, the first wave of Crusades sets out; in 1099, Jerusalem falls. Rudolf Steiner points to the fact that these Crusades actually arose from the heretical movement or, in any case, from movements at the time that were opposed to the official Church of Rome. He describes Godfrey of Bouillon, the leader of the first Crusade, as one who was initiated into the problems that had resulted from Rome's control over Christianity. There was a desire for the famous *Ecclesia non romana*, a non-Roman Church. People wanted to return to Jerusalem in order to found a Christ-centred Church there on the site of the Mystery of Golgotha. Those were the spiritual impulses. Liberation from the infidels was, so to speak, the exoteric aspect.

At that time there was a strong, rising tide of spiritual understanding for Christianity, as well as opposition to the rigid conditions of the beliefs and dogmas of the Roman Church. In connection with this, Rudolf Steiner says that the most important thing to come out of the Crusades 'are the Knights Templar'.[2] Here is the external history. When Jerusalem was conquered, Godfrey of Bouillon was offered the crown, and he said then and there that he would not wear a king's crown where Christ had walked. That was an expression of his character. Another Burgundian by the name of Baldwin then became the King of Jerusalem and, following his early death, his brother became King Baldwin II. Seven Burgundian knights (the number varies between five and nine depending on the historian) come to Baldwin II from the Burgundy region of France and ask for a place to live because they want to help protect the roads in the Holy Land from the continuing attacks of the Saracens.

As their living quarters they receive the site that was formerly the Temple of Solomon, and some time later they name themselves the 'Poor Brothers of Christ and of the Temple of Solomon'. After a few years they return to France, because in 1128 a great council is called at Troyes by Bernard of Clairvaux. At this council, the order of the 'Poor Brothers of Christ and of the Temple of Solomon'—referred to in short as 'the Templars'—was ceremoniously installed. Bernard of Clairvaux gives them a Rule, and then something quite astonishing takes place.

Within a very short time, one or two decades, these few knights who were actually not poor (among them was one of the richest feudal lords in France, the Count of Champagne) brought about an amazingly swift spread of the order throughout Europe. Princes endow the order with property, money, castles, and so forth. Many enter the order and it grows quickly; many young knights crowd into the order. Thus, over the span of two hundred years—we are still speaking only of the outer structure—the order cultivates a remarkable activity in Europe. Of course, it fights in Palestine and against the Moors in Spain, but quite obviously its real activity is directed towards Europe. In the end, at the peak of its development, it has nine thousand commanderies throughout all of Europe. A commandery is the centre of a certain district, a smaller castle or even a fortified manor with houses. In the end, twenty thousand knights belong to the order. It has an annual income of many millions. And the order has friends, the so-called affiliates.

The axe falls in 1307; members of the order are suddenly arrested on the orders of Philip the Fair, Philip IV of France. In a very modern, one might say secretive, Gestapo-like action, the castles of France are suddenly occupied. The order is accused, abolished by the Pope in 1312, and finally destroyed in 1314 with the burning of the last Grand Master, Jacques de Molay, on the Ile de Seine in Paris.

The Transformation of Europe into the Grail Chalice

Those familiar with the history of the Templars will soon notice that the preparation and inauguration of this order has a spiritual background, that it was called into life for a very specific task. Rudolf Steiner called this the task of raising Europe to a higher level,[3] essentially bringing European society into a form where a new, freer kind of Christianity could develop.

This is the same effort against Rome that led the army of the Crusade under Godfrey of Bouillon to Jerusalem. It is the complementary gesture to the Crusade and it is intended to bring Europe itself into a new situation.

Now the strange thing is that two great impulses are harmonized in this Templar order. The first is the Grail impulse, and the second is the Round Table of King Arthur, the Arthurian knights.

Everything about the Arthurian knights has been partially falsified by kitschy or romanticized depictions. They were a circle of initiates who had worked since the end of Atlantis. The name of Arthur—from a legendary king of the fourth century—was associated with the circle only much later. Rudolf Steiner says that it was the first Mystery school of the northern emigration stream from Atlantis, and it had great initiates as its members.[4] Until the time of Queen Elizabeth I, the Round Table existed in Wales; then, during the reign of James I, the successor of Elizabeth I, it was dissolved for political reasons. Rudolf Steiner adds that originally all ideas about power were derived from what came down from Atlantis.[5]

This Arthurian circle worked strongly into Europe, especially into everything connected with Celtic knighthood. Rudolf Steiner visited the Waldorf School while *Parzival* was being read there, and the Arthurian knights were mentioned. He remarked, 'Indeed, those were the knights of the sword. And what were the Knights of the Grail?' It is so nice the way the class fell silent; finally one spoke up and said, 'Those were probably the knights of the word.' 'Yes,' said Rudolf Steiner, 'absolutely correct. The Knights of the Grail were the knights of the word; the Arthurian knights were the knights of the sword.'[6]

In the Templars, what had come down as politically applied power—which was always intended to be spiritual—blends in a special way with the inner element of the Grail. The first Grand Master of the Templar order, Hugo of Payens, writes in a letter, 'It is an order in which, for the first time, the life of a monk is united with the life of a knight. The virtues of the knight and the virtues of the monk flow together into one form.'[7]

When we speak about a task in Europe, we must imagine how things were at that time. There were no states yet. France was cut up into an infinite number of large and small feudal domains. The realm of the King of France was quite small, limited to a specific region around Paris, and otherwise there were overlordships and vassal states—a patchwork quilt like the one we later came to know in Germany. Many maps show how the commanderies of the Templars are situated in this patchwork quilt, or how they slowly entered into it. We see that this cut-up, chaotic Europe is structured throughout by one unifying power—the Order of the Templars. The order was naturally united throughout all of its commanderies. This unity of the Order of the Templars leads to what is to be a higher level of Christianity in Europe.

To understand this, we come to the most fundamental motive behind the whole activity of the Templars, a kind of world-historic imagination. It was kept secret for a long time, intended only for the highest level of Templar initiation. It describes how the human being was originally meant to form his own religious and social life; together with others, he was meant to have religious and social sovereignty. But he lost his maturity as a result of the Fall of Man; and so he accepted the Pope as the authority over his religious life, and the emperor as the authority over his social life. The Templars said that the one—the religious life—is the *Vita contemplativa* of man, and the other—the social life—is the *Vita activa.* And what we want to accomplish is that the human being himself restore his sovereignty over the *Vita contemplativa* and the *Vita activa.* We want to shape Europe so that these results of the Fall of Man are cancelled out. From this comes a motto that has gone down in history, one that the Swiss are likely to inscribe on their banner even today: May Every Man Be His Own Pope and King!

However, this idea lived on in the view that European society must be formed so that it can take up the Christ. That actually was the foundation of the Templar imagination: Europe. European society itself must become the Grail, the Grail vessel. It must become the shell that can hold the pearl of the Logos.

The Templars in the Context of the Egyptian and Greek Mysteries

The so-called Templar initiation served this purpose. It was carried by two basic pillars, one that was long-term and continues through incarnations, and one that was apparently quite simple. The first pillar was the special relationship the Templars had to a genuine experience of the world of the stars, to the wisdom of the stars. This had begun when many of them were incarnated in Egypt and where they took part in the cult of Isis. They had participated in the Egyptian Isis Mysteries at that time as priests and as co-workers, and experienced there the goddess as star wisdom. Then, after they had been in the spiritual world during the second millennium before Christ, they experienced two significant events.

We have already considered the earthly aspect of the first event. Through the Queen of Sheba they experienced the passing of star wisdom from Solomon to Hiram. That was not just a superficial story, and certainly not as folkloric as the Old Testament might seem to indicate; it was a matter between gods and men. It is depicted in a simple imagination. The queen arrives and becomes engaged to Solomon. She then meets Hiram, changes her mind, and breaks off the engagement. She then turns to Hiram. But these are, in fact, quite sketchy indications of something in which the hierarchies and various beings, as well as many discarnate human beings, had a part. This whole story of Solomon, Hiram and the Queen of Sheba was a cosmic event from the point of view of the cosmos, and those Templars in the spiritual world experienced that. Their beloved star wisdom—the wisdom they had perceived as always flowing into the Abel stream, into the blessed priest-kings—passes over to actively working human beings.

Then came the next important life for the Templars. Many of them were incarnated in the Pythagorean School, either directly as pupils or within its sphere of influence. They took up something there that was infinitely important for their later work. In the School of Pythagoras, the harmony of the world was taught along with mathematics and other subjects. And the way the harmony of the world was taught demonstrated that access to it arises out of what takes place between music and mathematics. Music and mathematics are two sides of the same coin; through them we enter into the harmonic fabric of the world, later called the harmonies of the spheres. Hence a device originated from the Pythagorean School, the so-called monochord. The monochord is a longish sound box with a single string stretched across it; below this string runs a bridge that lifts the string a bit wherever it is positioned. And the tone created by striking the string is naturally either higher or lower, depending on how the bridge is moved. There are engravings on the monochord, a scale. And—if we run through the octave, from the prime, second, third, fourth and fifth—it becomes clear that the tones we hear are mathematical relationships.

This played an enormous role. Later it was discovered that these relationships correspond to the planetary intervals. Great works on the subject were written in the nineteenth century, works like *The Harmonic System of Antiquity* by Alexander von Thymus.[8] In these two thick volumes he approaches all of ancient culture from this point of view. This was continued in the twentieth century by Kaiser, Hase and others in *Harmonics*. A narrow stream was experienced with pre-intellectual power of imagination in the Pythagorean School at that time, a stream that many may find difficult to access today. The individual experiences the harmony of the universe through music in which mathematical laws exist; he experiences it through mathematics which reveals itself as the element of music.

Then, shortly after the Mystery of Golgotha, the second great event took place that was experienced from the spiritual world by these Templar souls. The Evangelist Mark lives as a bishop in Alexandria where he writes his Gospel, a quite cosmically oriented Gospel. The book *The Cosmic Rhythms in the Gospel of Mark*[9] by Hermann Beckh was republished not long ago. This Gospel of Mark demonstrates how all Christ Mysteries can really be understood only through cosmology. Mark is in Alexandria together with a high initiate of Isis, an initiated priest who becomes a Christian. And together Mark and Ormuz transform the entire ancient cults of Isis into a Christian Mystery cult. This is characterized quite precisely by Rudolf Steiner.

When a cultus is really transformed—both of the individuals who undertook this transformation were initiates in their way—then there is an effect that reaches right into the spiritual world. Many souls who had lived with the Isis cultus observed this event. Recasting one genuine cultus into another creates waves high up into the hierarchies. Thus the Templar souls experienced how their beloved Isis cultus now transforms into a Christian Mystery cultus. Rudolf Steiner emphasizes this: 'Mark and Ormuz were both disciples of Christ after His resurrection ...'[10] We recall that the Resurrected One passed through the Mysteries in order to transform them. Yet even apart from the emphasis Rudolf Steiner placed on this point, or the esoteric tradition that knew of this fact, we have the impression that Mark and Ormuz act under the inspiration of the resurrected Christ and with His cooperation; they do this as His pupils and His disciples.

The Templar Initiation

Now we come to those two centuries when these souls incarnate and join the Templar order. As Templars, they take up what was carried through the tradition of this transformed cultus and they continue it as the Templar ritual, as the Templar cultus. Through this cultus they rediscover their old goddess. Rudolf Steiner speaks movingly of the Templars. He begins the longer discussion of 1916 by saying that gazing at this Templar order is something 'to gladden the human soul'.[11] He uses quite wonderfully moving words when he comes to speak of the Templars. Thus he says, 'at the centre' of the Templars' teaching stood 'something feminine ... the divine Sophia, the divine wisdom'.[12] This is a key phrase for everything the Templars do. The Templars saw the Mystery of the Isis-Sophia as the great world-ether Mystery, now become essentially goddess-like. They observe the great world-ether Mystery in which the Isis-Sophia lives as something essentially goddess-like. They venerated Mary Magdalene as the earthly, human reflection of this being.

This cult continued in a modified form up to the time of Rudolf Steiner, who also practised it. Through his practice of this cultus, he once again affirms the whole story of Mark and Ormuz and its origin in the Isis cultus. During my time in Berlin I came to know several elderly people who had participated in the cultus. Through them, I own the last Templar sword used by Rudolf Steiner in the ritual. It is called a ritual sword, which means that it does not have a sharpened edge; but it is a real sword, and it was used by Rudolf Steiner in the Templar cultus. Rudolf Steiner always looks at the Templars from new perspectives. And he states that one of their principles was, 'We again take up the belief in the elemental forces of the world. We believe that the destinies of human beings are a result of the relationships among the stars, and that the human being himself was born out of the great relationships among the stars ...'[13] This is not to be confused with astrology, which has another background. This was the one great pillar of the Templar initiation—its view of the Isis-Sophia as essentially a goddess.

The other pillar is quite simple and yet quite powerful. It is their principle—and Rudolf Steiner cites this repeatedly: 'Our blood does not belong to us; our blood belongs to the Christ.' But that was not merely a credo. It was something lived out with the powerful might of faith, something lived out with more than courage. It was really the sacrifice of the illusion of the personal self.

Initially we live in this illusion out of necessity. We live in the body; we live in the blood. We are here and others are there. The world is out there, and we are an individuality simply because we feel more or less naturally at home in our skin. We must break out of this, as we have already heard in the Hiram legend with the three evil journeymen. Certainly every initiation had to deal seriously with this in some way; and the Templars lived it out in battle. In addition to what they began in Europe, they were also present at battles in Palestine and Spain. They took part in the *reconquista*; they joined in battle, and they situated their fortresses in Spain—for example, at Ponte Ferrada. This was the proving ground; they were greatly feared because they were unafraid of death and fought as though they were already dead. Rudolf Steiner says that they were not permitted to yield unless the odds against them were more than three to one.[14] It was an inner deed that was fulfilled in battle: 'I am not I. Everything that I am belongs to the Christ. The Christ works through me; the Christ works in my blood.' And Rudolf Steiner also says that many of these Templars were really initiated into the Christ Mysteries, that they underwent a truly Christian initiation.[15]

Jerusalem as a Centre of the Grail

There is yet another special background we must consider when we call the Templars the 'Emissaries of the Holy Grail'. We have already said that for their residence they were given the place high above on a rocky plateau where Solomon's temple stood. Rudolf Steiner says that the Templars 'built a place of wisdom on the site of the Solomonic temple, and after being prepared there, they become servants of the Holy Grail, they are initiated there by the Grail'.[16] Thus we said that the Grail impulse wanders; it goes from San Juan de la Peña, Montségur, upwards to Mount Moriah in Jerusalem. An archaeologist and historian writes, 'The Dome of the Rock, called *Templum Domini*, was transformed into a church. The Templars erected a balustrade around the holy rock, which still exists today, and an altar atop the rock.' Of course, this is a monstrous fabrication. An Islamic mosque was built around this rock—an octagon, the so-called Dome of the Rock—and after the conquest of Jerusalem, the Templars transformed it into a church. The plateau of the rock rises above ground—although not very high—and is actually a roof. From one side you can go under this rocky roof and find a space below, a shallow cavern where a person can stand. Here the rock is actually above the person. This is an ancient initiation site, the sanctuary of Melchizedek, where he had been active as King of Salem, Jeru-Salem. The Templars erected an altar atop this rock and they were initiated there by the Grail. Today we know that a Templar travelled to Jerusalem when he was mature enough—Rudolf Steiner says that not all of them were; there were exceptions. Many travelled to Jerusalem to this wisdom site, were initiated there by the Grail, and then returned to their work.

They took the principle of the Grail Knight from the Grail itself. The Templars actually emphasized this more than the Knights of the Grail. A living knight and a dead knight worked together. There is the wonderful Templar seal which has been reproduced and can be purchased. Two people sit atop a horse, one behind the other. I have drawn your attention to the fact that the Count of Champagne, one of the first seven Templars, was the richest feudal lord in France. Thus it was not out of poverty that two men rode one horse. This image says to those who know: Here are two people—a living person accompanied by a dead person who protects and guides his companion.

The Three Secrets of the Templars

There were several great secrets on which this particular Mystery was based. The first secret is the best known. They recognized and acted on the fact that there is a kind of universal formula; the individual has to master this universal formula in order to build the earthly temple. As Rudolf Steiner says, this universal formula was one of the three secrets that Solomon actually knew—the secret of wisdom, beauty and strength. The second secret that Solomon knew concerned the two Pillars of Hercules. And the third was the secret of light and darkness.

The Templars now become the ones who live and create with this universal formula. This is not at all easy to understand. Wisdom means that I become aware of how the entire world around me was created from primal wisdom. Wisdom is contained in everything—in the universe, in nature, in the build of the human being. This creation with wisdom came to an end; the creation of the world out of wisdom is complete, and in the future it is supposed to transform into a new cosmos. Rudolf Steiner says that the word 'strength' means the perfect social ordering of human beings among one another. Thus when we say that the 'cosmos of wisdom' develops into a 'cosmos of love',[17] we mean love as an organizing element for the whole universe, just as wisdom is currently an organizing element.

This is supposed to take place through the human being. The world of wisdom is at an end. Now it is up to the human being to create beauty, *Gloria*, out of this world of wisdom, to form the world of phenomena through piety and love—in so far as it is not a world-creating love, but the love between one person and another. This is what flowed into the social deeds of the Templars, defining their effect on European society over two centuries—allowing wisdom to pass over into beauty, into phenomena, through the creative power of the human being, so that love as a world-creating force can eventually grow out of the human experience of beauty. The world of wisdom is completed; it has its laws; it is defined. The cosmos of love, when it is completed, will be created out of love. Between the two is freedom. Here we could also pose the question—and now an ancient riddle surfaces anew—what role does art play for human beings?

The Golden Fleece

The second great secret helped to bring about the decline of the Templars; it is the secret of the Golden Fleece. This is a name that comes from the ancient Mysteries. What was meant by it within the Mysteries and in esotericism is the following. When I observe some kind of natural connection, an external relationship of the facts, then I can say to myself that something spiritual lies behind this natural connection. I can attempt to penetrate nature in order to arrive at the spiritual element from which the physically visible element has emerged. I arrive at a particular spiritual place. Then I can turn my attention to human relationships, to what occurs among people socially, and once again I can say that something spiritual is hidden behind human encounters, behind social forms. If I break through these social relationships, I also arrive at a spiritual element. It is the same spiritual element that I arrived at when I penetrated nature. Nature and human society have the same source. This is designated in various ways in the spiritual world—the creative gold of God, the creative sun of God, or the Golden Fleece.

It is not so difficult to understand this if we think about evolution. Earth and humanity were once united and then slowly separated. Humanity came into being as a social entity, as society; and below this, the kingdoms of nature—the plant, animal and mineral kingdoms—emerged from humanity. Thus I should not be surprised that I come to the same spiritual wellspring when I observe the kingdoms of nature and pass through them, or when I observe human relationships and pass through them. The secret here is that to alter something in nature, I must also alter it in the social realm; and to alter something in the social realm, I must also alter it in nature. Expressed in modern terms, ecology and sociology are two sides of the same coin. The Templars knew that physical gold has to be handled selflessly so that we can grow into the secret of the Golden Fleece in a Christian and humanly freeing way—and their whole activity was determined by this. The order dealt with money so that it was always used for the well-being of people. The order was wealthy; the individual knight owned nothing but his belt and his sword.

But there was also a dark secret. If I egotistically claim gold in the occult sense, desire it with greed and even with passion, then the physical gold will not lead me to the Golden Fleece; it will lead me instead in the opposite direction—downwards to the sun-demon, to Sorat. This principle remains true today, and that is why the expression 'the Golden Fleece' was used in two ways. The combination of certain alchemical processes is designated by the name Golden Fleece; the Golden Fleece is also an order created by Philip the Good, Duke of Burgundy. Only the pivotal rulers of Europe were to meet in this order to discuss how the society of Europe was to be formed in the best sense. It is also said that Philip the Good possessed the Philosopher's Stone.

Thus 'Golden Fleece' was the expression for the alchemical processes that are always present when we deal with nature, and for social processes as well. What this Philip IV—the so-called Philip the Fair—knew was: 'When I deal with gold egotistically, when I possess it as my property, then it leads me to those forces that teach me how to enslave people, how to exercise power over people.' He was a remnant of the dark, black magic Mysteries of Mexico. He had participated there in all the dark cultic rituals in which human beings by the hundreds were tortured, sliced open—there are the most horrendous old images from the Mexican Mysteries—and he was brought back with all the instincts and the knowledge of a black magician. Philip dominated the Pope, Clement V. Even Rudolf Steiner, who otherwise expressed himself quite civilly, called this Pope 'a ... creature'.[18] Philip dominated the Pope so that, acting through the Pope, he could ban the Templar order. He wanted the Templar's gold, but he also knew about the secret that the Templars actually wanted to abolish Pope and King.

Thus the destruction of the Templars came about precisely because of their intentions concerning the Golden Fleece. The Templars always used gold to serve the interests of human freedom, even in their so-called banking institutions. These institutions are external things that are often written of, and they are certainly important. A person could always deposit his hundred or five hundred gold coins at the Temple in Paris or somewhere else, and receive a receipt and a secret password. Then that person pocketed the receipt, travelled out of harm's reach to Jerusalem, and picked up his money from the Temple lodge there. That was a moment of freedom. Travelling with gold coins during that age of highway robbery was always a very risky thing; and so the Templars did much to put people in a position of independence, of freedom.

The Knowledge of Etheric Geography

The third great secret leads us to the most difficult Mystery questions. The third is the secret of etheric geography which the Templars mastered. By etheric geography, we understand the following. Various kinds of ethers can be differentiated—the warmth ether, the light ether, the chemical ether and the life ether. These are connected with earth, water, air and physical warmth. These ethers are present everywhere; but where the earth's surface is concerned, various kinds of ether dominate in certain places. There are areas where the light ether is dominant, others where the warmth ether is dominant and the other ethers less so; or areas where the life ether—or sound ether—is dominant. In fact, in a broad etheric landscape where the various ethers are evenly distributed, it is possible for a powerful beam of light ether to shoot out suddenly from a particular place into the starry heavens. Shrines were built at such places, menhirs were erected, cromlechs and dolmens. Churches were constructed on these sites at a later time, or temples at an earlier time.

The Templars now used this knowledge of the etheric geography for the shaping of Europe, the shaping of European soil. Added to this is their great alliance with the Cistercians, which even conscientious historians often deal with as incidental. Bernard of Clairvaux was Abbot of Clairvaux; he was the great spiritual leader of the Cistercians. Rudolf Steiner calls him 'the ... most important personality of the twelfth century'. He characterizes him as a person whose aura radiated far and wide.[19] In this context, far and wide actually means working out into many regions. A person could sense Bernard of Clairvaux even if he were sixty miles away.

It is the Cistercian order that actually cultivated the ground of Europe—France, Germany, the whole eastern region, parts of Spain and England. The Cistercians went where it was inhospitable, where there were swamps and primeval forests. The swamps were drained, lakes were established, fields were drained, and cattle breeding, fruit farming and fisheries were begun. We owe the fact that we live in a civilized Europe to the Cistercians and their esotericism, their secrets. The Templars—and this is also overlooked—laid down roads, they took care that markets were developed in certain places, they secured the roads; they were, so to speak, the social, legal aspect of the whole process. The Golden Fleece in

Europe is the result of Templar and Cistercian companionship; they called themselves 'companions', 'communal bread eaters'—shared bread was the image.

The Templars dealt with their ever-increasing stores of money in an absolutely selfless way, and remained personally poor; they used their gold for the freedom and interest of the human being, and the Cistercians did likewise. The Cistercian order naturally grew wealthy. If a cloister pursues farming and so forth for decades, naturally it becomes wealthy. The individual monk was utterly poor, and a historically documented story explains how seriously this was taken.

A highly esteemed monk dies; he was the brother of the abbot. His room is cleaned out and a copper penny is found under his straw mattress. He was subsequently taken out of the cloister and buried in a grave outside the cemetery. They threw the penny in the grave after him and cried out, 'May you be happy with your money!' There was nothing he could buy with the penny; but possession was so scorned and despised that, even in this historical case, a highly esteemed monk is tossed out of the cloister after his death. This story illustrates what Rudolf Steiner often says. We cannot imagine the enormous power of the heart and soul that prevailed at that time, nor the completely different realities concerning faith and conduct.

Through the cooperation between the Cistercians and the Templars, a Europe is shaped that might become a vessel for the Christ. The Grail intended the Christ to be taken up by the individual; the Templars intended Christ to be taken up by society.

Let us turn our attention again to the second secret. The earth was created out of the spiritual element. There came a moment in the astral-etheric element when the earth started to become physical substance; one might say this was the first point on the physical earth. Tradition says that this place was Mount Moriah. Emil Bock has researched this matter.[20] Then the earth condensed further, which is to say other points were created. From these points, more points arose across the earth. One of them is Vézelay. Others are located on other continents. Still other points are created around these points—in Switzerland, the Gotthard—and these are points in the phantom body of the physical earth, independent of any geological shifts. The phantom body of the physical earth arises as these points become denser and denser. Of course, these were things the initiates knew; the Altar of the Templars where the Grail initiation of the Templars took place was on Mount Moriah, the beginning of the physical earth.

Much could be said about this because this principle applies to the whole earth. We have a strong sense that there is a region in North America which is such a place. It is noteworthy that Rudolf Steiner says this is where the anthroposophical centre must be founded. This is also true for the other continents. Of course, Ayers Rock is where the point-by-point development began in Australia.

The third level, this level of the geographical secrets, leads us to the limits of what we are accustomed to think. In the so-called 'Astronomical Course', Rudolf Steiner speaks about the correspondences between the cosmos and the earth. He says, 'For example, we might come to think of Jupiter in this light and discover a counter-Jupiter in the interior of the earth.' He even draws it this way: there, outside, is Jupiter; below, in the earth's interior, is the counter-Jupiter. 'We arrive at something that works from the interior of the earth outwards, in the same way that Jupiter works from without.'[21] Now comes the decisive sentence that expresses almost incidentally one of the great world secrets. 'We arrive at a mirroring—in reality it is the other way around, but I will say it now in this way—at a mirroring of what is on the outside.'[22] It is not the stars that are reflected in the earth, but the earth that is reflected in the stars. The world of the stars is the reflection of the earth's interior. The Earth Mother, Eve, appears as the Heavenly Virgin, as the Isis-Sophia.

Of course, we can find a way to understand this if we consider that, at the beginning of Earth evolution, during the Polaric age, the earth was as large as the orbit of Saturn. Then the earth contracted and it might be said that it left the planets behind as it contracted. From a certain point of view, in the beginning, when the earth was as large as the orbit of Saturn, it had already left behind the physical aspect of the world of the fixed stars. When we look out at the stars, we are observing something that developed from the unity of Earth and the human being; the same is true when we look at the animals, the plants, and the minerals.

This is the Mystery knowledge that formed the basis for the relationship of the initiated Templars to their goddess Isis-Sophia, to their etheric secret of the cosmos. The problem of the present time is that we accept this world as naïve realists. We think that everything is exactly as we see it. That is why the present time is so materialistic. Someone can go to church every day, believe that there is a God Who encompasses everything, and that there was a Christ. If such a person takes this world to be real, he is a materialist. This is unmistakably expressed in the next to the last Class lesson of the School for Spiritual Science. But there had always been Mystery knowledge, and it was always known that what matters is spirituality. What we experience as the Earth Mother, as the Great Mother, comes to meet us once again from out of the starry world as the Isis-Sophia.

The Inauguration of the Gothic Style

All of this creates the background for the great cultural deed of the Templars, the inauguration of the Gothic style. Today it is an uncontested fact that the Templars were the real leaders of the lodges (German, *Bauhütten*). Rudolf Steiner says in general that the forms, the proportions of the Gothic style work in the subconscious, conveying a reflection of the music of the spheres. What we experience in the Gothic style is a reflection of that music of the spheres in which the angels associate with one another through music. Between the hierarchical beings, cosmic intelligence lives as the music of the spheres. Music is the language the angels use with one another; the harmony of the spheres is the language of the hierarchies among themselves.[23] In the Mars sphere, the dynamis direct what is orchestral; in the Jupiter sphere, the kyriotetes convey what is songlike, the logical element of music; and, finally, in Saturn, in the world of the thrones, the Cosmic Word resounds as music or music resounds as the Cosmic Word.

The Templars had learned this from Pythagoras and, in another way, they had already learned it in the Egyptian Mysteries. Thus, what is told as a legend of the order is also true. The inauguration of this order arose from circles of initiates and, according to the legend of the order, the Templars were sent to Jerusalem with the task of finding the Ark of the Covenant. Because the Ark of the Covenant has never surfaced—unlike the seven-armed candelabra that Titus carried back to Rome in triumph—the tradition has always existed that the Ark is hidden somewhere in the vast caves of the Temple Mount in Jerusalem. I have wandered through these caves myself, not to find the Ark of the Covenant, but in order to understand this. Above ground, there is this large plateau; at one point there is Mount Moriah, and then it slopes downwards into passageways and caves, artificial passages, natural caverns that are walled up and filled with rubble. The legend has always existed that the Ark of the Covenant was there below. The Templars find the Ark. There are indications from Rudolf Steiner that this depiction of the events is correct. Within the Ark are the primal proportions for the development of the structure of humanity.

For this reason, the Grand Master of the Templars always had the abacus as a sign of his office; it was a staff on which units of measurement of various kinds were engraved. The Grand Master knew which measurements were to be used for which purpose. We know this to be true. We know the dimensions of the pyramids, the dimensions of the Egyptian temple; we know that in the whole history of temple construction certain systems of measurement were always used. And now this is carried over to what becomes the primal system of measurement for the Gothic style.

Let us turn our attention again to the Council of Troyes. All the prominent figures in France were gathered at this council: the Archbishops of Sens and Reims; the Bishops of Chartres, Paris, Troyes, Orléans; and the Abbotts, Bernard of Clairvaux and the famous Suger of Saint-Denis. They hold the council, disperse, and immediately afterwards the Gothic style develops wherever there are people who attended the council. The first to build is Suger of Saint-Denis. He has a Gothic apse built in the church, invites the whole world to admire it, and even writes a great text in which he says, 'What we are attempting to do here is to reconnect with the Temple of Solomon.' Shortly afterwards, Henri Sangliers, Archbishop of Sens, builds the first Gothic façade, and soon after that, Godfrey of Chartres builds the first Gothic westwork; and so it continues. One can say that the whole Gothic style spreads throughout the Western world as a result of this Council of Troyes.

If we read Rudolf Steiner's description, we understand what actually happened there. He says quite emphatically that it was not just a matter of building a great house of God. 'The Gothic style has a much deeper foundation. Those who gave the first indications for the development of Gothic buildings in the world were knowledgeable about occultism, they were ... initiates ... The Gothic style ... cathedrals and churches trigger quite specific soul impressions.' They impress the soul into certain spiritual elements and, through these spiritual elements, into a certain morality. He says that architectural styles project from the great thoughts of the initiates far into the future. Souls who took up the Gothic style demonstrate ... in their next incarnation the expression of this inner state of heart and soul'.[24] Actually, the Gothic style was built for the next incarnation of the people who see it.

All proportions—the world-ether secret that is experienced through music and mathematics; the harmony of the spheres built into the Gothic cathedrals; rules and measurements—all have a spiritual-moral effect.

They were primal measurements that were carried over and now form the basis of Gothic buildings.

Rudolf Steiner describes the primal proportions for the building of the first Goetheanum. Two circles are given as the outline, one larger and one smaller circle, and the smaller stands in a quite particular relationship to the larger circle. There are mathematical concepts of intersecting circles; we can however state it very simply. When we inscribe a pentagon, a five-cornered figure, in the large circle, the corner points of one side are precisely the points through which the small circle passes. And then Rudolf Steiner says that this proportion, this relationship of the small circle to the large circle, has determined all the forms of the Goetheanum. He says that, had the relationship been a bit different, all these forms would necessarily have been different. This is an indication that can really occupy us for a long time, that we can ponder for a long time—proportions based on primal measurements determine what then results. We experience that many Gothic churches have primal elements, and everything that develops in them arises from these primal measurements.

Rudolf Steiner says that the Romanesque churches were always concerned with the relationship with the dead. As a rule they were always built over a crypt, thus they were always surrounding the dead and for the dead; through this connection to the dead, they were to serve as an entrance to the spiritual world. The Gothic cathedrals were built for the living, and the Gothic cathedral remains unfinished until throngs of people are praying in it.[25]

The Knowledge of America

The Templars were the architects of the Gothic style; they also financed it, specifically with silver and gold from America. This is already an open secret today; historians write about it without raising controversy. The Templars travelled regularly from La Rochelle in France to America. They knew about America from members of the order because the north of France was colonized by Normans, hence by Vikings who had settled there bringing with them knowledge of America. We must also take a look at how much was achieved. A modern historian describes it this way: 'In just two hundred years, over one hundred large churches and cathedrals were built.'[26] At that time, France had fifteen million inhabitants. All this construction was an enormous accomplishment because stone masons, sculptors, carpenters, bricklayers, and sophisticated logistics based on a highly-developed technical ability were necessary. In addition, cloisters, castles and secular buildings were also erected. 'Financing,' writes this historian, 'came from the Templars who had silver from America.'[27] The average work week was thirty-six hours long, and there were up to 190 holidays in the year during which no work was done.

Effects of the Eradication of the Templar Order

With the eradication of the Templars, something occurs that reaches into the present with both good and ill effects. Philip, using the truly dark arts at his command, had the Templars tortured, and under this terrible torture they confess to things they had never done. They had travelled the path of self-knowledge, of overcoming the self, of purification—because this was their path of schooling. Initiation was not just some ceremonial deed, but the outcome of years or decades of schooling during which they overcame an infinitude of urges, passions, vices, and so forth. According to Rudolf Steiner, through this torture at the hands of Philip, something quite frightful happened. Philip knew that when people are tortured they confess to exactly what they have overcome.[28] Thus, for example, while glowing coals were being laid on the bare stomach of a Templar, horrendous scribes sat nearby, writing down what the Templars cried out in their anguish—because they were confessing to what they had overcome. History, however, records these as the Templar's confessions of their vices. The other side of this was the Templar's heroic courage, their self-surrender for Christ.

As Rudolf Steiner points out, the effects from these unholy years (1307–14) continue up to the present.[29] Wherever people are tortured today and speak untruths during their torture—whether or not this is a brainwashing or something else—the old, evil impulse is present. And wherever people sacrifice themselves selflessly for the well-being of others, the good impulse of the Templars is present.

Today we stand at the second zenith of Sorat. The first had been Gondishapur, the attempt to destroy within the individual human being what can be received through the Christ. Around 1332 (twice 666)—we have to take the time as approximate, although Rudolf Steiner emphasizes the number—Sorat was active in a way that was intended to hinder the ability of human communities to live with the Christ.

There were people affiliated with the Templar order, not members of the Templar order, but private individuals who participated in the

Templar secrets. Dante was such a person. After the destruction of the Templar order, he writes down the secrets of the Templars in *The Divine Comedy*. He describes the great level of the *Inferno*, which is nothing other than a description of everything the human being must overcome. We can experience hell for ourselves when we observe our own laziness, or envy, and so forth. We can experience how this is really like hell. And when the human being has overcome what the *Inferno* depicts, then comes the *Purgatory*, the purification, the clarification. Finally, there is Paradise with the rose of heaven. Bernard of Clairvaux appears as the initiate of the great rose of heaven. Finally there is an image for the Trinity. At the end are the words that love holds the whole world together. At a decisive place along this pathway, the pupil Dante is told: 'Your will is free. Now be your own Emperor, your own Pope.' This is the origin of these words, which then worked their way far into the Western world.

The Survival of the Templar Impulses

The Templar order was completely eradicated in France. In other countries, the Templars remain viable but their wealth proves to be much too interesting, and authorities of all kinds appropriate it. Two great esoteric traditions continue. The first travels up to Scotland where the so-called Order of the Thistle arises; many Templars survive and pass on their secrets there. The other then radiates towards Portugal, where the Templar order is entirely transformed into the Order of Christ under the protection of the king.

James I then comes from Scotland. The anthroposophist Hildegard Wiegand wrote a book about James I entitled *Der kampf gegen den Tarnhelm* [The battle with the tarnhelm]; it is based on conversations with Rudolf Steiner. This book ends with an image. The supersensible Temple appears and three figures stand before the altar. One has a chalice—for the Grail. One has a sword—for the Templars. The third has a book—for the Rosicrucians. And she writes, 'We recognize as James I the figure with the sword.'[30] Rudolf Steiner said the most amazing things about James I. He was the founder of all the newer brotherhoods. He was a very advanced occultist. He 'immunized the British folk substance with ... an element it dare not lose if it does not want to open itself completely to materialism'.[31] Thus one tradition says that the Freemasons, especially the high degrees of Freemasonry, were inspired from Scotland; and another tradition says that in Portugal the navigator-impulse arises out of the Order of Christ. Henry the Navigator and his great school lived with the order, and Columbus was told, 'There is land over there.' Right up to the end of his life, Columbus believed he had discovered India. But today we know that all the material passed on to him, and perhaps also discussed with him, came from Templar knowledge. There were people who knew what he would find when he set sail.

After the destruction of the order, the great spiritual being connected with it withdrew; but all sorts of traditions were handed down. One of these traditions leads to a system of high degrees called the 'strict observance'. Goethe becomes a member of this 'strict observance'; he takes the old Temple Oath to Bernard of Clairvaux, and then the order dies out. It is as though the tradition was meant to survive until Goethe's time. The dead Templars have not vanished; Rudolf Steiner describes how they begin to inspire European spirits in a wonderful way. Goethe was someone who received particular inspiration from the Templars.[32] Prepared through outer circumstances, he took up what the Templars told him; one of the primary results of this inspiration is the second part of *Faust*. Rudolf Steiner says about it: There are an infinite number of secrets about European development flowing into this *Faust*, into the second part. Goethe knew the secret of the Templars.[33]

Many Templars are returning in the Anthroposophical Society. The image of Hilarius—the old Grand Master of the Templars who is there again in the Mystery Dramas—and the others who are with him, only hint at this reality. Something once appeared in a book title that can be applied literally to us: *The Templars Are Among Us*. Everyone who examines this fact is of one opinion. Today, Templars are people who enter into economic life, who are enterprising, like Hilarius with his factory. Hilarius brings new impulses into the economic sphere, into manufacturing, into social relationships. Above all, the universal mission of the Templars—the self-determination of human beings in religious and social matters—shines on and will continue to shine on.

That is what we actually mean when we speak of anthroposophy and threefolding: the achievement of self-determination in all spiritual matters through anthroposophy; and the achievement of self-determination in all matters relating to the social organism through threefolding.

Lecture 10

The Three Initiations of Christian Rosenkreutz

Manfred Schmidt-Brabant

In what follows we arrive at the threshold of the present time; in fact, we even enter into the present.

Rudolf Steiner calls Kaspar Hauser's teacher—Professor Daumer of Nuremberg—one of the last Rosicrucians; he referred in the same way to Privy Counsellor Karl von Eckartshausen, who wrote highly spiritual-esoteric works. Thus, what was prepared in the far distant past continued into the nineteenth century.

What takes place in Rosicrucianism is that outer paths become inner paths; everything that had guided mankind externally—through the Grail, the Camino, the Templars—is changed into an inner experience of the human being. Questions become crucial; it becomes crucial for the human being to grasp an initiative inwardly. External events will no longer set the individual in motion. If he hopes for outside help, then he hopes in vain. Taking the initiative to ask a question becomes decisive; the outer path becomes the inner path. This is a sign of the age of the consciousness soul, and as part of the consciousness soul it is a sign of modern knowledge—especially modern scientific knowledge. We move from question to question. The question finds an answer through research, and new questions arise from that answer.

At the same time, through a growing awareness of the inner path, it becomes clear that what we are considering here is not a matter of book learning but of our individual, inner reality. We are inwardly constituted in one way or another by what has occurred throughout history; that is our reality. It is about the reality of our inner soul life. Much of what Rudolf Steiner has said becomes a hint, a signpost, a conceptual source of light—and all of what he said would merely be paper if we could not relate it to our own inner, soul-spiritual reality.

The Three Rosicrucian Texts

The Rosicrucian movement begins exoterically with three well-known publications. In 1614, a work appears in Kassel, *Fama Fraternitatis* or *The Revelation of the Brotherhood of the Laudable Order of the Rose Cross*; one year later, in 1615, the *Confessio Fraternitatis* or *Confession of the Laudable Brotherhood of the Esteemed Rose Cross*; and finally, in 1616 in Strasburg, the great primary text, *The Chymical Wedding of Christian Rosenkreutz 1459*. We know that in 1604 the *Chymical Wedding* was already being circulated in manuscript, and that the author was Johann Valentin Andrae, a seventeen-year-old theology student.

These three texts have an extraordinary effect. They are quickly circulated; a sensational hysteria of anticipation and all sorts of speculation spread throughout Europe. Many publications follow. Nothing further was known; there was only talk of an Order of the Rose Cross. And as a result mystifications arise; there are many who write about the Rosicrucians as if they knew them, or as though they themselves were members. Then comes the counter-attack with the claim that all this is merely an invention, that Christian Rosenkreutz never existed, that it is a prank perpetrated by a young theology student. Others are more clever and say that the expectation of the entire age is expressed in these writings because they discuss a 'general reformation'. Here we must also remember that Martin Luther gave rise to Protestantism in the sixteenth century, protesting against the omnipotence of the Pope. He posted his ninety-five theses in Wittenberg; in 1520, he authored his great epistle, 'To the (Christian) Nobles of the German Nation'. Shortly thereafter, in 1534, the counter-attack took place with the founding of the Jesuit order, whose goal was the Counter Reformation. These Rosicrucian texts appear in a climate of anticipation that a new age had to begin; initially, these texts lend this anticipation an esoteric form.

The Rosicrucian Principle of Atlantis

Rudolf Steiner spoke frequently about Christian Rosenkreutz and the Rosicrucians. He says that Rosicrucianism already had its Mysteries in Atlantis. He distinguishes between the historical Rosicrucianism that goes back to the personality of Christian Rosenkreutz, and the Rosicrucian spirit, Rosicrucian esotericism and spirituality. The latter already had its Mysteries in Atlantis. During Atlantis, the life of the Mysteries was organized as we later experience it with Solomon and Hiram, namely, into what the planets above the sun took up as pure spirit out of the spiritual world; into the Mysteries of the planets below the sun that were concerned with the relationships on the earth; and into the Sun Mysteries in which the elements both above and below came into balance. When Rudolf Steiner looks at the impulses presented here, he always considers the sun together with the planets beneath the sun, spiritual knowledge in connection with an experience of the earth which was just beginning at that time.

This means that we already have in Atlantis the beginning of the principle of Rosicrucian schooling—spiritual life is being developed but in conjunction with earthly activity, with earthly experience. The first great, significant demonstration of the spirit of Rosicrucianism occurs in the figure of Hiram. He is the one who works on the earth. He builds the Temple so that what is physical leads mankind into the spiritual interior. This impulse then works into the Mysteries of Dionysus.

The Gathering of Three Bodhisattvas

Rudolf Steiner says that a decisive moment for humanity happens in the fourth century when three representative Bodhisattvas meet in the spiritual world. The first is the legendary Scythianus, a hidden initiate. Even today he remains hidden behind lofty initiates; he is the 'keeper of ancient Atlantean wisdom', the wisdom which contributed to the creation of the physical body throughout the Atlantean period.[1] Shorter periods were sufficient later for the cultivation of the sentient body and the etheric body in India, or the sentient soul in Egypt. The whole of Atlantis contributed to our physical body until it emerged essentially as we know it at the end of Atlantis. The keeper of all of these Mystery secrets is Scythianus.

The second is Buddha. In this context Buddha is called the second 'Keeper of the Seal of the Wisdom of Humanity'.[2] The third is Zarathustra, the keeper of all cosmological Mysteries. These three are called together by a fourth, Manes, who appears as a higher initiate in relation to them; it is said that Manes appears among them like a 'lofty messenger of the Christ'.

In this conference a kind of decision is reached. This must be imagined in a totally spiritual way, but also in a way that such beings discuss among themselves the fate of humanity. Their decision, made for the sake of the future of humanity, is to take all the wisdom previously carried by the Bodhisattvas and transfer it to the Rosicrucian Mysteries yet to come. What then becomes the concrete, historical Rosicrucian Mysteries emerges from this supersensible resolve made in the light of the Mystery of Golgotha. Led by the lofty messenger Manes, the three leading Bodhisattvas decided to bring over all of the Bodhisattva wisdom—that is all of the Mystery wisdom—into the Christian stream of future earthly Rosicrucian Mysteries.

It is in this spirit that we understand why Rudolf Steiner often speaks of Rosicrucians of the eighth and ninth centuries. There is a wonderful depiction in his work of how pupils of the Rosicrucians in the seventh and eighth centuries, pupils who had been taught in the Rosicrucian temples, travel about as rhapsodists. The effect of this can be felt right down to the troubadours; they sing songs, and Rosicrucian wisdom is brought to the people through the content of the songs. There are fairy-tales and legends, but presented in song. These songs are then sung over and over again, and handed down from person to person in this way.

Lazarus—The Transformation of the Etheric Body

The historically verifiable individuality of the being we call Christian Rosenkreutz—named after one of its incarnations—has its first important and visible incarnation in the figure of Hiram. Christian Rosenkreutz was the master builder Hiram, not in his first incarnation but in his most decisive incarnation of this sequence. Hiram was an earthly man, not a superhuman being like Manu who led the Sun temple, nor a Bodhisattva. He had undergone many and extensive experiences on earth and, according to Rudolf Steiner, he arrives as Hiram 'on the verge of initiation'.[3] He is killed and is reborn as Lazarus—as the Lazarus who is awakened from death by Christ in a public deed.

This was an image of the old initiation which took place in the Mysteries, but in complete secrecy. The person who was to be initiated fell into a deathlike sleep so similar to death that the etheric body was considerably loosened. The danger always existed in these old temple initiations that the bodily members would tear asunder and the neophyte would actually die. Very slender connections remained that were clairvoyantly supervised by the initiates; and then the initiation was completed in the loosened bodily composition. The supersensible members of the human being were affected magically, and when these members returned to the physical body the candidate was enlightened, initiated. All of this took place in secrecy. And now the initiates of the Hebraic Mysteries witness the Christ performing in public the awakening of a human being to consciousness out of the death sleep of initiation.

The awakened Lazarus, who looks into the spiritual world as a result of the awakening, becomes the 'disciple whom the Lord loved'. He becomes the John who writes the Gospel and the Book of Revelation. Christ, dying on the cross, entrusts Mother Earth to this soul. I quote here, because we need to know these words of Rudolf Steiner's:

> Now ... as the great Sun Spirit had descended to the earth and lived in the body of Jesus of Nazareth, Christ Jesus Himself laid the seed of new life in the heart of the reborn Hiram Abiff. Through Christ Jesus Himself, Hiram was awakened to spiritual life; he was born again in the disciple whom the Lord loved. The human ego was enlivened by the divine ego and elevated to a higher existence. Afterwards, this disciple could become the author of that Gospel which has as its starting-point the human and the divine ego. And the development of this human ego throughout the post-Atlantean cultural periods and into the future until the end of earthly days was revealed to him in the way he presented it in the Apocalypse. It is told in his Gospel how Christ Jesus entrusts this disciple to his mother with the last words that sound from the cross. This is not his physical mother. As a son, He gives the human ego to the Earth Mother after He has enlivened it with His forces. He gives the earth as a mother to this ego so that the son would give its powers to the mother. The human ego is to redeem the earth, lift it up into spiritual regions with its forces, in full consciousness that without this earth, the ego could not develop into what it is and should become.[4]

This is the ancient secret of the Rosicrucians: If the earth does not become spiritualized, the ego will not be able to develop into what it should be.

The Transformation of the Astral Body

After the incarnation as Lazarus/John, a series of what are called 'quiet incarnations' ensue—these enormous experiences must settle into the soul. Some are female incarnations, because the emotional deepening of the soul is easier in the feminine incarnations; there are also some simple ones, perhaps as a workman. Only those people who met him in such an incarnation might sense: this is someone very special! But nothing about this quality appeared outwardly; it all took place as an inner process.

And then comes the second initiation. While the first initiation is wholly connected with life, with the etheric body, now comes an initiation that fully transforms the astral body of this individuality. At an unidentified location in Europe, a child grows up, and this child is educated by twelve initiates. Of course, the infant was also cared for. But when the education of the child begins, twelve great initiates become very quickly involved. They represent the seven great Atlantean periods of development; they represent the post-Atlantean cultural epochs; and the twelfth represents the present age. They allow all the wisdom they have to give to flow into this growing child.

We can reflect on what such an education looked like, since it was conducted not merely through lectures and theory. We can reflect on how one initiate led the boy though nature, perhaps showing him the plants, the minerals, the animals; how another initiate showed him the starry heavens, introduced him to cosmology. Thus a kind of idealized Waldorf education takes place until the time the boy became a young man, which we can assume occurred around the age of twenty-one or twenty-two. Then, over the course of a shorter period, these initiates once more allow all their teaching to be impressed upon the young man in a form that is mantric and songlike. We can imagine that this might have had a certain cultic character, that again and again the initiates mantrically sum up in speech and song what they had taught him throughout the years.

Now something wonderful happens, which Rudolf Steiner says 'could only take place once in history'.[5] The young man again sinks into a deathlike sleep and his body becomes completely transparent. All ashen components fall away, and the restored phantom appears fully visible in the world. The pure, white diamond which the physical body should actually be arises before the twelve. As the young man returns again to himself, a completely new version of all the teaching that he received from the twelve sounds from his lips; ancient primal knowledge streams forth from the thirteenth in their midst as a new life of wisdom.

Soon after, the young man dies, and the twelve initiates indicate in figures and symbols what they heard from this thirteenth after his awakening. These indications were preserved and disseminated in Rosicrucian circles. In 1785, they were published in Altona near Hamburg by one of the last successor organizations of the Rosicrucians, the Order of the Gold and Rose Cross; they had been collected by Hinricus Madathanus Theosophus. They were published again during the First World War, and yet again after the Second World War; they are still available today. Rudolf Steiner says what streamed forth from the thirteenth as a new body of knowledge lives in these drawings and images expressed in the symbolism of that time.[6] We are still able to look at such images. We have at the Goetheanum an old example of drawings from the early Rosicrucian period. It is not a mechanically reproduced copy; someone has made these drawings with humility and care in pen and black ink on ancient, handmade paper. There are thirty or forty pages with complicated drawings, especially of the central figure of the Rosicrucians, that wonderful figure, the heavenly virgin Sophia. We see how she opens below and the whole of creation, even God and Christ, emerge from her cloak, from her very being. And we recall that it was always said that the Sophia was already present when God created the world because she is His wisdom. The whole world originated from her, from the wisdom of God, from Sophia.

We see this Sophia in these images. First we see the great developmental strides—the elements coming into being, the planets, and then the whole world below. There are many small circles—human beings, the craftsmen, death and hell are at the very bottom. All this is the Virgin Sophia of the Rosicrucians.

The Initiation through the Ego of the Christ

After some time, the young man is reborn. In 1378, he begins the incarnation of the human being who, in this life, we call Christian Rosenkreutz. He travels widely throughout the world, visiting the old Mystery sites. The experience Paul had on the road to Damascus is renewed for this young man when he experiences the Resurrected One in the restored phantom. Now, as an earthly man, he takes up all the wisdom of the world at that time, and then he enters into his third initiation. The first initiation of Lazarus occurred out of the life forces of the ether body; the second initiation of the youth brought about such a complete purification of the astral body that all the ash present in the physical body as a result of the Fall of Man was eliminated; and now the third initiation takes place. He is eighty-one years old. Rudolf Steiner confirms the date; he is initiated by Manes in 1459. Manes, 'a lofty messenger of Christ',[7] himself completes the third initiation of Christian Rosenkreutz. In this initiation, Christian Rosenkreutz is the first to be endowed with the ego of the Christ from the chalice of the Holy Grail. First there was the penetration of the ether body by the Christ and then the penetration of the astral body by the Christ. In his third initiation, Christian Rosenkreutz receives the ego of Christ itself.

We should not necessarily take this to mean that Manes stands at a higher level, but rather that one great initiate completes the initiation of another great initiate. A kind of lofty, spiritual collegiality holds sway in this process.

This initiation is described imaginatively in the *Chymical Wedding*. In it, a long process is depicted in images. At this level, the one to be initiated is no longer merely passive; he is also an active participant. We could say that both Manes and Christian Rosenkreutz complete the implantation of the Christ Ego in Christian Rosenkreutz, and through this lengthy, active deed, Christian Rosenkreutz unites the ancient Atlantean Tao wisdom with Christianity.

In Atlantis the human being lived with the whole world as though with something spiritual. People looked into everything that occurred in nature; in all the events of nature lived the great spirit, the Tao. Rudolf Steiner recalls how the Indians still maintained that the Great Spirit Manitou was to be found in all things. For Atlantean people this spirit was their own existence; at the time, the physical body was not seen in the same way we do today. The individual lived outside—the human being was out there and the body was only a point of reference, because an individuality needs some point of reference. People lived within the world. The spirit of the world is united through Christian Rosenkreutz with the deepest inner experience the human being can have, with the 'Not I, but the Christ in me'. This experience is found in the meaning of this initiation, and makes it applicable to the whole future of the earth. The human being is united inwardly with what is outside, outwardly with what is inside.

Until the year 1484, the Order of the Rose Cross is being established through the work of the eighty-one-year-old initiate, 'Father Rosenkreutz'—as we like to call him; he lives to the age of 106 years in this incarnation. There is an important secret that is associated with the creation of the first Rosicrucian community. Rudolf Steiner emphasizes frequently that this was a very small circle, fewer than ten people. What kind of people were they? First, Rudolf Steiner says, 'At the awakening of Lazarus, the spiritual being of John the Baptist entered from on high into the earlier Lazarus, reaching down into the consciousness soul ... and from below, the being of Lazarus entered, so that the two merged into one another. As a result, there stood before the Christ a human being who reached from the depths of the earth to the highest heights of heaven, who carried within himself in perfection the physical body through all other members, including the spirit members Manas, Buddhi, Atma; this condition can only be developed in the far distant future by all mankind.'[8] However, he indicates this is still not the whole story. Actually, at the awakening of Lazarus, every part of his body is another being. In the intellectual soul is the Hiram-ego, and all the other soul members are other beings. The sentient soul is Mary Magdalene, and the consciousness soul is John the Baptist, the Adam-ego.

These beings, or individualities, that had made up the bodily members of Lazarus, create the first Rosicrucian community. Thus it can be said that Christian Rosenkreutz, as the Hiram-ego, has around him those beings that experienced with him in Lazarus the first initiation by Christ.

This circle works into the world. There are seven members, according to Rudolf Steiner, and each of the seven has a further seven around him. An external Rosicrucian brotherhood also arises. But again and again, reference is made to the historical nucleus, to a kind of core group that continued to develop during the subsequent two centuries.

Christian Rosenkreutz at the End of the Sixteenth Century

At the end of the sixteenth century, Christian Rosenkreutz had returned and he convenes two conferences—a somewhat larger conference of the most important initiates in Europe at that time, which is spoken of as a 'physical conference'; and a short time later, a smaller conference comprised of perhaps only four or five initiates. In this conference he presents to his friends his concern, his concern about the coming age of the consciousness soul.

This consciousness soul age has a dual nature. The human being has now ascended through the sentient soul and the intellectual soul to the point of developing the consciousness soul. This consciousness soul borders above on the Spirit Self, on the world of spiritual existence, on the spiritual world; at the same time, however, it is developed through the fact that the human being depends on his physical body. The sentient soul required the astral body as a foundation for its own development; the intellectual soul required the etheric body for its development; the consciousness soul requires the physical body. Now Christian Rosenkreutz and other initiates were concerned that mankind might be torn apart, that there might be spiritual human beings devoted only to the spiritual experience made possible by means of the consciousness soul in conjunction with the Spirit Self, and that another part of humanity would fall completely into the isolation of the physical body, into the egoism of the body, into materialism.

Human beings were still connected with one another in the intellectual soul because the etheric body is not so differentiated. Here are our physical bodies; a knife could pass easily between them. Our etheric bodies are already interwoven with one another; the etheric body depends on water, on the moisture that is abundantly present and surrounds us. The astral body requires air; there human beings are as one, but the physical body is separate. Egoism, isolation in material existence, begins in the physical body. In the words of a modern author, Arthur Koestler: Humanity threatens to tear itself apart into the yogi and the commissar,[9] into the manager—into those who manage practical life—and into those who flee practical life and turn only to the spirit. Were this to happen, mankind would be at its end; it would lose the ego-element, the commissar in matter, the yogi in spirit.

Christian Rosenkreutz poses the question: What must happen? Two things happen, both puzzling in their own way. The decision is made to send forth into the cosmos a member of their circle—one of the greatest ones—in order that he might give a gift to human souls who are inclined to incarnate, who are descending again to the earth from what is described as the cosmic midnight, so that they are able to stand firm on the earth. This great being is the Buddha. Christian Rosenkreutz instructs his friend and pupil to depart for Mars in order to work in the Mars sphere so that that the souls who are returning to earth not only bring with them from there the wild and warlike impulses living on Mars—who is not so unjustly named the god of war—but also what enables them on the earth to hold the middle ground between the outer world and the inner world. And what they bring is the spiritual word, the spiritualized human word—Mars is also the planet of language—but not just the spiritualized word; along with the spiritualized word, they also bring the ability to meditate. On Mars, as we returned again to this incarnation from the cosmic midnight, Buddha was the one who taught all of us to meditate.

One of the most difficult questions is: Do we see the 'Martian' Mars, or do we only see the earthly Mars? Do we extrapolate earthly existence to such a degree that the planetary sphere appears to be merely what we see with earthly eyes? The physical can appear in a variety of manifestations, so we must imagine there is also a kind of physical constitution that cannot be experienced from the perspective of the earthly constitution—that there is, so to speak, another level of vibration at which we must enter into a different reality. We can simplify this by saying that what Buddha does there takes place in an etheric realm, which is something *Discovery* will never be able to photograph. There are strange stories which reveal how much these things occupy people. For example, there is a short anecdote about how two Martians are having a conversation and say: 'There come those folks with their space ship. Such old-fashioned people—they still go in for space travel. We have been in energy bodies for a long time now. Let's put a few stones out to make them happy, some we once brought back from earth.' This story expresses something like a deeper perception. What is photographed there cannot be the whole picture. There is another layer of reality!

The first decision reached by this conference concerns the activity of the Buddha on Mars. The second concerns the decision to make public the most important Rosicrucian impulses. Hence the writings we have already discussed here appear. European humanity was to be given an impulse so that it would occupy itself intellectually with this kind of spirituality.

The Thirty Years War

There ensues the great counter-attack. All of the Rosicrucians' activity for Central Europe is eradicated. The Thirty Years War breaks out (1618–48) and leaves behind it, in the broadest sense, a ravaged Central Europe. The population drops by seventy per cent, whole regions die out; cities, cultural institutions, cloisters are burned to the ground. An unprecedented human hardening sets in; each person only cares about his own survival. In spite of the wide dissemination of the Rosicrucian writings, it was impossible to speak of any spiritual life they might have engendered. Rudolf Steiner speaks explicitly about the fact that initially the Rosicrucian impulse was devastated by the Thirty Years War. Today we can scarcely imagine the effect Martin Luther had. This effect has always been kept secret for good reason. All of Austria had become Protestant; thousands of priests had converted to Protestantism; there were few Catholics remaining in southern Germany. There were pietistic communities everywhere in Bohemia and Moravia. Rudolf Steiner calls attention to how the piety of the earlier Rosicrucianism lived on in these pietistic communities. Actually, everything was once again being prepared in the mood that an *Ecclesia non romana*, a spiritual Christianity, a general Reformation of the old state of affairs, was necessary. People were experiencing the beginning of the age of the consciousness soul. The Roman Church knew that if it wanted to continue it had to eradicate Central Europe.

In the end, the religious Peace of Augsburg decided that everyone must believe what the prince believes, so that some sense of order is achieved out of the chaos—*Cuius regio eius religio*, you must believe in the faith of the one who rules you. A very strong sense of nationalization was also connected to this. When the Thirty Years War comes to a close with the Peace of Westphalia, we arrive at the enormously destructive birth of the national state. At the beginning of this time stands that Innocent III who destroyed the Cathars, who did not want people to find the true Christ through the Church. He sends his influence outwards from Italy; Rudolf Steiner depicts explicitly how Innocent III inaugurates the national state. It works its way over into France; it works its way further so that the dominant principle during the Thirty Years War is the national state. It is often said that the Thirty Years War started as a religious war and ends as the victory of national states.

Rudolf Steiner explains that the spirits that want to block the path to the Holy Grail work out of nationalistic chauvinism, because nationalism and sexuality are two sides of one and the same thing.

> ... what lives in this national emotionalism, these national feelings? ... Exactly the same thing that lives in the sexual arena, except it works in one way in the sexual realm and in yet another way in national emotionalism. The sexual human being conducts his life between these two different poles. Chauvinism ... is nothing more than the development of sexuality in the framework of a group. We could say that nationalistic chauvinism is present to a greater degree where human beings are more firmly in the grip of what the sexual element has left behind; for the force found in reproduction also expresses itself in national emotionalism.[10]

At the end of the seventeenth century, Europe is still quite devastated; nevertheless the Rosicrucian path begins to prevail. It is the path that becomes the path of the consciousness soul, the path that we also travel in anthroposophy.

The Rosicrucian Path of Initiation Today

Today the Rosicrucian path of initiation rests upon two pillars. The first pillar is the assertion that everything that proceeds from knowledge is founded in thinking, that a question follows from knowledge founded in thinking, and that everything that will be understood about the world, everything that is also to appear as spirit, is subject to the authority of knowledge founded in thinking. Something quite important has emerged since the time of the Rosicrucians. Everything arising from the physical body in a somehow mediumistic way is rejected, not only because it is considered harmful, but also sinful. All those things that can somehow emerge from the body as a result of the Fall of Man are declarations of Lucifer and Ahriman. This is true for everything that appears today in the way of channelling and the like. Today, humanity is contaminated to an almost incomprehensible degree by all sorts of statements made by means of the physical body. These statements are thought to be as good as gold. This does not mean we cannot find our dreams interesting, nor does it mean that they cannot reveal interesting things to us. What it does mean, however, is this activity does not pass under the authoritative scrutiny of thinking.

We are surrounded by all manner of demons, by all manner of beings who try to delude us, perhaps with earlier incarnations or interesting connections. Everything must go through the test of knowledge. More than ever, we must be aware of the danger known in the Nordic Mysteries as the Fenriswolf. The evil of the Fenriswolf is so powerful that it survives the whole Twilight of the Gods and can only be defeated by Vidar. Rudolf Steiner says that 'the Fenriswolf represents ... the power of atavistic clairvoyance'.[11] Human beings will be granted all manner of atavism, and Lucifer and Ahriman will not be the only ones at work in this atavism. Through Lucifer and Ahriman, the Sorat-being will be active as well. We know that Rudolf Steiner calls Christian Rosenkreutz the greatest martyr after Christ. But Christ suffered as God. Christian Rosenkreutz has been the greatest human martyr over the last one or two centuries because people will not decide to develop initiatives within themselves, because they do not meditate, because they expect the truth to come to them from outside in some passive way. Throughout his whole sequence of incarnations, Christian Rosenkreutz prepared a way of knowing that depends entirely upon human beings developing initiatives within themselves—questioning, knowledgeable initiatives. He has sacrificed his whole being in this way, and he suffers under every human being who does not develop this initiative, who expects leadership and teaching from outside himself.

For this reason, Rudolf Steiner strongly emphasizes the second pillar of Rosicrucian teaching: Never interfere in the free will of another human being! You may say anything if you present it as the truth as you have experienced it. If other people wish to accept what you say, they must decide to do so out of their own freedom. Unconditional, deep respect for the free will of another person, avoidance of every sort of influence—this is the second pillar of genuine Rosicrucian spirituality.

Alchemy and the Healing Arts

Everything that constitutes the core of Rosicrucianism—which is alchemy—flows into this path of schooling and initiation. The founding of alchemy is attributed to the legendary Hermes. Originally, alchemy was a teaching about the spirituality of matter, about how the spirituality of matter is interconnected. This teaching was prepared for the Rosicrucians over a long period of time. The Rosicrucians live with two images. The first image is contained in a simple sentence in the book *Occult Science, An Outline*: 'Even the mineral realm ... was created as a result of being expelled ... from the evolution of humanity.'[12] The realms of nature were expelled so that the human being would be purified, so that he would become a 'cathar', a 'lily' in the Grail. Now the human being becomes aware that what was taken away must be absorbed again, that he must take the wildness of the beasts of prey into himself and tame it; he must take in the indolence of the plants and enliven it; and he must also take into himself the mineral realm. The Rosicrucians call the beginning of this process the re-humanizing of matter. That was the Mystery of their alchemy; it can also be referred to as the 'permeation of matter by the Christ'.

They did not look at matter as elements, in the modern way, but more as processes. They observed the salt process, called it *Sal.* And in all these salt processes they saw what purified the passions and drives of the human being, just as the mineral salt can be used externally to counter spoiling and decay. They saw the thoughts of the gods at work in this *Sal.* When they considered the processes of dissolving, the processes of the liquid element they called *Mercury*, they saw in them the love of the gods at work. They attempted to experience how that resounds in human beings. They recognized lower and higher processes of dissolving, in the same way that the human being knows lower and higher forms of love. Then they observed all the processes of combustion, and called them *Sulfur.* They saw in them the sacrifice of the gods and felt themselves called to be prepared to sacrifice themselves. Their laboratory was a lens for the thoughts of the gods, the love of the gods, and the sacrifice of the gods. The crucial part was that it did not take place without a parallel activity occurring both inwardly and outwardly. *Ora et labora*—the oratory was part of every laboratory—you cannot work in the laboratory without simultaneously lifting your heart to God, praying, meditating. And the inverse is just as true—all your praying will be to no avail if you do not immerse yourself in an understanding of the material world.

Thus the alchemical process was always two-sided. What happened externally in crucibles and retorts had to be completed in the soul of the adept as purification, sublimation, combustion, liquefication, sedimentation. What was being sought was achieved only if the process on the laboratory bench, in the laboratory, was accompanied by a process in the oratory of the innermost soul.

Today modern physics has arrived once again at the point of view that the observer is himself a part of the experiment. We cannot think the observer away; we cannot act as though something happens objectively and ignore the person observing it.

The preparation of medicaments was also developed out of this alchemical activity. The Rosicrucians travelled throughout many countries as healing practitioners and what they offered from their laboratory was produced with the intention that it would lead to a humanization within the soul of humanity. It is perhaps easiest for us to imagine this in homoeopathic processes. Whenever we take silver and dilute it to a D12 solution, it does not remain as material silver; it is the silver process of creation. It is prepared so that the silver process undergoes a humanization, an elevation to human existence, when it enters into the human being. There are some exceptions, but generally speaking we have not yet reached the point today of being able to do what the Rosicrucian doctors and healers did. When they administered these materials, they told the people fairy-tales or legends, showed them certain symbolical drawings. They knew that the humanization of matter, the humanization of the gift they bestowed, would only properly proceed if images lived within the person, if something took place within the person that is similar to what happens in the oratory. Many say that anthroposophical medicine must come to the point where we not only give medicaments to the sick, but we are able to advise the patient about what he should alter in his soul, to offer advice that is so effective that the medicaments in him rise to the stage of humanization.

We realize from this why James is the patron saint of alchemists. An inner and outer experience—that was the Camino. People experienced nature, the elements, the forces of the planets—which also means the forces of the metal, the gold, silver and lead processes, and so forth—and simultaneously they experienced the inner path of prayer, the inner oratory. The legendary Philosopher's Stone is nothing more than the product of physical matter made transparent—made humanized—at least somewhere in the world; it is the outcome of returning one small piece of physical matter to Paradise.

This is also connected to activities of the spirit. We develop imagination in the astral body, inspiration in the etheric body. In early editions of *Occult Science, An Outline*, the next step is called the acquisition of intuition or work with the Philosopher's Stone.[13] Intuition is achieved where our physical body also becomes a bit transparent, where a bit of the material in the physical body is humanized and elevated.

Words that had lived in secret for centuries, that had been a hidden cosmic formula, became exoteric in the *Fama Fraternitatis*. In the *Fama Fraternitatis*, the discovery of the grave of Christian Rosenkreutz is described, and in this grave are the words: 'Ex deo nascimur, In Christo morimur, Per spiritum sanctum reviviscimus'—'From God we are born, In Christ we die, Through the Holy Spirit will we be resurrected.' (In the original: 'Ex deo nascimur, in Jesu morimur, per spiritum reviviscimus.') This was printed for the first time in 1614. Before 1614, this was an inner secret of the whole stream. It says that the Trinity is to be experienced dynamically, that a stream of movement goes through the Trinity, and that the human being himself stands in the stream of movement expressed in these words.

In the *Chymical Wedding*, with its abundant imagery—hence in the 'alchymical wedding', which means the initiation of the soul through alchemy—everything is led by a virgin guide called Alchemia. The candidates who come to the wedding are weighed to determine whether they have the right qualities of soul. Many fail completely and are thrown out, and are even whipped as they leave; others just barely pass. Christian Rosenkreutz is portrayed as humble. 'I am too old for this; I don't have these virtues', he claims. Then the virgin says, 'Just for fun, let's weigh you.' This is all immersed in a wonderful spiritual humour. Christian Rosenkreutz allows himself to be weighed and he is so heavy that all seven counterweights shoot skyward. He weighs so much that he can redeem another person, the emperor who has built the Karlstein castle near Prague where the secrets of the *Chymical Wedding* are depicted.[14]

Rudolf Steiner says that these virtues are the virtues of the Seven Liberal Arts. In order to learn Grammar, I must develop a quite specific virtue; in order to learn Rhetoric, another virtue, and so on to the highest virtue, Music. Because these virtues have to be acquired in the sensory realm, there is a test in the *Chymical Wedding* of whether or not the individual has achieved these virtues on earth. We have to acquire these virtues in the sensory realm, but we must bring the virgin *Alchemia* from the spiritual realm.

These observations revolve around something that we never want to define, around the Queen of Sheba, the Isis Sophia, the Sophia, Natura, the Earth Mother Eve, Alchemia; they revolve around the wonderful secret of the great goddess who appears in so many images. A volume just appeared with many of Rudolf Steiner's meditations, and in it there is a whole group of meditations that begin with the exclamation, 'Maternal cosmic spirit, paternal soul of the earth!'[15] The cosmos is apostrophized as the goddess, as the maternal being that envelops everything.

Thus in alchemical writings we often find pictures where the alchemist is being taught by the goddess Natura sitting before him as a winged, naked woman wearing a crown with the seven planets, the seven planetary metals.

The Founding of Inner Brotherhoods

Rudolf Steiner describes how small Rosicrucian groups often consisted of three plus four Rosicrucians. It was understood that three Rosicrucians had a particular connection with the spiritual world. They wandered among the stars, learned the secrets of the stars, and brought them back; however they were only able to express these secrets in symbols. The groups of four were capable of bringing these symbols into language; they could go among the people with these words and they could bring to the people the wisdom of the other three through fairy-tales and legends. They were dependent on one another. The three would not have been capable of anything; they would only have been able to stammer to the world. And the four would have been without content if the three had not brought the secrets down to them from the stars. Thus the principle of the inner brotherhood of the soul was founded.[16] Again and again, this rising into the world of the stars and this translation into the language of earth took place in the smallest circles. We find it again in the relationship between the School for Spiritual Science and the General Anthroposophical Society. The School offers forms of the experience of the spiritual world; the Society offers ideas and conceptual language of our time.

And then, according to Rudolf Steiner, there came a moment when something was accomplished in a solemn, cultic deed. At that time, the Rosicrucians said that human beings had entered too deeply into physical matter because of the Fall of Man. Now it was necessary for them to find free will; star wisdom had to withdraw. Thus, through this solemn, cultic deed, the sacrifice of star knowledge was made. The Rosicrucians who could wander among the stars surrendered their star knowledge to non-human beings who accepted it for certain purposes. With this, the life of Rosicrucianism came to a halt, even though in their souls people experienced the contents of its symbols through Rosicrucian traditions for a long time after.[17]

Lucifer

The Rosicrucians had a precise and intimate knowledge of Lucifer; they affirmed his cosmic activity as a being of wisdom saying: 'We need Lucifer so that through Lucifer we can truly know and understand the Christ. We seek the Christ, but we also seek to know and understand the Christ; and for this knowledge and understanding we need Lucifer. Lucifer becomes for us the star that guides us to the cross; he becomes the light that illuminates Golgotha.' Christian Rosenkreutz returns in a later incarnation as the Count of Saint-Germain. Rudolf Steiner says that this Count of Saint-Germain possesses a copy of a document buried deep in the archives of the Vatican.[18] This document contains the secret that the Holy Spirit is to be born in human beings and that this Holy Spirit is in fact Lucifer, risen again in new glory. The human being permeated by the Christ begins to redeem Lucifer when—permeated by Him—he understands the Christ through the wisdom of Lucifer. Lucifer streams through human beings and arises as the Holy Spirit. Therefore the circle of Bodhisattvas is referred to as a wreath of luciferic beings and the Holy Spirit at the same time. This is a preview of what is to happen in the evolution of the Trinity itself.

Making Work a Sacrament

The Rosicrucians continue to be active. They are at work in the emergence of spiritual brotherhoods; we know today that they are the real inaugurators of the genuine, early Freemasonry as it existed before 1717. They carry Templar impulses into Freemasonry—the impulse for the independence of human beings so that we are able to determine our religious and social life in freedom. But they also bring something else quite different into it. Their position in regard to the emerging technical world said: This technical world will come; we must do everything to make it a human technology. Today, wherever there are attempts at ecology and the like, where people talk about a humane technology, about humane power, light and heat production, Rosicrucian impulses are behind it. They tried to prepare this through something that was then taken from their hands by the counter-forces. They wanted work to be made a sacrament in the context of Freemasonry. People were supposed to come together as masons; masons were understood to be all professions, all active people. They were to gather together in order to create from this gathering spiritual power for their activity in the world of work. Rudolf Steiner had created a similar organization through his own words before the First World War. This motif is very clear in his words: We are in the temple in order to gather forces for our work in the world, to create something from wisdom, beauty and strength that enables us to make any profession, whatever it might be, into a sacrament.

Jakob Böhme and Paracelsus worked out of these impulses; Rudolf Steiner calls them Sun initiates and, based on their writings, revealers of the highest cosmic secrets.[19] In 1575, at exactly the same time the second Rosicrucian conference is taking place, there appears in Basel a small work, the so-called *Arbatel*, a theosophic, magical work, 'On the Magic of the Ancients, or the Loftiest Study of Wisdom'. In it are presented Mysteries of Olympus, Mysteries of Hesiod, Roman, Sybilline and Pythagorean Mysteries, as well as Mysteries of Apollonius; and at the end there is a chart. In this chart it says, 'All of these occult sciences can be divided into bad sciences and good sciences; and the bad sciences can be divided into the kakodaimons and the kakosophias. The kakosophias are the contempt for the word of God; and the kakodaimons are black magic. And the good occult sciences can be divided into theosophy and anthroposophy.' On the last page—in the language of our time—it says: Theosophy consists of the knowledge of the divine word; and anthroposophy consists of spiritual natural science and spiritual sociology. The Golden Fleece is present again in spiritual natural science and in the spiritual understanding of what people achieve together.

The Rosicrucian Temple

The Rosicrucian impulse actually continues today in a particular way. Rudolf Steiner drew attention to the fact that each of the three great spiritual movements had an idealized temple building. He says that the Grail temple was always a circular building with the Grail secret in the middle, and around this circular building sat the participants in the Grail event.[20] In *The Mission of Michael*, he even draws on the blackboard this ideal Grail temple—which, of course, never existed in this way on the earth. Then came the churches of the Templars which had something quite peculiar about them. They had the round Grail temple, and attached to it is a nave with an altar at the back. Thus they actually had two altars, one in the middle as with the Grail, and another that symbolized their working into the world. Anyone who goes to Segovia in Spain will find a Templar church, Spirito Sancto, the Church of the Holy Spirit, outside the gates of the city. In its central building, there is a wonderful, second, raised cupola with an altar; and above the altar there is a large opening. From there a person can look down at a second altar that lies to the east in the usual east-west alignment.

Rudolf Steiner notes the form of the true Rosicrucian temple, one that never really existed; but, as he himself says, he is speaking for the initiates. It was characteristic of the Rosicrucians that they actually worked inwardly in the quietest way, and in the most simple, unassuming meeting spaces. And yet Rudolf Steiner speaks of the 'true Rosicrucian temple' that is characterized by the fact that in it, lengthwise from back to front, the temple manifests the evolution of the world through seven great pillars—as he then constructed it in the first Goetheanum. All of this continues into the present where, since 1998, the seven pillars of the Rosicrucian temple have stood once again at the Goetheanum—in pairs, from back to front, leading from the earth's past to its future.

Many people may ask: 'Am I connected to this Rosicrucianism? Do I have a relationship to Christian Rosenkreutz?' There are two answers. If someone has experienced in life that he was in mortal danger, that he would surely have died if a voice in him had not called, 'Stop! Go no further!'—experienced that he stood before an abyss or some other mortal danger—in that moment, Christian Rosenkreutz called to him. If someone perhaps forgets such an experience, or does not know if he had such an experience, and questions whether or not he belongs with Christian Rosenkreutz, then he should try to place before his imagination the image of Christian Rosenkreutz sending the Buddha to Mars; he should try to imagine in a living way how the friend and pupil of Christian Rosenkreutz ascended into the sphere of Mars. Then, if inwardly the words somehow arise, 'O Man, you are not only an earthly being; you are a cosmic being,' if these words are felt, then that person may feel himself to be a pupil of Christian Rosenkreutz. Because then he knows that he is finding the path from the earthly Christ to the Cosmic Christ, and that the Cosmic Christ will have led him to the Christ Who became the Earth ego and the ego of mankind.

Lecture 11

Rosicrucian Impulses in America and their Repercussions on Europe

Virginia Sease

A question confronting the Church around 1250 was: How will Christianity gain a foothold? There was to be no misunderstanding about what this meant. Other large questions facing the Church were: What will we do about the conquests by the Arabs? How will the question of the varying liturgies be resolved? Can they be reconciled, or will we be plunged into a great religious war? Although virtually all the heretics had been burned by 1250 or had met with an otherwise unfortunate end, the Church felt the insecurity of its position, and continued its conduct of oppression in one form or another until the time when the Templars were suppressed.

Journeys to America in the First Millennium

Rudolf Steiner put a much earlier date on connections to America than was common until a few years ago. Already in 1917, he said these voyages played an important role even as late as the sixth and seventh centuries after Christ, '. . . because during the earlier centuries of European development, ships sail continuously from what was then Norway across to America'.[1] They sailed to America not once or twice, but again and again before the sixth or seventh centuries, and later. We know from history that Eric the Red made his voyage around 982.

There is enormous controversy surrounding the date of the earliest journeys. Barry Fell, a historian and Harvard professor, wrote a book entitled *America BC*,[2] in which he shows that petroglyphs already exist in pre-Christian America, and what they depict is almost identical to petroglyphs in the Nordic countries. An example of such petroglyphs is found north of Toronto in Peterborough, Canada (Illustration 25). Barry Fell dates this petroglyph to pre-Christian times—and it is strikingly similar to petroglyphs in Sweden. It depicts a sun ship, which has the task of bringing the sun across the heavens to illuminate the world each day.[3]

25. Petroglyph, pre-Christian (?) (Sketch of the original)

The sun ship revealed a deep symbolism and pointed—like a promise—to the coming Christ. In the Gnosis, there is also the image of the sun as a ship for the third emissary, for the Christ. And the moon was a ship for Jesus. In the Mysteries, initiates all over the world—on the Black Sea, in the north, the south, or even in America—were able to communicate with one another, naturally through supersensible experiences. They spoke a common language at that time. When seafarers travelled from Norway to America, or from Greenland, they arrived at the northern coast of North America near Canada—where they encountered the local Indian population. However, the Indians with whom these seafarers dealt were initiates, and thus the seafarers also were exposed to the Indians' knowledge through these encounters.

From the ninth century onwards, the Church wanted to bring this connection to an end for a variety of reasons. Rudolf Steiner addresses this in the context of geographic medicine. He says that one reason they wanted it to end was so that the forces of the earth present on the North American continent might not affect Europe; and for another, so that the secrets of these earth forces—the forces of 'the double' (German *Doppelgänger*) as Rudolf Steiner calls them—and their medical effect might not be brought back to Europe. Nevertheless we find an echo of this medicine, this healing, actually practised up to the time of Paracelsus.[4]

The Rediscovery of America

The third initiation of Christian Rosenkreutz in 1459 coincides approximately with the beginning of the age of the consciousness soul.

America was rediscovered shortly after the death of Christian Rosenkreutz in that long incarnation. Today, people speak more often about the rediscovery of America and less about the discovery of America in 1492. Christopher Columbus thought he had found another route to India; therefore he called the indigenous people he encountered Indians. Descriptions of these indigenous people are contained in letters he sent home to Portugal. Christopher Columbus wrote that he was absolutely convinced the beings he found were human, even though they looked completely different. He sent a letter of warning to the court in Portugal so that they would be prepared for the appearance of the Indians he was bringing back as examples.

A Church council meeting in 1494 concluded the famous Treaty of Tordesillas which divided up the world. Spain would have possession of everything west of the Cape Verde Islands, and everything east of the islands would belong to Portugal. Portugal was quite pleased with this arrangement because, of course, everything that lay eastward was the civilized world; Spain took some offence. No one knew yet—they only suspected!—that west of that line lay the whole of North America and practically two-thirds of South America. It is interesting that the line of the Treaty of Tordesillas falls almost exactly between the region of the life ether and the region of the chemical ether, the sound ether, according to Günther Wachsmuth's determinations of the etheric regions of the earth.[5]

Four Paths to the Wisdom of the Rosicrucians

During this time, after the third initiation of Christian Rosenkreutz and even a bit before it, there were four main paths by which people came to Rosicrucian wisdom. On one path, a person could establish a connection with the rhapsodists. From the sixth and seventh centuries onward—thus at the time when the individuality of Christian Rosenkreutz had quiet incarnations after the awakening of Lazarus-John—the rhapsodist-singers were already going from village to village to spread the news of the spirit. People did not simply take this up. It was a calling. The rhapsodists received a spiritual call. The souls of those who heard the rhapsodists experienced thought forms, but ones people took up in their feelings and perceptions. The songs of the rhapsodists made souls inwardly warm. Rudolf Steiner mentions that people who experienced this—and there were many of them in Central and Eastern Europe—are today people who experience a longing for spiritual science.[6]

In later times—after 1250—there were those who belonged to this stream and had received their initiation from the twelve teachers. They brought sayings and stories into the humanity of Europe. We find the final echoes of this, for example, in the Grimms' fairy-tales. The wisdom in them is so true that it would be senseless to alter them merely because some people might think they contain cruelties unsuitable for children.

In addition to this, there was a second path through the Rosicrucian schools. Their goal was the development of soul capacities in their pupils, which they achieved through dramas. In these dramas, the pupils were able to experience all sorts of situations that stirred their emotions. This schooling consisted of experiencing the emotions fully, but not surrendering oneself to them. It was a matter of mastering the images of these dramas through knowledge.

A third path was through a contemplation of symbolic drawings passed along from person to person. The drawings served as windows through which people could gaze into the spiritual world. These insights of knowledge were absorbed by the soul in a latent form and awakened later. The drawings were published in 1785, and are known as *The Secret Symbols of the Rosicrucians from the Sixteenth and Seventeenth Centuries.* People spent long periods of time in deep, quiet meditation on such a symbol. In the two examples provided here (Illustrations 26 and 27), we see that the form of the one figure is somewhat simpler; but if we immerse ourselves in it and try to experience it inwardly through its forms, we discover that this is a complicated undertaking. If we were to try to do this in eurythmy, we would see that it is not quite as easy as it seems.

The fourth path through which this Rosicrucian wisdom was spread involved an actual meeting with Christian Rosenkreutz himself, either in a situation of danger—when the person had the experience of hearing an instruction or his own name—or through meditation. A mighty radiating power streamed—and streams—from the etheric body of Christian Rosenkreutz.

Jakob Böhme

One individual in the stream of this radiating power is known to us by the name of Jakob Böhme. Jakob Böhme also had a strong radiance emanating from him when he began to work. We hear various stories about him from his boyhood, particularly how he always listened. He lived intensely in his hearing, in the ear, and absorbed all sorts of stories. We

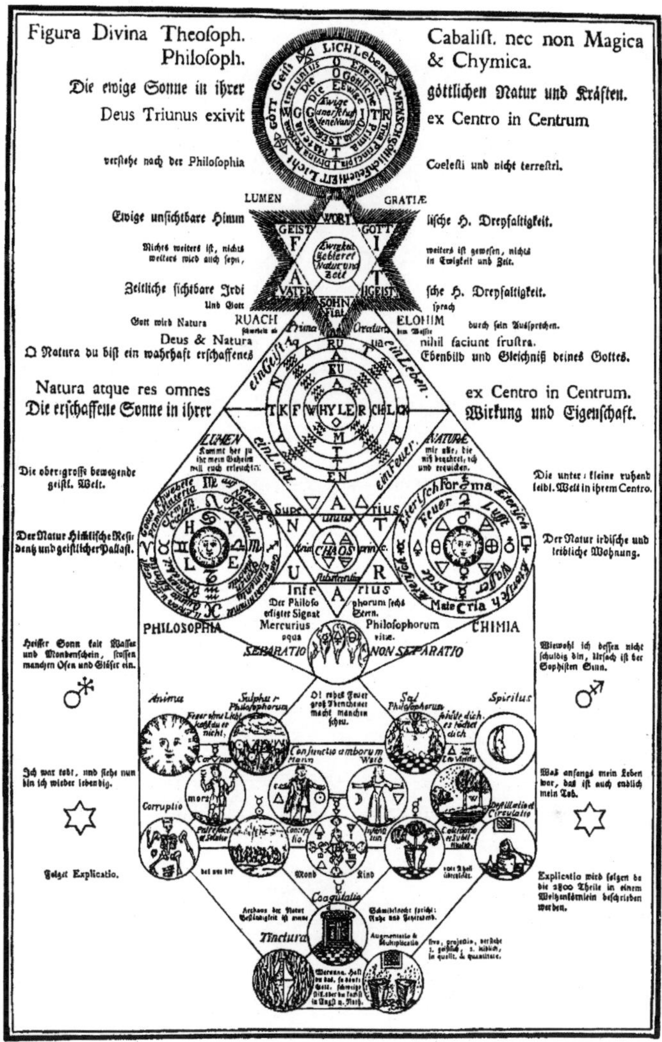

26. From: The Secret Symbols of the Rosicrucians from the Sixteenth and Seventeenth Century

have to imagine that the stories he heard about the wisdom of nature, the teachings of the heavens, were stories that had been spread about in the world by Christian Rosenkreutz himself. Then Böhme underwent a formative experience. He was an apprentice cobbler. His master and mistress went away, but before they left they told him he must not sell any shoes in their absence. He was alone in the shop when a person entered;

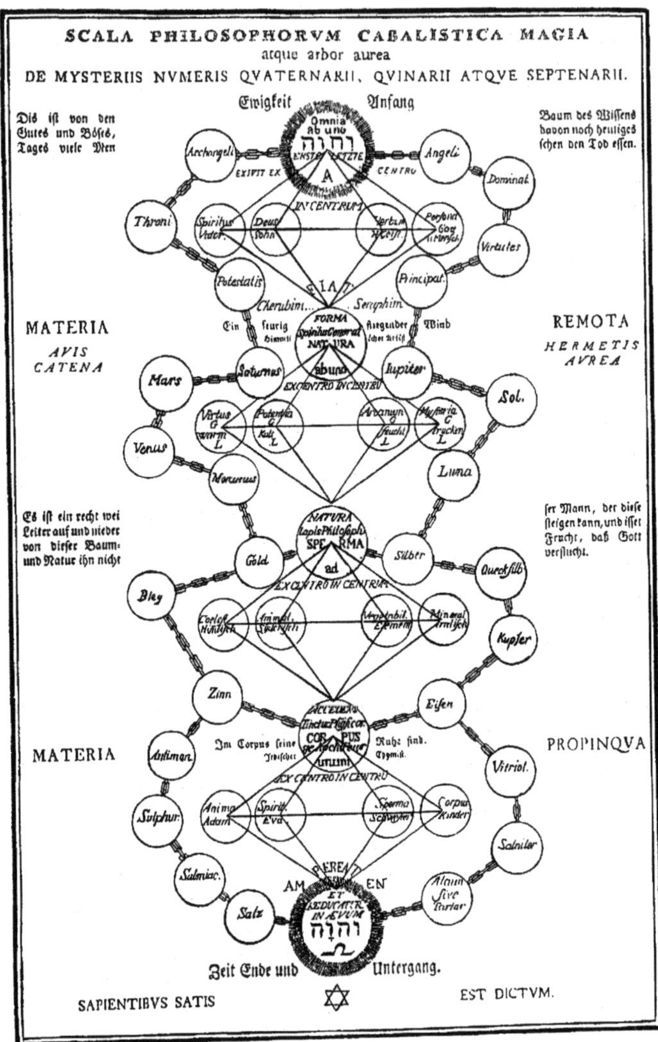

27. From: The Secret Symbols of the Rosicrucians from the Sixteenth and Seventeenth Century

but Jakob sold him nothing. The man went outside and is supposed to have called loudly, 'Jakob, come outside!' This is the story according to tradition. Of course, we recall the words, 'Lazarus, come forth!' However, Rudolf Steiner says that this person actually said to him, 'Jakob, you now are small, but one day you will be great. You will become a person whom the world will encounter in amazement.'[7] A secret affinity remained between Jakob Böhme and this person, who was a great initiate. The mighty inspirations of Böhme originated with him.[8] Rudolf Steiner does not indicate that this initiate was Christian Rosenkreutz; however, later it becomes clear through other indications that it was indeed Christian Rosenkreutz.

Jakob Böhme was a Sun initiate; he was a Sun human being, inwardly permeated by Sun forces.[9] He did not undergo initiation during this incarnation. All of that occurred before birth. He was given this Sun initiation as he entered into his incarnation. He was born in 1575 and died in 1624. He had a vast power of memory; he was able to remember being in Paradise with Adam and taking note of the Christ-being. He always claimed that everything that came from him resulted from his connection with the Christ. Truly, he was deeply Christian.

He had a large circle of people around him. This is a significant phenomenon. Outwardly, he was very simple—a cobbler—and nevertheless he wrote many texts like *Aurora* [Dawn arising], *De signatura rerum*, and other works which he also published. The circle of people around him came from all classes of society—from the nobility, partly from Church circles, and from simpler circumstances. Abraham von Franckenberg's biography of Böhme gives a clear picture of how wide this circle was and how Böhme later served as inspiration for people like Angelus Silesius and the important, but less known—yet great—poet, thinker and philosopher, Daniel von Czepko.

Böhme's writings spread quickly, also in England. Twenty-five years after his death, his writings came to the attention of a particular woman in England by the name of Jane Lead. She herself was a clairvoyant. She read these writings in a translation given her by an Anglican priest named John Pordage. She felt quite connected with them and claimed that Böhme's wisdom had been a great help to her in holding onto her own visions. Jane Lead and John Pordage then founded the Philadelphia Society, a reference to the Philadelphia in the Apocalypse. There is a remarkable continuity here when we look at this and follow its thread back to Jakob Böhme, Christian Rosenkreutz and John the Evangelist—the author of the Book of Revelation. Jane Lead is simply mentioned in religious history as a Böhmist (when her name is mentioned at all). But she is an important link in a chain of destiny.

Johannes Kelpius

There was a young theology student named Johannes Kelpius who had a very short life but an important mission. He studied with Christian Knorr Baron von Rosenroth, famed for having translated the Cabbala from Hebrew into Latin. This was important because his translation of the Cabbala made the text available to the academic world; before that, it had been inaccessible to most. Christian Knorr von Rosenroth, who lived in Sulzbach, near Nuremberg, was known as a great scholar during his time. He was also known as a Böhmist, since his work was strongly influenced by Böhme's, and he lived in the great radiance of Jakob Böhme. When he first studied with Christian Knorr von Rosenroth, Johannes Kelpius was just sixteen years old, which was not unusual at the time. Kelpius then found a connection with a Pietistic stream. Pietism, this inwardly pious direction, began to blossom as an effect of Lutheranism. What Luther had contributed by way of interpretation was experienced by many as somewhat dry, and so the Pietists arose. We have a good description of them in Goethe's little story in *Wilhelm Meister's Apprenticeship*, 'Confessions of a Beautiful Soul'. Susanne von Klettenberg was a Pietist. If you immerse yourself in this story, you can experience the mood that lived in Pietism.

In 1694, when Johannes Kelpius was twenty-one, he led a small group of Pietists to America. At that time, the Pietists in Germany were not at all threatened; nonetheless, he took this group to America. The first stop on their journey was London. One tradition says that they had to wait there for their ship, which might well be true. Another tradition says that they used this time to visit with Jane Lead; it also says that they received esoteric training from her through the way she took up Böhme's interpretations, but also through her own insights. Then this small group travelled to America, landing in Philadelphia on 24 June 1694—St John's day. This fact appears like a raying back towards Böhme, towards the Sun initiate, almost like a rune.

The German Pietists in America

The Pietists arrived only a century after the first settlements of Europeans in America. But these new arrivals found that the city of Philadelphia was too wild, too noisy and too populous. They moved about six miles away to a small place, Germantown, which was only seven years old in 1694. Germantown was actually a very new town, founded by Germans who had come to America from the Rhineland. They settled by a creek with an Indian name, Wissahickon Creek—it was not even a river—where they felt at home.

The whole thing is very mysterious. These Pietists are mentioned in every history of colonial East Coast America, but most often the name of Johannes Kelpius is not mentioned. Most of the time they are described as a kind of German hermit group, quiet and pious. In fact, they really did not converse with one another very much. When we then think of Kelpius himself, we must recall Rudolf Steiner's words about how a silence of thinking prevailed among some people in the fourteenth and fifteenth centuries. He said, 'And no one has a real concept of the character of this period who does not know how much happened in the silence of thought in which people exchanged their souls, not merely their words.'[10]

Now the question is this: Did Johannes Kelpius have a mission in the New World? The Pietists were not being persecuted. Was there a visit in London with Jane Lead, a follower of Jakob Böhme and, therefore, a connection with Christian Rosenkreutz? A great American occultist who died some years ago, Manley Palmer Hall, says that this visit in London is not authentic, and that these people had absolutely no identification as any kind of an order. Moreover, they lived in poverty so they could not have been Rosicrucians. Although I value Manley Hall's research in many areas, I think this can be seen differently. There is much that speaks for the fact that this small group came from Germany with an important mission—evidence exists in the testimony of their contemporaries, available in manuscripts or old books, and in oral traditions that still live on when people talk about this group on Wissahickon Creek. Besides, there is proof that *The Secret Symbols of the Rosicrucians* circulated among the Pietists in manuscript form. We also see from their writings how seriously they took this. The unpublished prayer book of Kelpius is profoundly Christian, deeply permeated by every Rosicrucian principle.

My assessment is that this whole region was suffused with the attitude of Pietism, of piety, and that shortly thereafter, on this very site in America—in Philadelphia—great events played themselves out. Through their moral way of life, the Pietists spread something like a spiritual aura over this region. Philadelphia was the place where the United States was founded, from where it declared and achieved its independence from England.

The Quakers in America

The Quakers came to America a few years earlier with William Penn—the state is named after his father, Admiral William Penn (Penn's Sylvania means Penn's Woods).[11] Penn himself was a Quaker, deeply connected with Böhme. From the middle to the end of the seventeenth century, Jakob Böhme's writings were read diligently in England, in translation of course. One element of the Quakers was connected with the Cathars and harkened back to Manichaean principles. The Quakers at that time referred to themselves as 'Children of the Light'; and their striving was to leave themselves free enough and unburdened enough by daily life that they could be open to the light. And when they conducted their usual dialogue, called 'queries', which took the form of question-answer, question-answer, like a test of conscience, the focus was always on whether a person had left the soul open enough so that the light could radiate into the darkness of corporeality. The Quakers lived right in Philadelphia. Here we differentiate between two influences. The Quakers go back to Böhme and therefore had a Rosicrucian element; direct Rosicrucian elements came from Kelpius and his so-called Pietists.

The etheric aura of Philadelphia had already been prepared. We have looked at Kelpius and William Penn, but many people from Germany settled in the area around Philadelphia at the beginning of the eighteenth century. A strong musical culture also developed—through Conrad Beissel, for example. Many of the communities that were developed felt closely connected through music, for example the Ephrata Cloister under the leadership of Beissel. Then, in its turn, this early Rosicrucian, Böhmist stream has an effect on Europe.

Benjamin Franklin

A powerful individuality entered into this whole situation, and it was as though a cradle had been prepared there for him. His name is Benjamin Franklin (1706–90). We have a good description of his life until 1757 (age 51) through his famous *Autobiography*. He was born and lived in Boston until the age of seventeen. His father soon discovered that Benjamin was an avid and gifted student; but as he saw no financial prospects for furthering an academic career for his son, he apprenticed him under bondage to his older son who was a printer. In time Benjamin Franklin experienced the relationship as intolerable and secretly fled to New York to try his luck in the printing business. Finding no possibilities there, he went on to Philadelphia—all this travel took place by ship in an adventuresome manner. He writes in his autobiography that he will describe his first entry into Philadelphia so that 'one may compare such unlikely beginnings with the figure I have since made there. I was in my working dress ... I was dirty from my journey; my pockets were stuff'd out with shirts and stockings, and I knew no soul nor where to look for lodging ... I was very hungry; and my whole stock of cash consisted of a Dutch dollar and about a schilling in copper.' With his meagre fund he bought three 'great puffy rolls ... and having no room in my pockets, walk'd off with a roll under each arm, and eating the other. Thus I went up Market Street as far as Fourth Street, passing by the door of Mr. Read, my future wife's father; when she, standing at the door, saw me, and thought I made, as I certainly did, a most awkward, ridiculous appearance.' This story takes on special interest for us when we recall the indications Rudolf Steiner gives in the karma lectures about how Garibaldi was aboard a ship at sea and saw his wife on land through a telescope. Benjamin Franklin's encounter is strikingly similar.

A printer by trade, Franklin went to England when he was eighteen years old. He absorbed many impressions of England's cultural and scientific life, and then returned to America. It was characteristic of his biography that he had ready access to all kinds of groups and people. He was the one person in all of Philadelphia chosen to print the constitution of the Freemasons; early in his life, he became a Freemason. He also found his own karmic group there. We often notice that when people have a task, they are able to undertake this task through a connection with a group of other people. For example, we think of Garibaldi; in his small karmic group, he came together with Cavour, with Victor Emanuel, and with the writer Mazzini. Benjamin Franklin's small karmic group was made up of George Washington from America, the English writer and journalist Thomas Paine, the French Marquis de Lafayette, and later a few other individualities.

In 1753, Benjamin Franklin negotiated a treaty with the Iroquois. This treaty was necessary so that people could continue to work together in the environs of Philadelphia unhindered by the fear of a sudden attack from the Iroquois. The Indians still possessed a great and vital spirituality at this time. The Iroquois said: 'We are negotiating a treaty, but we will decide with whom we conclude that treaty.' The person they wanted was Benjamin Franklin. Then, ten years later, Franklin negotiated the treaty at the end of what Europeans call the Seven Years War; in America, we refer to it as the French and Indian War, since many Indians had taken part in the fighting.

This is actually a turning-point. In 1763, as a result of this treaty, it was finally settled that English would be the language of North America.

Before that, it was uncertain whether French or English would prevail in the region later to become the United States. This is quite significant when we think about Rudolf Steiner's indications that it is extraordinarily important for the consciousness soul to come to expression in our age: 'I want to say this. Actually, it is only the people of the English-speaking population who are prepared in our time through their blood, through their birth, through their heredity, to have the consciousness soul impressed into their humanity. That is just how humanity is differentiated.'[12] He goes on to describe how this is prepared through the circumstances of blood, birth and heredity. It is not the case that the English-speaking peoples have a greater spiritual predisposition for the consciousness soul; but it must and will be carried for the most part by the English language. Of course, today when English is often used only as a language of information, we also see its shadow side.

Benjamin Franklin is best known as the inventor of the lightning rod. This is an important image. According to Rudolf Steiner's description of the electromagnetic forces in the North American earth, these forces offer a very fertile ground for ahrimanic beings. Rudolf Steiner describes these beings as geographic doubles (German *Doppelgänger*). Naturally, every human being has a geographic double, not only the Americans. It is just that the conditions of the earth in America are such that the doubles are really fed by these forces. We can imagine lightning striking the earth from the heavenly hierarchies, and the lightning then going down into the earth. But the lightning rod—thus Benjamin Franklin—is standing there between the hierarchies and the forces of the double.

We have heard how, in earlier times, the impulses of Rosicrucianism lived on through Freemasonry. Benjamin Franklin was most deeply connected with the trinitarian impulse of the Rosicrucians, with this triad of freedom, equality and fraternity for all of humanity. Even today many Freemason lodges in North America believe in the principle of the immortality of the soul. That was certainly not a problem for Benjamin Franklin and his circle. When we read the writings of these men, we find frequent allusions to the immortality of the soul and to reincarnation. Thus this idea of reincarnation is introduced to America through the writings of these men. Benjamin Franklin wrote his epitaph very early in his life. He created it simply as a joke; nevertheless it demonstrates his humour, his genius, and also his spirituality. It says:

B. Franklin, Printer
(Like the Cover of an Old Book

Its Contents torn Out
And Stript of its Lettering and Gilding)
Lies Here, Food for Worms.
But the Work shall not be Lost;
For it will (as he Believ'd) Appear once More
In a New and More Elegant Edition
Revised and Corrected
By the Author.

The Declaration of Independence of the Thirteen Colonies

Benjamin Franklin was seventy years old when the Declaration of Independence was written and signed. Around this time, he met with two mysterious events. The first is handed down as follows. George Washington and Benjamin Franklin were together to consider how the flag for this new nation, for the United States, should look. They met in the house of a lady who was to design it. This woman had an old professor as a guest. The professor was very friendly, very nice, ate little, and spent most of the time in his room. But he engaged Benjamin Franklin in conversation; and afterwards the design for the flag of America arose. The old man disappeared, and was never referred to in any other way than as 'the professor'—as very wise and very helpful.

Another event is more widely known. All fifty-six individuals who were to write the Declaration of Independence were gathered together; fifty-three of them were Freemasons. It was an unusually hot July day in Philadelphia, and they were in a closed room to decide whether or not to carry out this declaration of independence. What they were intending to do was considered high treason, so they debated back and forth behind closed windows and doors. Suddenly, someone came down from the gallery and spoke to them with passionate words: 'Look, do not hesitate! It must be signed and there must be independence. Don't waste a moment!' The men rushed forward to sign the document. Then as they came to themselves, they looked around; everything was still locked tight. They had posted guards at the doors—yet the man who had spoken to them was no longer there! A tradition with both stories is that it was the Count of Saint-Germain—an important incarnation of Christian Rosenkreutz—who had taken part.

Benjamin Franklin in France

The thirteen colonies declared themselves independent of England, and the world was thus divided and organized. Later, Benjamin Franklin went to France. There he was viewed as a specimen from the New World, something completely unfamiliar. He was genuinely a common man. There were no members of the nobility in his family; he was a self-made man, open to everything. He had such a way about him that he was welcomed everywhere, and also served as an advisor to many officials in France. He took part in a number of conferences, especially with foreign ambassadors, but also within France itself. Lafayette returned to France from America and worked with him there. Franklin knew all the leading men, even those who became so destructive later. He had hundreds upon hundreds of conversations, and he wrote hundreds of letters. He was in the great Freemason Lodge of the Nine Sisters, and was friends with Voltaire, for example. He believed that, with his advice, France would arrive at a solution to its problems through a new constitution. With others, he laid out plans for this new constitution; then, at the age of eighty, and nine years before the blood-bath of the French Revolution, he returned to America, greatly relieved. He wanted to be in his beloved homeland once again. He died there in 1790. He gave his best efforts based on this deep Rosicrucian principle embodied in him. He was without doubt a great individuality—Schiller and Goethe affirmed this as well. As far as I know, Rudolf Steiner never spoke about Benjamin Franklin. However, he did make a notation in the original 1912–1913 *Calendar of the Soul*, in the actual calendar portion which precedes the verses of the *Calendar of the Soul*. The note reads: 17 April 1790, Benj. Franklin died.

Helena Petrovna Blavatsky

Rudolf Steiner says that approximately every hundred years it is possible to experience Christian Rosenkreutz exoterically. We find such a manifestation in 1785 with the appearance in print of *The Secret Symbols of the Rosicrucians*. Then, around a hundred years later, another manifestation is visible in connection with the Russian Helena Petrovna Blavatsky.

She was born in Russia in 1831. Early in life, she showed herself to be quite clever, fearless, articulate and adventurous. As a young woman, she travelled alone throughout the world, which was unheard of at the time.

She also fought with Garibaldi's army in Italy and afterwards loved to wear the red shirt, which was considered quite conspicuous behaviour in those days. Then she came again to America, and in 1874 a decisive karmic meeting took place. She met Henry Steel Olcott. Olcott was already well known in America as a lawyer and journalist who, after the assassination of Abraham Lincoln, was asked to investigate the assassination because he was someone the government could trust not to be bribed. He was also interested in supersensible phenomena and was visiting a Vermont farmhouse to investigate spiritualistic phenomena, when he met Helena Petrovna Blavatsky.

Rudolf Steiner describes the situation of humanity around the middle and end of the nineteenth century in the following way. People who somehow wanted to school themselves in spiritual or soul matters had to look to the East out of necessity. There was nothing suitable in the West for a spiritual schooling. A brotherhood in the East took note of this, and felt that people in the West should nevertheless try to experience that a spiritual world stands behind the natural world. The brotherhood acted to bring this about and was quite surprised when a whole movement of spiritism arose rather than the kind of thinking they hoped for.

Then, as Rudolf Steiner describes it, the teachers of humanity looked further. At that point they could find only one person to fulfil a great task for the spiritual awakening of humanity—and that was Helena Petrovna Blavatsky. Rudolf Steiner calls her a 'world event' and said in unpublished notes, 'Helena Blavatsky opened the gates of spiritual life, and in light of this, all else that could be said for or against her seems quite insignificant.'[13]

How did she open these gates? For one thing, she stated that the human being is not dissolved into a general spirituality after death, but instead remains the entelechy that he is. Secondly, she said there is a spiritual world and there are spiritual beings in this spiritual world. Both of these concepts are the basis for an understanding of Christianity, although Helena Petrovna Blavatsky never contributed to Christianity. That is what is tragic; she was diverted.

In September 1907, Rudolf Steiner and Edouard Schuré were in Barr in the Alsace; there Rudolf Steiner described to Schuré how Christian Rosenkreutz worked out of his stream in relation to Helena Petrovna Blavatsky. Rudolf Steiner referred there to her work *Isis Unveiled*, written between 1875 and 1878. 'The things that are said in *Isis* are true; but the way in which they are said is a distorted reflection of the truth. The truths themselves are inspired by the great initiates of the West, who are also the initiators of Rosicrucian wisdom. The distortion is the result of the inappropriate way these truths were taken up by the soul of H.P. Blavatsky.'[14]

The Founding of the Theosophical Society

Rudolf Steiner also explained that Christian Rosenkreutz was present at the founding of the Theosophical Society. The proposal to found a Theosophical Society came not from Blavatsky, but from Olcott. Olcott thought they should found a society for people who seek spiritual knowledge and who also want to know the secret laws of nature. Thus they founded the Theosophical Society in 1875. He was the president and she was the recording secretary. Rudolf Steiner greatly respected Olcott. After Olcott died in 1907, Rudolf Steiner gave a wonderful eulogy for him.

After the founding of the Theosophical Society, work began on *Isis Unveiled.* Olcott describes how it came about. During the day, Olcott attended to his job as a lawyer. When he returned home in the evening, he worked virtually through the whole night with Helena Petrovna Blavatsky. He believed she was not in a trance state but could simply push her own personality aside. She wrote, and he corrected the English phrasing and so forth. Thus he was the first to perceive these inspirations which came from Christian Rosenkreutz through the possibilities offered by Blavatsky. Three years later, they went to India with other theosophical friends and founded their permanent centre there in Adyar. However, a little before that, Christian Rosenkreutz had withdrawn and was no longer inspirationally active. That is a mysterious and complicated matter. We must keep in mind that Christian Rosenkreutz worked for three years in New York through Helena Petrovna Blavatsky. Theosophy was first conveyed through the English language, then spread quickly throughout Central Europe. After that, through the Theosophical Society in Berlin, it served as the bridge for Rudolf Steiner in 1900. Twenty-five years after the founding of the Theosophical Society, he could make use of this vessel, and that was decisive for him. Once again, there is a direct connection to the inspiration of Christian Rosenkreutz.

We can see the spiritual aura of New York City as similar to that of Philadelphia—as prepared by a similar radiance. New York City is only ninety-two miles from Philadelphia. There has always been a lively exchange between these two cities that were allowed to experience the influence of Christian Rosenkreutz in their histories.

If we look at the history of America, we can perceive how various spiritual effects radiated into it from Central Europe. We think of the very early seafarers, the initiates from the North, who probably learned many secrets through their contact with the Indian initiates and then brought them back to Europe. In the seventeenth century, the effects of Jakob Böhme came to America by way of England with the Quakers and the Pietists. Anthroposophy arrived in America in 1910. Interestingly enough, the first home for anthroposophy in America was in Carnegie Hall, very near the place where Helena Blavatsky and Olcott had worked. Musicians, especially singers who had experienced Rudolf Steiner, first brought anthroposophy from Germany to America.

A complete picture appears before us: Central Europe—the German region—worked in the direction of England; then—with the English language woven in—it made its way across to America; what is truly American arrives in France with Benjamin Franklin. In a completely different way and yet together with Christian Rosenkreutz, Helena Petrovna Blavatsky, a Russian, is spiritually active in America, then India. From India, the effect of theosophy travels to Europe, first to England and then later to Germany, to France, and so on. And then the connection is made through Rudolf Steiner with the new Christian spiritual science, anthroposophy.

Lecture 12

The Anthroposophical Art Impulse under the Protectorate of Christian Rosenkreutz

Virginia Sease

Immediately after independence was declared by the thirteen original colonies, Benjamin Franklin carried his Rosicrucian, Freemasonry insights and experiences to France where he worked vigorously for a bloodless reformation through a real constitution. As the story goes, he had many conversations with the Count of Saint-Germain. In spite of Franklin's efforts, the French constitution failed to materialize. In America, he had been able to find a measure of success when the Declaration of Independence became a reality; but that had been accomplished with much bloodshed during the Revolutionary War. He experienced that first hand, and then went to France with the aim of helping this reform to take place peacefully there.

The French Revolution can be seen as one of the greatest turning-points in human history. Until then, humanity had been able to find guidance in the context of the Mysteries, or later through the esoteric Christian brotherhoods. These were the Templar brotherhoods, the Rosicrucian brotherhoods, the Grail brotherhoods and, later, the good Freemasonry brotherhoods. This principle came to an end with the French Revolution. The individual human being had to arrange his own spiritual, political and social matters; he had to take them into his own hands. For this reason, this whole period is also called the age of the Atlantic Revolution. Whether in America or France, the events are seen as a whole.

As new relationships were definitively established after the French Revolution, it became possible for other developments to take place. We saw that an individuality emerged towards the end of the nineteenth century—Helena Blavatsky—who could bring something new into humanity. Although that new element arose partially as the result of a distortion because she did not have a logical soul, she nevertheless played a decisive role in the development of modern spiritual science.

The Munich Congress of 1907

In May 1907, Rudolf Steiner said emphatically, 'Only in our time has it once again become possible to open up the sources of Rosicrucian wisdom and allow them to flow into the general culture . . .'[1] This was made possible by Rudolf Steiner and Marie Steiner. It did not happen by itself; rather Rudolf Steiner was able to open up these sources.

We will now look at this from a chronological point of view—because it will help us to enter somewhat into the Akashic images for ourselves. In 1904, Rudolf Steiner founded the 'Esoteric School' independent of the Esoteric School in the Theosophical Society; in other words, he was asked to lead the Esoteric School in the German-speaking countries. He was responsible for *his* people; Annie Besant was in charge of the other group in the Esoteric School. Through the possibility afforded him by the Esoteric School, Rudolf Steiner developed a particular method of working. When he wanted to bring something very intimate and esoteric, and when he thought the time was ripe for it, he frequently introduced it first in the Esoteric School, sometimes through lectures, sometimes through indications for meditation.

Afterwards, he gradually opened these stores of wisdom to the general membership. There was an obligation of silence in the Esoteric School; the members were not allowed to speak about what happened there. When this wisdom had taken hold in the souls of the School's members, it could gradually be made more public—public in the sense of the membership of the Theosophical Society, and then, as a next step, the general public.

With this substance prepared in the souls of the early members of the Esoteric School, we come very quickly to a turning-point in 1907. At that time, many treasures hidden in the indications, meditations and paths of schooling of the Esoteric School were brought into the open through the Theosophical Congress in Munich. This Theosophical Congress had become an annual event; the previous year it had been in Paris, still earlier in Holland, and in 1902 it had taken place in England. With his friends, Rudolf Steiner had accepted the task of arranging the 1907 Congress in Munich. This Congress signalled a breakthrough. It can truly be said that it was a world event. Only now are we gradually beginning to understand what this Congress was really about; and it will take a long time before we are in a position to penetrate what took place there, what was brought into the world as a seed for the development of science, art and the structuring of society. It was the Congress of the Federation of the

European Sections of the Theosophical Society, and it is well documented—which is indeed fortunate.

In the account of a young student, E.A. Karl Stockmeyer, we can read how he experienced it.

> ... The so-called Kaim-Saal, later called the Tonhalle, at the corner of Prince Ludwig and Türkenstrasse, was completely decked out in bright red fabric. Even the ceiling was clothed in red. The large galleries were curtained. Thus a rectangular space was created with a rather wide floor plan, without windows; it was a purely interior space.
>
> The red fabric walls were completely smooth. Only at the front of the room was a simple, rectangular, slightly deeper stage area left open, its floor a good yard higher than the floor of the room. There above was a long table (towards the front) for the leaders of the Congress, covered in red as well, and decorated with the signs of the zodiac. Next to it, and a bit in front of it, was the lectern.
>
> Over the opening of the stage hung a picture, *The Great Babylon*, by the Munich painter Hass. Under it, on pedestals, stood the busts of the great German idealists Fichte, Schelling and Hegel. To the left and right of them were two pillars, one red with a J on it, the other blue with a B on it. The pillars were inscribed with the sayings:
>
> J
> In pure thinking you find
> The Self that can sustain itself.
>
> When you transform the thought to image,
> You will experience creative wisdom.
>
> B
> When you condense feeling into light,
> You reveal its forming power.
>
> When you objectify the will as being,
> You create in cosmic existence.
>
> The two side walls and the back wall were decorated with seven pillars, each about eight feet high and painted quite simply on large boards. They show ... in their capitals the motifs of the later Goetheanum pillars. The planetary signs were affixed to them. In the spaces between the pillars were affixed the seven apocalyptic seals. Both pillars and seals were painted according to Rudolf Steiner's sketches ... [2]

'Pillars and seals ... were painted according to Rudolf Steiner's sketches.' Rudolf Steiner later described these seven pillars as the doubled seven-pillar rows that could be experienced in the Rosicrucian temples.

The Revelation of Rosicrucian Secrets

The Munich Congress was not only concerned with the decoration of the room—there was also a production of Schuré's *The Sacred Drama of Eleusis*. Through it, there was a connection to the past history of the Mysteries. Marie von Sivers (later Steiner) rehearsed the drama after Rudolf Steiner had revised its language for production. For the most part there were no professional actors in the cast. Even the printed programme was an expression of the Rosicrucian intent of this conference. On the cover of the programme was the black cross; around the black cross, the radiant red roses. In a dark blue oval were ten letters, the initials that had been kept secret throughout the ages: 'E.D.N.'—*Ex Deo Nascimur*—'I.C.M.'—*In Christo Morimur*—'P.S.S.R.'—*Per Spiritum Sanctum Reviviscimus*. Prior to this, these letters and their meaning had been secreted away in the Esoteric School; and now they appear on the programme, like a call. Rudolf Steiner remarked about these letters in a report about the Congress, 'These are the ten initial letters of the words through which true Rosicrucianism is summarized as a statement of purpose ...'[3]

Not every participant was pleased with this arrangement. As Rudolf Steiner wrote later in *The Course of My Life*, they did not understand that '... the main thing was that the Congress had the element of art in it. An artistic element signalled the intention that, from then on, spiritual life could not exist in the Society without the artistic.'[4] From that moment, the artistic element was connected at the deepest levels with anthroposophy, with the Anthroposophical Society. I believe that the Anthroposophical Society as well as the anthroposophical movement differentiate themselves from all other movements precisely through this will to be connected to the arts—which appeared fully for the first time at the Munich Congress of 1907. In looking back, Marie Steiner understood this event as an 'inner dividing up of souls'. Many theosophists did not want the art. Inwardly, they completely rejected this kind of art in a Rosicrucian form.[5]

The Congress was a great deed condensed into a brief period of time. Often the greatest events in world history occur in a very short time. This was the case here as well. The Congress took a long time to prepare, but it lasted only four days. Immediately afterwards, Rudolf Steiner gave lectures on the theme 'The Theosophy of the Rosicrucian'. In them, he describes the task and the attitude of the Rosicrucians, which is to seek not a withdrawal from the physical world, but a spiritualization of the physical world.

How do we spiritualize the physical world? As an old theosophical concept described it, spiritualization is when material substance grows thinner and thinner. But that is really not the point. It is not that the material substance becomes thinner and thinner, but it is a matter of its complete transformation, a metamorphosis. The physical substance—a colour, a sound, a stone, or what we can bring about physically through the word, through movement, through sound by way of our bodily nature—is transformed so that it becomes different. This is the spiritualization of matter.

The Esoteric School and the Masters

In 1907, the Esoteric School had already existed in the German-speaking world for three years under the leadership of Rudolf Steiner. Ten days after the closing of this Munich Congress, he indicated to the pupils of the School that they needed to make a decision. It is a unique occurrence in spiritual history that the teacher asks for a decision from his pupils. Previously, pupils had been chosen, called for a spiritual schooling.

Now the pupils had to decide of their own free will whether they wanted to remain with him, with Rudolf Steiner—which meant with the teachers he always called 'the Masters of the West' in those days—or whether they wanted to stay in the old, familiar relationships with Annie Besant, with the Eastern Masters. It was a matter of an inner decision. Many went with Rudolf Steiner; however, there were also many who chose Annie Besant. He said that this should not be thought of as some kind of disharmony among the four Masters he always addressed for this movement; but rather it was a distinction that simply needed to be made between the Masters of the East and the Masters of the West. From a loftier perspective, the Masters always live together in harmony.

Later Rudolf Steiner no longer used the word 'Master' but always said 'helper of humanity' or 'teacher of humanity'. He reworked this concept, just as in other cases when he changed the theosophical vocabulary—often based on Indian phraseology—to a Western means of expression. Rudolf Steiner says that the Masters who teach the West are Christian

Rosenkreutz and Master Jesus, whom he also frequently refers to as Zarathustra in this context. They are the Christian esoteric Masters of the West.

The two Masters of the East are Master Kuthumi and Master Morya. In the Theosophical Society at that time, Rudolf Steiner always drew a connection among these four Masters. Now he introduces a distinction between the realms of their tasks.

There are also teachers of humanity, Masters of humanity, connected with the middle and the south: Master Hilarion and the so-called Venetian Master. Then there is a Master individuality who moves among these realms. This Master is not discussed very explicitly in Rudolf Steiner's writings; however he does appear in conversations so that we can mention this Master here with a fair degree of confidence. His name is Serapis, and in conversations Rudolf Steiner identified this Master individuality with Scythianos.[6]

These Masters had certain tasks in the history of humanity. Rudolf Steiner described the tasks and periods of activity for some of these Masters. For example, the change from the Egyptian cultural epoch to the Greek—hence from the third cultural epoch to the fourth—occurred under the leadership of Master Kuthumi. The Greek cultural epoch was under the protection of Master Hilarion, the Master of the middle region. Then came the transition from the fourth to the fifth age, to our own age; Rudolf Steiner designates this period as the Germanic/Anglo-Saxon/American epoch. This transition took place through Master Jesus, who made this change possible. Our entire epoch is now under the leadership of Christian Rosenkreutz. The sixth epoch, the Slavic epoch, lies far in the future, and will be led by Master Morya. There is no definitive information for the seventh epoch.

There are actually twelve teachers of mankind, or Bodhisattvas as they are also called. Only seven of them work during a particular period on the earth. Three—Scythianos, Buddha and Zarathustra—were teachers in the Rosicrucian Schools through all the ages; and Manes, as the lofty emissary of Christ, works through the twelve Bodhisattvas as the thirteenth. This brief summary is necessary in order to describe precisely where the Munich Congress belongs spiritually—under the protection of Christian Rosenkreutz.

Christian Rosenkreutz and the New Art Impulse

This Munich Congress was also of great importance for Rudolf Steiner. It was connected to his task, because he had to discover: Who is coming with me? Whom can I count on? It was really a dividing up of souls. As a result, Christian Rosenkreutz finds a way into the modern age. After three years as the inspirer of Helena Petrovna Blavatsky, Christian Rosenkreutz had withdrawn for mysterious reasons. Now with the Munich Congress, this individuality begins to appear more and more. Two years later, in 1909, two important events took place. The first is the creation of a small model building in Malsch, Germany, not far from Karlsruhe. In it we see how the impulses for three-dimensional art were developed further through the new possibilities of form. This building still exists and can be visited. The second event occurs when Rudolf Steiner creates something unique in world literature. In October 1909, the members arrive expecting to hear a lecture about 'The Being of the Arts'. But Rudolf Steiner tells them an unusual fairy-tale. It is long and complicated and, to the people who heard it, it seems to be a call from the spiritual world. Such a call from the spiritual world is always taken up by some human souls; once taken up, it is in the aura for all human beings whose souls are somehow open to it, open to the fact that the arts must really be understood out of their heavenly origin so that these arts can take on form in a new way.

The soul is warmed by this fairy-tale, just as it was by the deeds of the rhapsodists in the seventh century and later, and it is wonderful when told by someone in speech formation. It takes place in a snow-covered landscape.

> It is evening. The sun has already set ... Within our realm stand two female figures. And from the evening glow of the sunset an emissary is born ... an emissary of higher worlds who places himself before the two women and listens attentively to what their mouths express about their most intimate feelings, about their most intimate experiences.
>
> One woman standing there clasps her limbs to her body; she holds herself and speaks the words, 'I am cold'.[7]

The other woman experiences only the beauty of the landscape. She experiences not the cold, but the beauty. She is art, while the first woman is science without warmth.

This fairy-tale—I call it that, but naturally it is much more than a fairy-tale—is meant for the future. It is connected with the higher senses of the human being. We have the impression that Rudolf Steiner worked intimately with Christian Rosenkreutz on this poetic form. The helpers of humanity always work together. We already touched upon this when we set forth Manes' task of bringing reincarnation and karma into connection with Christianity. It is a task of Christian Rosenkreutz to offer his help so that human beings can have the experience of Christ in the etheric realm. Rudolf Steiner is assisting in this work of mankind.

The Mystery Dramas

For twenty-one years, Rudolf Steiner carried a Rosicrucian inspiration inwardly; then this inspiration bursts forth—in Munich the first Mystery Drama is written and produced in 1910, only three years after the Munich Congress. It was described by Rudolf Steiner in the following way: '*The Portal of Initiation.* A Rosicrucian Mystery through Rudolf Steiner.' We could perhaps even say, 'through Rudolf Steiner with Christian Rosenkreutz'. In the first drama, we see immediately how his great task is presented on the stage. In a great artistic moment, Theodora proclaims Christ's presence in the etheric world.

Forward-looking people saw these Mystery Dramas. Those in Rudolf Steiner's circle of friends report that there were to have been seven dramas, but only four were written. The First World War broke out, and this summer activity in Munich had to come to a halt. Christian Morgenstern describes a production of the Mystery Dramas as: '... a new level, a new epoch of art. This epoch itself is still far away; hundreds of years may pass before there are enough people who want this purely spiritual art so that, for example, Mysteries of this kind can be worthily offered and received in every city. But here in *The Portal* is its historical starting-point; we are present here at its birth.'[8] A poetic soul like Christian Morgenstern was able to feel all of that.

We are looking here at a short time during which much comes together; the year 1911 is an especially important step in this evolution. The second Mystery Drama was produced that summer. Following that, in autumn, Rudolf Steiner gave important indications about the relationship of Rosicrucianism to anthroposophy, which was still called theosophy at the time. It is a period of increasing concentration on the individuality of Christian Rosenkreutz. This individuality—and not just the general Rosicrucian element—is addressed again and again. For example, Rudolf Steiner describes how the Rosicrucian element and its impulses must be formed differently in every age. This is understandable only if we recall that the whole fifth post-Atlantean epoch stands under the protection of Christian Rosenkreutz. Thus, the forms of expression naturally change according to the needs of the time.

The Endowment for Theosophical Art and Way of Life

On 15 December 1911, Rudolf Steiner called together a small group of his esoteric pupils. It was not until 1947 that Marie Steiner circulated private copies of information about what transpired at this meeting. She called it 'An Impulse for the Future Given through Rudolf Steiner, and What Has Become of It'.[9]

It was 'a call ... to humanity', a direct communication from the spiritual world; thus it was an 'attempt not to found, but to endow a community of people'. This endowment incorporated a method of working, with the individuality of Christian Rosenkreutz as its starting-point. The document by Marie Steiner describes how something had already been created as an 'artistic representation of Rosicrucian occultism'. What form should this method of working now take? This creative effort ought to be based on an interpretation of spiritual intentions. For his part, Rudolf Steiner was in a position not only to bring this interpretation into the world, but also to accompany those who wanted to join in it. They were to be free—working out of their own will—but there had to be some way to recognize their work. Later, we again find these two aspects in the Anthroposophical Society. Marie Steiner was appointed to gather together the people who wanted to participate. Its method of working also required that people base their work only on the 'principles of becoming'. This means that what already exists should never determine what wants to come into being—in other words, they should base their work on the strongest artistic and esoteric principle imaginable. The further development of this endowment never took place. Rudolf Steiner said about it in a lecture a few years later: 'The way in which the matter was taken up in one particular case made it impossible. It was an attempt.'[10]

Eurythmy

At the same time, in December 1911, the mother of a young woman by the name of Lory Smits approached Rudolf Steiner. The mother was one of Rudolf Steiner's esoteric pupils. She asked him for advice about the future of her eighteen-year-old daughter whose father had just died. Soon afterwards, Rudolf Steiner came to Kassel, where in January 1912 he gave instruction to Lory Smits, who wanted to do something with movement. Rudolf Steiner's conversation with her was embedded between two powerful lectures about Christian Rosenkreutz; and that conversation was the very first seed for the development of eurythmy. It is quite worthwhile to read the details of these events in Magdalene Siegloch's book about Lory Maier-Smits.[11]

Lory Smits had lessons with Rudolf Steiner during that summer, with Marie Steiner always present. During that time, the first foundations for this art were laid; the name 'eurythmy' was also found. In fact, Rudolf Steiner had experienced the birth of this new art almost as a surprise. He described it: 'Eurythmy actually grew up on the soil of the anthroposophical movement like a gift of destiny.'[12]

The development of eurythmy went hand in hand with the development of the forms of the first Goetheanum. If we immerse ourselves in these forms—we are delighted that this has become more possible for us through the newly renovated Great Hall in the Goetheanum—and then attend a eurythmy performance, we can experience how both these two artistic developments are quite intimately connected with one another.

The Calendar of the Soul

The *Calendar of the Soul*[13] was a direct outcome of the attempt at an 'Endowment for Theosophical Art and Way of Life' that never came to pass. Rudolf Steiner formed this *Calendar of the Soul* in preparation for Easter 1912; it proceeds through the year from Easter to Easter. Many have worked for years with these meditations. The *Calendar* is unique in the realm of art, if we want to think of it primarily as art; and it is unique in the history of mankind, because it is comparable to nothing else. Rudolf Steiner mentioned that it did not come about quickly; instead, he says: 'Long occult experience and research is concentrated in these fifty-two formulations that can serve as chronological formulations for an inner life of the soul, and thus connect it to the processes of divine-spiritual experience.'[14] Through these sayings, these meditations, we enter into the realm of the hierarchies. During the First World War, Rudolf Steiner had the *Calendar of the Soul* and the four Mystery Dramas[15] printed small enough that they would fit in a pack of cigarettes that could then be sent to soldiers at the front.

Work on the Mystery Dramas continued, and enormous occult realities found their way into humanity through these dramas—for example, the way the Guardian of the Threshold speaks. How should a person undergoing a spiritual, occult development find a relationship with his karmic group? How should he arrive at the threshold of the spiritual world? How should he meet this Guardian of the Threshold? This is discovered very clearly in his instructions for the staging; it is also discovered in the language itself, which is not an arbitrary language. The language of the dramas is structured in such a way that it works as a seed in the soul of the observer.

Art at the Beginning of the Century

It is like a minor fulfilment of Christian Morgenstern's poetic promise or prophecy that work on the Mystery Dramas was already being done at the end of the twentieth century, with translations into many languages, and many amateur groups performing the Mystery Dramas in part or in their entirety. This is especially the case in the English-speaking world; for example, all four dramas have already been performed in Los Angeles and Sacramento, California, and in Spring Valley, New York. In England as well there has been active work with the Mystery Dramas over the years.

At the threshold of this new century, we stand before a grave question: What must art based on anthroposophical sources accomplish if it is to continue developing its work 'under the protectorate' of Christian Rosenkreutz, as it was called in the 'Endowment'? As we saw in the case of Helena Petrovna Blavatsky, it cannot automatically be assumed that once inspiration flows from Christian Rosenkreutz it will continue forever. He can also withdraw. That would be a great misfortune, because the impulses in art brought into the world through Rudolf Steiner are so new they will need a long time to be cultivated by the spiritual world and from the human side.

I think it is quite important here to continue taking seriously the original indications from Rudolf Steiner, namely, indications for eurythmy, for the Mystery Dramas, for the art of jewellery making, for speech formation, for dramaturgy. These are not indications meant for a few decades, but for centuries; they correspond to occult realities with which Christian Rosenkreutz is also creatively in agreement. For example, Rudolf Steiner wrote in a letter to Marie Steiner: 'There is basically only *one* correct form for a poem.'[16] He gave many eurythmy forms for poems, for musical compositions, which are the *one* correct form, when seen from an occult perspective, when seen spiritually. Artists naturally create their own forms where no form has been given yet. With it they come close or not so close to the actual form of a poem or a piece of music as that form lives in the spiritual world.

Spiritual faithfulness in a person's artistic work cannot lead to slavery if the person approaches these indications individually, out of his own selfhood, and works through them, experiences them thoroughly, and practises, practises, practises. These are spiritual realities, and these realities are just as valid for the one human being, for the one artist, as for any other human being—even if we approach these realities from different points of view.

Buddha and Christian Rosenkreutz

In 1911, when Rudolf Steiner speaks about Rosicrucianism and the task of Christian Rosenkreutz, he also speaks about the task of the Gautama Buddha. He calls him the good friend and pupil of Christian Rosenkreutz. Rudolf Steiner mentions that the Gautama Buddha—whose task, seen from a cosmic perspective, is connected to Mars—lives and works within our movement. Since he works in conjunction with Christian Rosenkreutz, this means that he works in a special way in regard to art, particularly in connection with the arts of speech and music.

When Buddha was a Bodhisattva during his final incarnation on the earth approximately six hundred years before the Mystery of Golgatha, he bestowed upon human beings the possibility of developing the sixteen-petalled lotus blossom. Rudolf Steiner also called lotus blossoms 'spiritual organs of perception' which are embedded in the astral body of human beings. Half the petals of the sixteen-petalled lotus blossom have already been developed, and the human being must himself develop the other half. He must also train certain qualities in himself so that they then become capacities.

There are eight qualities for the sixteen-petalled lotus blossom—we also know them as the eightfold path—that are always described with the adjective 'right'. The first quality is that the person develops the 'right' opinion, without sympathy or antipathy. This is done so that from the 'right' opinion he arrives at the 'right' judgement; this in turn leads to saying the 'right' word; so that, in regard to his actions he has a 'right' way of acting. This leads him to find the 'right' point of view, so that he acquires 'right' habits that are beneficial for his spiritual development, without separating him from his surroundings. The seventh is 'right' memory so that he does not forget what he had once learned—not what he had learned intellectually, but what he has taken up into his soul-spiritual constitution. And then there is the 'right' attitude of contemplation so that, for example, the individual is not tripped up by what accompanied him from previous incarnations, but takes it as a foundation to develop the 'right' attitude of contemplation for the here and now.

According to Rudolf Steiner, in about three thousand years these qualities will necessarily be accessible to all human beings. The sixteen-petalled lotus blossom is situated in the region of the larynx; in the future the human being will transform the larynx and bring forth his own kind from that region. This means there will be a new kind of human reproduction in the future. We can sense the decisive importance for the future of humanity represented in the arts that have to do with the word—the word that is formed, the word that is sung, with eurythmy as visible speech, as visible music.

One task of the Gautama Buddha lies in this sphere. However, the task of the Bodhisattva—the successor who will rise to the position of the Buddha in about 2500 years—is also connected to the word. One important incarnation of this Bodhisattva took place about one hundred years before the Mystery of Golgatha. In the Hebraic tradition he is called Jeshu ben Pandira. Jeshu ben Pandira was associated with the Essenes; he was put on trial, condemned as a heretic, stoned and hanged. One day he will become the Maitreya Buddha who will bring the most sublime word into human culture. Language and word will be permeated by a 'magical morality', where what is good will be called forth by the word. That is a task for the future.[17]

Christian Rosenkreutz's Commitment to the Arts

We could ask: Why, among other things, is Christian Rosenkreutz especially interested in the arts? When we follow this individuality into the past, we find—according to Rudolf Steiner's indications—the Hiram incarnation and the building of the Temple. And we see that this continues far back into the distant past. When this individuality is present as Lazarus, a transformation occurs through the Christ-initiation. We read in the Gospel how seemingly far away the dead Lazarus was; the physical body was beginning to decay. From this perspective, he could see what the laws of the ether body are, how these rhythms come together to bring life to the physical body. He could, so to speak, experience the arithmetic and the geometry of the etheric body, and how it can impress itself into the physical body. And that would also be a kind of description for eurythmy. Rudolf Steiner coins the phrase, 'God geometrizes', for eurythmy. Almost two thousand years ago, this experience took place in Lazarus-John with his own etheric body and its laws—and much later came the birth of this new and still very young art.

Then in the Middle Ages, around 1250, the initiation took place through the twelve initiates working together. The individuality of Christian Rosenkreutz, free of its corporeality, experienced everything connected with the Fall of Man, and how the Fall formed the astral body. After the awakening of Lazarus, he had had a number of quiet, withdrawn incarnations in which everything he experienced was internalized, and during which he also purified himself. Then, after the initiation by the twelve, he returns in a fully purified astral body. This is related to star wisdom. He experiences star wisdom and how the stars are connected with human beings. Here we think of the words Rudolf Steiner once wrote for Marie Steiner who, as a great artist in collaboration with Rudolf Steiner, was able to bring to the world a completely new art of speech—speech formation.

Stars once spoke to humanity,
That they grew silent is cosmic destiny;
To perceive their growing silent
Can bring suffering for earthly man.

Yet, in the mute silence ripens
What human beings speak to the stars;
Perception of their speaking
Can bring strength for spirit man.[18]

We sense here what is connected with this medieval initiation and also with the initiation through Manes in 1459, when Christian Rosenkreutz experienced an initiation in the ego. If we view this artistically, we see that these ego forces are connected at the deepest level with music. The development of music out of the spiritual realm is the most future-oriented deed for the new age, as shown by Rudolf Steiner's words concerning music and the Christ Mysteries:

However, the element of music is capable of one day placing this Christ impulse before the world in formed tones, in soul-permeated, spirit-permeated tones. If music allows itself to be inspired by anthroposophical spiritual science, it will find ways to do this ...[19]

Lecture 13

The Supersensible Michael Cultus and the Being of Anthroposophia

Manfred Schmidt-Brabant

By the middle of the Lemurian period, a quite distinct pair of streams had developed within the evolution of humanity. Humanity—still without the gift of the ego, but nascent as physical body, ether body, astral body and soul form—had 'emigrated'—as it might be described—to the planets. The encrusted moon forces became too strong; the bodies, which still reproduced out of themselves at that time, became too hard. This left only one stream on the earth, which Rudolf Steiner once called 'a kind of primary couple'.[1] Another time, he simply says that a distinct, especially strong bodily stream remained on the earth; and now, as the souls were returning, they could connect to it. This primary couple, these two human beings, thus became the parents of incarnate humanity. As the souls returned in their first incarnation from the various planets as well as from the sun, the elohim, the exusiai bestowed the ego upon them. With that, the incarnations of an evolving individuality really began—because the ego was still very indistinct and vague then, still without shape and contour.

Old and Young Souls

A number of souls soon came to the earth from the region of the planets and the sun. They began to take on bodies in repeated incarnations on the earth—in Lemuria, and then throughout the period of Atlantis. We call these souls 'old souls', because they have many incarnations behind them. Other souls remained for a longer time in their cosmic homeland and descended much later into their first incarnation, often not until the end of the Atlantean age. Hence we refer to these souls as 'young souls'.

It is not that old souls are the clever and experienced ones who have already endured a lot here, and that young souls are less intelligent. Each has a different spirituality. The old souls have had many earthly experiences, but the young souls participated in the same experiences from the spiritual world. They descend full of spiritual perspectives on Earth evolution.

These old souls are often called Platonic souls. Within their whole attitude of soul they found an affinity for what later developed as Platonic philosophy, for what had already been prefigured in the Mysteries, and for what Plato brought to thought, to human beings seeking knowledge. Young souls found an affinity for the Aristotelian attitude, for the attitude towards knowledge that was then brought into the School of Athens by Aristotle. Here, once again, are the old, prototypical gestures: Plato, gesturing upwards with his hand to the world of ideas; Aristotle, pointing to the earth in order to find there the spirit in earthly work.

After the end of the Atlantean period, these souls pass through the most varied Mysteries, and we find them again in the Middle Ages. We see that the old souls, the Platonists, are connected with the School of Chartres, with the Cistercians, but also with other streams. There were many souls who were connected long ago with the sun, human souls who had experienced their exile in the cosmos in the spiritual region of the sun. A quite distinct stream crystallized out of this stream of sun souls. There are the Platonists of the School of Chartres, but there are also the Platonic souls who live with the Cathars and in other movements quite outside the School of Chartres, quite outside the Cistercians, and—this is very important here—they were absolutely not all in agreement with each other. Alanus ab Insulis, the great teacher at Chartres, was a significant Platonist, yet he wrote in the most pointed and scathing way against other Platonists, against the Cathars. This was always a matter of life and death at that time. It was essential that certain biases were formed, because strengths were also formed through the biases. Essentially the last of the young souls descended somewhat later and connected themselves with the whole stream related to the Dominicans—with scholasticism—but also with streams other than the Dominicans. In all, there are twelve great groupings of souls—seven different groups of Platonic souls, five of the Aristotelian souls.

Cosmic Intelligence

A quite distinct and smaller number of sun souls were connected with Michael, especially with a particular activity of Michael. Michael had worked as the Sun Intelligence from the time of the exile, and since then a number of souls had connected themselves closely with what is called his 'administration of cosmic intelligence'. Cosmic intelligence is that aspect of cosmic wisdom through which the patterns of the hierarchies' mutual activity come to expression. We are reminded here of Dionysius the Areopagite who later brought all this into a comprehensible form: how angels, archangels, archai form one grouping, the third hierarchy; how the elohim (the exusiai), the dynamis (the spirits of movement) and the kyriotetes (the spirits of wisdom) form the next higher grouping, the second hierarchy; and finally, how powerful cosmic beings—the thrones, cherubim, and seraphim—form the first hierarchy.

These beings stand in differing relationships to one another; they associate with one another, and this existence in relation to one another is cosmic intelligence. This cosmic intelligence lives among the hierarchical beings as the music of the spheres. They send one another sonatas or small symphonies—what we might think of as communications. This sounds from one being to another, to a third and a fourth, and resounds back again—that is their intelligence. Rudolf Steiner says composers like Mozart, Beethoven and Bach heard the music of the spheres. In earlier times, there were always human beings who could actually listen to this chorus—at least as much as was possible through the openness humanity still had at that time.

The souls who were especially connected with Michael's administration of the cosmic intelligence were later found where people turned to anthroposophy. After all, that administration consisted of maintaining a mutual balance and equilibrium in the cosmic order—in everything the individual planets bring forth as spirituality.

One aspect of this cosmic intelligence suffered a quite specific destiny. The Christ-being had been on the sun, and souls had experienced that. Michael was the sun-intelligence, but the Christ-being—that Being who encompassed everything—also resided on the sun. The souls had experienced—partly in the spiritual world—how the Christ-being descended to the earth, how He connected Himself with the earth, with mankind. Then they experienced a second event. Centuries after the Mystery of Golgotha, the cosmic intelligence as an expression of cosmic wisdom began to move its centre from the sun to the earth, following the Christ. All the souls in the spiritual world who were connected with Michael experienced this, and saw in the descent of the cosmic intelligence the great danger that it would fall prey to the ahrimanic forces on earth. This was sometimes clairvoyantly perceived in the physical world as well. For those who knew, it was obvious that evolution would enter a realm in which the etheric forces would also withdraw, in which nothing but the physical forces would be active in the age of the consciousness soul. It was clear to the initiates that humanity would step into the world of death, the sphere of Ahriman, after the fifteenth century.

Thus the question stood before these souls: What will become of the cosmic intelligence when humanity enters the world of death, the world of Ahriman? The initiates of these streams of old and new souls, the leaders of both streams, turned to Michael. Something Rudolf Steiner compares to a council, a kind of supersensible council, was held. Souls expressed their concerns to Michael and asked something of him. They called for a connection to be made with the cosmic intelligence through which it could once again find its central focus in the Sun with Michael; they called for anthroposophy, for what we would later call—in any case, since 1575—anthroposophy. They sought what would prevent cosmic intelligence from sinking into the realm of death, what would instead reclaim the spirituality of cosmic intelligence.

Michael, it is said, responded favourably to their appeal. Thus arose the great supersensible Michael School. It became a school in which all the old Mysteries nourished by the cosmic sun-intelligence—by the sun, by Michael, by the Christ—were reworked so they could be understood by *the* cosmic intelligence that followed the Christ to earth.

The Michael School

Two noteworthy events have always been a riddle, a secret, for those with research interests in this matter. At precisely that time, the youth known as Christian Rosenkreutz in his next incarnation was initiated below by the twelve, while above, the supersensible council takes place with its focus on the appeal for anthroposophy. As the solemn, cosmic opening of the Michael School takes place in the middle of the fifteenth century, the third initiation of Christian Rosenkreutz—the bestowing of the Christ Ego from the Holy Grail—takes place on the earth.

We portray the event in earthly terms initially. But when we go somewhat deeper, we say to ourselves: There is no above and below in the regions we are talking about; there is nothing spatial about them. They may have spatial aspects—but what is essential takes place in the realm of the spiritual. For example, in the spiritual realm the sun sphere is everywhere. The sun appears as only a point to us, but the spiritual sun sphere permeates everything, just as the spiritual Mercury sphere and the spiritual Saturn sphere permeate everything. Often the image of the physical planet is used—and here the orbiting planets are meant—to indicate only the place where the whole sphere that permeates everything is located. As a result, something always remains unresolved for those who pursue this question: Is there perhaps a close connection between the council and the initiation of the youth by the twelve initiates? Is the solemn opening of the Michael School perhaps intimately connected with the third great initiation of Christian Rosenkreutz?

Later, those souls taking part in this Michael School will find anthroposophy—from the twentieth century into the coming centuries—in whatever form it presents itself. They were on the earth during the time we discussed in these lectures. Rudolf Steiner once spoke to a large gathering of anthroposophists and said: Many of you were incarnated between the sixth or seventh and the twelfth or thirteenth centuries.[2] In fact, all our experiences and observations have shown again and again that virtually every anthroposophist lived during this 'lofty time'—as Rudolf Steiner once called it—in one of the forms we have looked at: as a Cathar, as a Cistercian, as a pupil at Chartres, as a member of the Dominican order, and so on.

Thus these souls had previously gone through many incarnations in which they had Mystery experiences, and now they find themselves in this Michael School that lasts for centuries—until around the end of the eighteenth century. Two elements characterize this School. As Rudolf Steiner expresses it, Michael 'dealt with' the old Mysteries in it; and he demonstrated how a common seed lived in all these Mysteries, a seed they shared because they were nourished by the cosmic intelligence. Whether the Venus Mysteries, the Mercury Mysteries, the Mars Mysteries, the Saturn Mysteries—all were infused with cosmic intelligence, and thus with cosmic wisdom. For those on the earth who were mature enough, the guides of the planets—the great archangels, Samael, Zachariel, Oriphiel and so on—served as the mediators of what stood open on the earth as the archangels' Mystery sites—as Saturn Mysteries, as Mars Mysteries, as Mercury Mysteries. The primal wisdom of the essence of the Mysteries was lifted up in this Michael School. The second characteristic element was that Michael showed how the primal wisdom of all the Mysteries now changes, undergoes a transformation, through the fact of the Mystery of Golgotha.[3]

The Christianizing of all the Mysteries—beginning with the primal cosmic principle—was one content of the supersensible Michael School. A second content was that all the human beings from the various Mystery streams must learn to set aside what they had created—for whatever reason—as one-sidedness. One-sidedness had always existed—it had existed among the Cathars, but also among the teachers at Chartres. In the Michael School, the people who came out of the Mysteries would learn to differentiate between what is essential and what is nonessential. They would learn to look back and say: This was actually the essential element, that was only secondary. They look back into the Dionysian Mysteries, the Apollonian Mysteries, the Persian Mysteries, the Egyptian Mysteries—not only at the Isis Mysteries, but at others as well. Everywhere they see that one-sidedness had to come about in those Mysteries because people were still closely connected with the blood and the soil. An Egyptian had to develop a different Mystery quality than a Greek or someone from the Scandinavian regions. Many of the Mysteries—no matter how large, no matter what their revelation of the cosmic secrets—were one-sided because of what was based on the blood and the soil.

The souls in the Michael School now learn to see this clearly: We were one-sided in Egypt, most especially in the late Egyptian period, but also in Greece, in Eleusus and Delphi. We had to be. But, precisely here in this place—beyond corporeality, beyond the relationship to the soil, beyond the blood—the non-one-sided, the all-sided truth of the Mysteries arises before humanity. This place is well described in the image: The sun shines for all humanity. It was quite decisive that the essence of the Mysteries itself went through a catharsis, through a purification in the supersensible Michael School.

Anthroposophia—An Invisible Human Being

The Michael School closes with a great cosmic celebratory deed. Over the course of about thirty-three years, and under the direct leadership of Michael, all the members of the School celebrate a mighty, supersensible cosmic cultus in the presence of all the hierarchies under the guidance of the Christ. Rudolf Steiner says that we always have to use earthly words to indicate something which, by its nature, has a quite different character. If, in terms of earthly conditions, we imagine the loftiest, most solemn religious cultus celebrated with the greatest intensity and fervour, we have only a pale reflection of what occurred in the sun temple at that time. It was something that shook the whole universe, sounded throughout it, resounded through it, sent power through it. All of the hierarchies took part in this cultus, worked in it and into it.

A being is born in this supersensible cultus, brought forth from the powers of the whole cosmos. It is a supersensible human being, invisible to sensory eyes; it the being of Anthroposophia. This being has lived with and among people since this cosmic cultus. It became possible to experience it after the souls who took part in this cultus had descended into incarnation at the end of the nineteenth century and the beginning of the twentieth century, and when they sought this being based on their knowledge of the earth. Henceforth and far into the future, this being will walk among human beings; it will be there for all who seek it, and it will answer all those who ask something of it. It is an invisible human being because it carries in itself the perfectly purified phantom body. There is no ash to make it visible. It carries the resurrection body, which can exist everywhere. The phantom is not subject to the classical law of spatial relationships that says if a body is here then no other body can be in the same place, or if the body is here it cannot be anywhere else. The phantom—and with it the entire being of the supersensible human being, Anthroposophia—can be experienced anywhere in the world just as the resurrection body of the Christ could be experienced. Paul saw that body of the Christ on the road to Damascus; those who later experienced it saw it elsewhere.

This being of Anthroposophia is a cosmic being. Rudolf Steiner speaks about the fact that cosmic substantiality and cosmic forces stream into this being; and what the Rosicrucians had sacrificed in a most solemn cultus—their star knowledge received from superhuman beings—now became a formative force for this being.

The New Christianity

With complete justification we say that 'Anthroposophy is star wisdom'; or, as Rudolf Steiner likes to say, 'Anthroposophy is cosmosophy'. However, in Arnheim, the Netherlands, he characterizes this being with another, seemingly abstract phrase. He says: What was born here as a being is 'the new Christianity'.[4] It is not a teaching, not a doctrine, not a particular interpretation of the Gospels, although any of these can arise from it; the new Christianity is a being, a bearer of the Christ, as was Jesus of Nazareth. From this cosmic moment on, and from the beginning of its activity in the twentieth century, this being has wanted to bring the Christ-being to people in accord with the will of the Christ-being Himself. We look back at endless conflicts, at Constantine, at Julian, at

Justinian, at the later battles surrounding the Grail, at the battles against the Templars, against the Rosicrucians, at the battles in the Christian Church. In terms of what we are discussing here, all that lies behind us. Now something arises from the cosmos, a being that wants to bring a Christianity that will do justice to all human beings, a Christ that all religions can embrace. What resounded like a promise—that the Christ might emerge in other confessions, that He might go to the priest-king John—becomes cosmic reality during these thirty-three years of the Michael School at the beginning of the nineteenth century. This is a reality we will begin to experience when people in Buddhism, in Islam, in other religions, receive this Christ of anthroposophy.

More and more people will do this. In Japan there is a large Shinto society with two million or more members and an executive council of high priests. Some members of this executive council are members of the Anthroposophical Society. We sensed in conversations with them: This Christ represented by anthroposophy can also be received by a Shintoist, or a Buddhist, or anyone who participates in another religion. For that reason the Anthroposophical Society has members of the Buddhist faith, the Islamic faith, and so forth.

This mysterious event that took place during those thirty-three years was something like a loftier Jesus-Mystery in relationship to Golgotha. If we say that the Christ will not return to the earth because that would render His previous mission senseless—He had only one physical, earthly incarnation—and that He is instead returning in the etheric realm, then we know that He finds this supersensible, invisible human being in the etheric realm, a being who will become a bearer for Him, just as the physical Jesus became a bearer for the Christ.

In earthly images, this cosmic cultus takes place on three mighty altars. They are the altar of the future Jupiter condition of the earth, the altar of the future Venus condition of the earth, and the altar of the future Vulcan, the last stage of Earth evolution. Time is different in the spiritual realm than here on earth. Contradictions necessarily arise if we use only earthly time to measure events like those we are looking at here. We must resolve these contradictions by understanding that there are various levels of time. There is the lowest level, earthly time, at which everything goes from the past into the future, and a future event cannot have already taken place in the past. But then we leave this layer and enter another. Rudolf Steiner even says: Recognizing that layer is the general prerequisite for clairvoyance, for perception in the spiritual world.[5] This second level shows that there are two opposing streams of time. There is one stream of time that comes from the past and goes into the future; and there is a second stream of time that comes from the future and goes into the past. Only through the meeting of the two, in the intersection of both, do we understand time from a higher perspective. Then there is a third level in which the observer stands above the stream of time; this is the view of the Akasha of the whole of time. Time becomes like space—the future is there, the near future is there, the near past is there, the distant past is there. At this level, the human being can look at the stream of time in all its detail.

Now we can come to understand the fourth level. Everything that will happen in the future, that happened in the past, that happens in the present, rests in a being, and this being says, 'I am the past, the present, and the future. No mortal can lift my veil.' It is that Isis-Sophia, that God-being, which contains in itself everything that was, is and will be. Rudolf Steiner says: Indeed, that is how it was in the old Mysteries, and he who dared to lift the veil had to die. But today we must speak of this differently; today we must view this being so that we hear what it says just as we did back then. At that time, this being said, 'I am everything; I am the past, the present, the future. No mortal . . . has lifted my veil.' Today this being says, 'I am the human being. I am the past, the present and the future. Every mortal should lift my veil.'[6]

The Trinity

From one perspective we must therefore say: Lucifer will transform himself into the Holy Spirit in the Christ-permeated human being. And at the same time, we look at this event and say: The Holy Spirit already came to the disciples at Pentecost. Looking far into the distant past, Rudolf Steiner even speaks of the circle of the Bodhisattvas—and says: That is Lucifer, the luciferic world. Then, in the next breath, he speaks of the circle of the Bodhisattvas and says: That is the Holy Spirit.[7] We could also say that what we analyse here below as past, present, future—what took place then, what is taking place, what will take place—converges above, as in a pyramid. The higher we go, the more everything happens simultaneously.

In light of these questions, we must also consider, for example, how far we will get in understanding the Trinity with our human comprehension. We talk about the Holy Spirit as we would about a certain Mr So-and-so. Is he here now, or is he there? There is a wonderful story. The illustrious

Alanus ab Insulis was a powerful teacher. His students loved him, and he was a very great man. One day, he announced in the Sorbonne, in the University of Paris, that he would speak about the secrets of the Trinity. Before his talk, he goes for a walk along the banks of the Seine in order to prepare. There he sees a small child who had dug a hole and was scooping water from the Seine with a little spoon and pouring it into the hole. Alanus stops and asks: 'What are you doing there?' 'Oh', said the child, 'I'm scooping the river into this hole.' Alanus says somewhat pompously: 'But it will take forever to do that!' And the child looks at him, beaming, and says: 'I will be finished with this long before you are finished with your explanation of the Trinity.' With that, the child disappears.

Alanus was a very smart man. He knows who had spoken to him. So he goes into the lecture hall; it is jam-packed. Everyone is there to hear Alanus speak about the Trinity. He climbs to the podium and says: 'My dear friends, for today you will have to be satisfied with having seen Alanus.' And then he left—shaken. He went to the Cistercians to live among them in anonymity as a swineherd. One day, a delegation from the cloister where he was living was sent to Rome. For some reason, the swineherd is also needed; he was to go with them to carry baggage and so forth. The delegation arrives in Rome; very tricky theological questions are being discussed. The small group of Cistercians is present; Church dignitaries are there, along with learned men. And the disputation takes place. The Cistercians get into a little difficulty; the swineherd injects himself into the discussion, guides it, and argues them all down, until one of them says in horror: 'Who are you? Either you're the devil or Alanus ab Insulis!' After this incident, he began to teach again.

The story is also moving because we sense how the Middle Ages wrestled with the question: How do we approach divine secrets with human understanding? Anyone who reads the works of the early Church Fathers—Origen or Clement of Alexandria—is left breathless by the force of the power of thinking called forth at that time in order to take up such questions.

The Opposing School of Ahriman

While this powerful cultus is taking place above in the sun temple, something completely opposite is taking place on an entirely different cosmic plane. As the Michael School developed, the ahrimanic beings became terribly agitated. As a result of this agitation an opposing ahrimanic school was developed in the interior of the earth. This should not be imagined topographically; spiritually speaking, mighty ahrimanic forces massed together within the earth in order to infect souls and inspire spiritual beings with the content of their school. To this day, much continues to emerge from this opposing school of Ahriman that is intended to hinder—and occasionally succeeds in hindering—the spread of a new Christianity, or the spread of the being of Anthroposophia. This is one aspect of the battlefield on which we stand. When the supersensible cultus took place, the forces of this opposing school of Ahriman were assembling into a great ahrimanic counter-cultus. Above, the birth of Anthroposophia is celebrated, while below, in the depths of the earth, a counter-cultus takes place in which the sun-demon, Sorat, is active, and in which preparations are made for his third culmination.

The French Revolution

The supersensible cultus streams into earthly history at this time, and is reflected in Goethe's *Fairy-tale*; likewise, the counter-cultus also begins to stream into earthly history. One of its first and most evil effects is that all the nobility and goodness actually present at the beginning of the French Revolution is stifled and destroyed. A young anthroposophist in America recently remarked, 'What lived in Benjamin Franklin—the independence of the human being in religion and government—was actually a Templar ideal.' In France, the meeting of the Estates-General in 1789 is also a kind of declaration of independence. Members of the good, humanitarian Freemasons took part in both revolutions, and only wanted the best. Benjamin Franklin had carried the best impulses of American independence into the developing French Revolution. It is moving to read reports from that time about how this was welcomed; how people, weeping with emotion, said: A new time is beginning! The old repression is at an end! This is why a figure like Benjamin Franklin was held in high regard by Goethe as well as Schiller. Schiller himself, filled with enthusiasm for the French Revolution, becomes an honorary citizen of France.

However, elements of black magic occultism based in evil powers force their way into the situation. They appear in people like Robespierre, Saint-Just, and the others who took part, and they are responsible for the fact that this general reformation of the constitution and all of French society—begun with such joy and hailed by all of Europe—sinks into a blood-bath. Not only Schiller, but all of Europe, turns away shuddering from this French Revolution. But, from a certain perspective, the revolution is also a great turning-point. The human being becomes responsible for himself. The Templar ideal was now supposed to become reality, and we can only imagine what the French Revolution could have made possible for all of Europe had this intrusion of Sorat forces not occurred—an early form of the Threefold Social Order with freedom, equality and fraternity. Because, as Rudolf Steiner says, those were Grail ideals![8] In them were things that had been hidden away for a long time and now they had arrived for humanity: to be free, to be equal, to be fraternal.

The Fall of the Spirits of Darkness

The second great intrusion of this black magic occultism took place when everything that had so nobly and humanely carried American independence as well as the early French Revolution, everything that had existed as Rosicrucian-inspired Freemasonry, was thoroughly corrupted and twisted. Certainly, during the time of Goethe the lodges were already no longer very spiritual, although a spiritual element remained in some. Mozart and his librettist, Schikaneder, were both members of a Rosicrucian lodge in Vienna, and *The Magic Flute* is an outcome of their participation. However, all of the lodges were humanitarian, even if they were often no longer so spiritual. Their philanthropy resulted in the building of old people's homes, orphanages, hospitals; their actions were always anonymous because they knew that a part of selflessness is the donor keeping his name a secret.

In the middle of the nineteenth century, an event took place that the occult world refers to as the 'fall of the spirits of darkness'. A great host of ahrimanic beings was thrown from the spiritual world to the earth by Michael. The spiritual world was opened up for those human beings who can now find their way there. But the earth is filled with ahrimanic beings. For the most part, the counter-cultus guides these beings into various kinds of lodges, not only Freemasonry lodges. The power politics, corruption and group egotism of Freemasonry does not begin until the middle of the nineteenth century. When one condemns Freemasonry, often with justification, one must look closely at what is meant. Not all lodges were corrupted, but the fact remains that, from the middle of the nineteenth century, many were.

Sorat's Effect

The third intrusion strikes directly at our hearts. Rudolf Steiner speaks about it in 1924—he predicts it very precisely, but indicates only the year. He says that the beast from the depths will be present in a phenomenon like Adolf Hitler—through him, with him, through what he does. Not just Hitler was permeated by these Sorat forces, but also a person like Stalin. There are peculiar events never mentioned by most historians. Stalin is supposed to have said: 'If we are victorious, do not touch Hitler. Bring him to me alive, my brother Adolf Hitler.' Suddenly we become aware that spiritual beings of a mighty kind are speaking there. It is still impossible, even today, to measure what Stalin did to Russia, what Hitler did to Germany. These are profoundly damaging deeds that reach far into the future. I often have the impression that just as the Thirty Years War prevented the blossoming of Rosicrucianism, National Socialism prevented the ability of anthroposophy to blossom into the world from Germany.

Cultic-Symbolic Work

In the outer world, the culmination of Sorat was being prepared. It took place in 1998, which is three times 666 years, and every 666 years is like a culmination—preparations were long underway, and will continue to have their effects. As this culmination of Sorat was actually starting to become apparent at the beginning of the twentieth century, Rudolf Steiner was creating in silence, in a hidden sanctuary, the rite we refer to as his cultic-symbolic rite. With a small group of participants—there were probably only seven hundred in all of Europe—and in a form appropriate for the time, he celebrates the cultus of Mark and Ormuz, who earlier had recast the Isis-cult into something Christian; he celebrates ritually what the Templars had practised, and what was once again prepared by the Rosicrucian Masters in an appropriate way for the age of the consciousness soul.[9] For example, this cultus was practised by the Templars who rode on horseback into their great round churches and stood in a circle astride their horses while the cultus was celebrated in the centre of the circle. Linguistically, Rudolf Steiner brings a form that is simple, and yet usable in any space that can be transformed with a few changes into an image of the Temple (as happened at the Munich Congress).

In this cultus, the participants are placed in the great stream of the

Mysteries. A vast amount of material appears in a new linguistic form, in a new image-form. Only fragments have been handed down and published;[10] the whole was much more extensive. Within this immersion in the course of the Mysteries of humanity, there is a fraternal unity—both practised and articulated—with all initiates, with all the hierarchies up to the Christ-being, whom we may call 'Brother'. This unity with the Mystery stream of humanity was expressed in a great prayer. Hundreds of people who took part have said this prayer throughout their lives, and many more said it after it was published. Each time we hear it, we always think that the Mysteries appear—the brothers in the Mysteries, the great initiates, the spiritual beings, past, present and future. The prayer—Rudolf Steiner definitely calls it 'a prayer'—says:

> *Brothers of ages past,* may your creating become our wisdom; we receive the compass and the plumb line from your hands. May your accomplished work be strength for our soul, be strength for our hands.
>
> *Brothers of the present,* as you are wiser than we are, let your wisdom radiate into our souls, so that we may become revealers of your thoughts of God.
>
> *Brothers of the future,* as you carry the building-plan in your will, may your strength stream into our limbs so that we may become a body for great souls.[11]

As though in an image—for it was celebrated at three altars—the supersensible cultus shines in. It then shines into the Mystery Dramas through the image of the sun temple, as well as through the image of the Rosicrucian temple and its three altars.

Sleep and Karmic Memory

This experience of a fraternal unity with all the Mysteries is related to a quality of the human constitution that Rudolf Steiner revealed relatively late, but then with extraordinary clarity. It is the fact that in every sleep we go through all our past incarnations, back to the first ego; he even says we go back a bit into the exusiai.[12] Here we arrive once again at the riddles of the stream of time. During sleep, physical body and ether body remain behind in our bed or wherever we are sleeping. Astral body and ego lift themselves out; they are above time. It is as though the spiritual human being now looks at a tableau and says: 'I have lived there and there and there.' It is as though this spiritual human being goes through these lives as it reviews them, experiencing them once again in reverse. Naturally, there was an implied objection during the lecture: 'But what if I just take a quick nap?' Well, says Rudolf Steiner, then it is as though you are just skimming over the tableau. The process occurs even if you take a quick nap for half a minute or a few seconds during a lecture. But then it is just like gliding past the image. And he adds: Those who can observe this can see quite clearly how these images exist in the spiritual organization of the human being.[13]

During the night, in normal, extended sleep, we go through our earth lives, and we also go through everything we experienced in the Mystery cultures. We go through quiet incarnations and through those incarnations when we sat in the Pythagorean school, in the Platonic academy, in Egyptian, Persian, Indian Mysteries. Souls who have lived on the earth for a long time took part in the oracles of the Atlantean age; we go through the incarnations of the Middle Ages, look at our life as a Cathar, at our Dominican life, our Templar life, at our Grail encounters, or only at what we experienced on the Camino. We awaken in the morning and enter with all of this into what we are as a human being today. We know nothing about it, and yet it is there; the past of the Mysteries lives in us. When we speak about the Mysteries, we speak about the soul-spiritual element within us just as someone might say: Take note that you have a heart, lungs and a liver. They are reality, not merely pictures in an anatomical atlas. They are inside you and you must pay attention to them! It is the same when we speak about the old Mysteries, although there are differences for each person. One person was in this Mystery, another was in that one. These things affect us in varying ways and determine our karmic relationships to other people.

There are those with whom we were together as Templars, and with whom we perhaps sat in the school of Dionysius or in the Platonic academy. There are others with whom we became enemies. A Dominican might sit here, and there sits a Cathar who says: That man burned me last time! This must not remain as animosity; this must not happen. We take the wrong direction with this if we say: I cannot stand him! Who knows what he might have done to me? That would be too arbitrary; we have to see the finer fabric that is woven among us. Our connection to people is not merely a matter of superficial sympathies and antipathies. These connections are structured in a variety of ways. One person always moves us to do certain things; another we listen to with pleasure; and we somehow always seem to have work to do with a third person. Let us just take note that the karmic relationship of one person to another is itself like an individuality; we do not have the same relationship with any two people. The relationship between two people is always quite individual, never the same.

The Apocalyptic Seals

Here an insight emerges that is expressed and strongly emphasized at the end of *Occult Science, An Outline*. The apocalyptic motifs begin there. Rudolf Steiner draws our attention to the fact that the sensory conditions in which we live and the soul-spiritual element of our destiny form two completely separate streams of development. Literally he says, 'Supersensible knowledge must seek the development of human forms and the development of soul destinies along two completely separate paths.' To mix them up is a dangerous materialism—and here we begin to understand some of the apocalyptic images. We read at the end of *Occult Science*, 'The forms of "evil humanity" arise through the forces inherent in the sensory stream.'[14] These are the two great apocalyptic images which characterize where the Mystery path is going, where the great decisions lie.

The 1907 Munich Congress was an extraordinary event. There are the planets in the pillars; there stand the Pillars of Hercules, Jachin and Boaz; and behind them is the zodiac. We recall our image of the path, the Camino: senses, temperaments, elements, planets, the Pillars of Hercules, ocean, the fixed stars. In Munich, the so-called apocalyptic seals hung between the planets, and that is a reference to Christian Rosenkreutz. The Book of Revelation does not describe particular seals, but rather various images. Six apocalyptic seals are quite familiar to us: the Horsemen of the Apocalypse, Christ with the double-edged sword, the woman with the dragon at her feet, and others. Up to that time, the seventh seal had not been known outwardly by any human being. It became public for the first time in 1907 in that room; it is the Grail seal, the expression of the New Jerusalem, when the earth and the human being form the Grail, when they become the Grail. We see a large, transparent, crystal-clear cube, an image of the body, of the earth. We remember the Brazen Sea and the transparent body of the youth. The earth is a clear crystal. Two snakes coil out of the six sides of the crystal. They are sitting, curving upwards, with one of their pointed tips touching each of the six sides. They are an image of what emerged from the crystal so that it could become transparent. A form similar to the staff of Mercury arises from the mouths of these snakes, the forces that were expelled now transformed into the spiritual, the purified lower forces. These purified lower forces come together above to create a chalice open towards what is below. Below the chalice we see the white dove of the Holy Spirit; next to the chalice and the doves is the rainbow as a symbol for the gate to the spiritual world. In a circle surrounding the seal stand the initial letters of the Rosicrucian words.

Rudolf Steiner speaks about this to the Munich Congress, and says that the chalice opens below, and thus is formed from above. This is an image for the fact that the New Jerusalem will be built from above to below.[15]

The Whore Babylon

We must place another image next to this one, one in which all manner of evil forces converge. In it, at the end of the earth, Christ the Lamb will unite with all those who found Him. This is the 'marriage of the lamb'. However, the sun-demon will also arise and drag with him into the abyss all the evil powers and souls that have developed—and those will be all the souls who fell prey to the being of the counter-Grail, the being into whom flows what lived in the age of Herod, and around Klingsor and Philip the Fair. That is the great evil being of the Book of Revelation, the whore Babylon.

She is really portrayed as a being of the counter-Grail.

> There came one of the seven angels who had the seven vials, and spoke to me: Come! I want to show you the fate of the great whore who sits on many streams of water, with whom the kings of the earth fornicated and from whose impure wine the inhabitants of the earth are intoxicated. And he led me on a spiritual level into a wilderness. There I saw a woman sitting astride a scarlet beast. The beast . . . was covered with the names of blasphemy of the spirit, and had seven heads and ten horns. The woman was clothed in purple and scarlet robes, dazzlingly decorated with gold and gemstones and pearls. She held in her hand a gold vessel full of horrifying forms and impure beings, the result of her fornication. And on her forehead a name was written, a mystery: The great Babylon, the Mother of all whoring and every horrifying form on the earth. And I saw the woman intoxicated with the blood of those devoted to the spirit and with the blood of the witnesses of Jesus.[16]

Rudolf Steiner discusses her in his course on Revelation. She is the one in whom is gathered everything Rudolf Steiner calls 'fornication with matter'. Human beings are meant to give form to the material world, permeate it with art, purify and humanize it, as the Rosicrucians wanted to do. They should not become devoted to it, dependent on it, nor submit to it, because that is the 'fornication of the spirit'.

The Grail

Thus the Grail and the counter-Grail stand at the end of Earth evolution and also at the end of all the paths that begin in the present, where what is external is to become what is internal. In the last century the great demand of the spiritual world began anew; Rudolf Steiner refers to it this way, 'The path to the Holy Grail will have to be found through work on the interior of human souls. That is a task of knowledge; that is a social task.' 'Because, if we understand the true, inmost call of humanity, we are still seekers of the Holy Grail, and must be seekers of the Holy Grail.'[17] This path leads to that great Mystery that has occupied us the whole time: What is external became internal, the outer paths became the inner paths, outer landscapes of the Mysteries became inner landscapes. Today there is the inner Camino, there is the inner Compostela, there are the inner Mystery sites, and above all, there is a most holy place within the human being.

Rudolf Steiner finds wonderful words for this place with which we will close:

> In the temple of the human body is located a holy of holies. Many people live in the temple without knowing anything about it. But those who sense it receive from it the power to purify themselves so that they may enter into this most sacred place. There is the sacred vessel which was prepared through epochs of time. There rests the holy chalice which was prepared throughout the epochs of time so that it would be ready when the time came to hold the blood of Christ, the life of Christ. When the human being has entered this place, he has also found the path to the holy of holies in the great earth temple. Many on the earth live there, too, without knowing it; but if the human being has found himself in his innermost sanctuary, he will also be allowed to enter the great earth temple and find the Holy Grail. Carved as though from wonderful gleaming crystals that form symbols and letters, the chalice will first appear to him; then gradually he will sense its holy

content, so that the content itself shines for him in a golden radiance. A human being enters into the Mystery place of his own heart, and then a divine being emerges from this place and connects itself to the God without, with the Christ-being. This divine being lives in the spiritual light that streams into the chalice, hallowing it.[18]

Notes

Editor's Note: The references to Rudolf Steiner's works listed below are to the original German editions, with a literal English translation of the title shown in brackets. These quotations have been translated directly from the original German. The 'GA' numbers given refer to the catalogue number of the *Gesamtausgabe* or Collected Works in the original German, as published by Rudolf Steiner Verlag, Switzerland. The dates of Rudolf Steiner's lectures are also given. To facilitate the identification of official English translated editions of the cited lectures, a bibliography of such books follows on page 242.

Citations are given in full the first time they appear in each lecture. Works cited only by title and GA number are by Rudolf Steiner.

Lecture 1

1. Cf. *Der Orient im Lichte des Okzidents: Die Kinder des Luzifer und die Brüder Christi* [The Orient in the light of the Occident: The children of Lucifer and the brothers of Christ] (GA 113), lecture of 28 August 1909.
2. *Vorträge und Kurse über christlich-religiöses Wirken* [Lectures and courses on Christian-religious work], Vol. 5 (GA 346), *Apokalypse und Priesterwirken* [Revelation and the work of the priest], lecture of 9 September 1924.
3. *Die Geheimwissenschaft im Umriss* [Occult science in outline] (GA 13), chapter on 'The Present and Future of Cosmic and Human Evolution'.
4. Ibid., Preface to the sixteenth edition.
5. *Geheimwissenschaft* (GA 13), chapter on 'The Present and Future of Cosmic and Human Evolution'.
6. *Die Tempellegende und die Goldene Legende* [The Temple Legend and the Golden Legend] (GA 93), lecture of 4 November 1904.
7. Ibid., lecture of 2 December 1904.
8. 1 Kings 11:1–13.
9. Matt. 12:42; Luke 11:31.
10. Cited in Rolf Beyer, *Die Königin von Saba* [The Queen of Sheba] (Bergisch-Gladbach, 1987), p. 35.
11. Ibid., p. 36.
12. Ibid., p. 193.
13. Ibid., p. 34.
14. Ibid., p. 35.
15. Ibid.
16. *Der Mensch im Lichte von Okkultisimus, Theosophie und Philosophie* [The human

being in the light of occultism, theosophy, and philosophy] (GA 137), lecture of 12 June 1912.

17. Ibid.
18. *Das Johannes-Evangelium im Verhältnis zu den drei anderen Evangelien* [The Gospel of John in relation to the other three Gospels] (GA 112), lecture of 28 June 1909.
19. See note 6 and *Zur Geschichte und aus den Inhalten der erkenntniskultischen Abteilung der Esoterischen Schule von 1904 bis 1914* [On the history of the cognitive-cultic section of the Esoteric School 1904–1914, and from its contents] (GA 265), p. 366.
20. Ibid., p. 395.
21. Wolfram von Eschenbach, *Parzival* [Parzival], trans. Karl Pannier, based on the original edition by Karl Lachmann (Leipzig, 1926), Book 9: 479.
22. Cf. Gen. 1:26 ff.
23. Cf. Gen. 2:21 ff.
24. J. W. von Goethe, *Faust*, Part 1, 'Walpurgisnacht', l. 4119.
25. *Drei Perspektiven der Anthroposophie* [Three perspectives of anthroposophy] (GA 225), lecture of 22 July 1923.
26. *Geisteswissenschaftliche Menschenkunde* [Spiritual-scientific knowledge of the human being] (GA 107), lecture of 22 March 1909.
27. *Wege zu einem neuen Baustil* [Paths to a new style of building] (GA 286), lecture of 12 December 1911.
28. *Zur Geschichte* (GA 265), p. 415.
29. *Die Pforte der Einweihung* [The portal of initiation] in *Vier Mysteriendramen* [Four mystery plays] (GA 14), Scene 4.
30. *Geheimwissenschaft* (GA 13), chapter on 'The Evolution of the Cosmos and the Human Being'.

Lecture 2

1. *Aus den Inhalten der esoterischen Stunden* [From the contents of the esoteric lessons] (GA 266/1), p. 491.
2. Exod. 3:14.
3. *Die Verantwortung des Menschen für die Weltentwicklung* [The responsibility of humanity for the development of the world] (GA 203), lecture of 1 January 1921.
4. Salcia Landmann, *Jesus starb nicht in Kaschmir* [Jesus did not die in Kashmir] (Munich, 1996).
5. *Die Geheimwissenschaft im Umriss* [Occult science in outline] (GA 13), chapter on 'The Evolution of the Cosmos and the Human Being'. The previously mentioned painting by Bosch is in the Prado.
6. Emil Bock, *Kindheit und Jugend Jesu* [Childhood and youth of Jesus] (Stuttgart, 1980), pp. 100 ff.
7. Matt. 14:6–11.

8. *Das christliche Mysterium* [The Christian mystery] (GA 97), lecture of 29 July 1906.
9. 1 Cor. 15:14.
10. *Verantwortung des Menschen* (GA 203), lecture of 28 March 1921.
11. Friedrich Ueberweg, *Geschichte der Philosophie* [History of philosophy] (Berlin, 1926), 1:518 f.
12. Rudolf Steiner, *The Philosophy of Freedom: The Basis for a Modern World Conception*, trans. Michael Wilson (London, 1970), chapter 5.
13. *Mysterienstätten des Mittelalters* [Mystery sites of the Middle Ages] (GA 233a), lecture of 13 January 1924.
14. *Bausteine zu einer Erkenntnis des Mysteriums von Golgatha* [Building stones for a knowledge of the Mystery of Golgotha] (GA 175), lecture of 27 March 1917.
15. Emil Bock, *Paulus* [Paul] (Stuttgart, 1981).
16. *Die Theosophie des Rosenkreuzers* [The theosophy of the Rosicrucian] (GA 99), lecture of 6 June 1907.
17. *Das Johannesevangelium* [The Gospel of John] (GA 103), lecture of 19 May 1908.
18. Heten Wilkens, *Paulus* [Paul] (Dornach, 1994), p. 59.
19. *Perspektiven der Menschheitsentwickelung* [Perspectives in the development of humanity] (GA 204), lecture of 15 April 1921.
20. Ibid.
21. Bock, *Paulus*.
22. *Esoterische Betrachtungen karmischer Zusammenhänge* [Esoteric studies of karmic connections], Vol. 4 (GA 238), lecture of 14 September 1924.
23. *Der Tod als Lebenswandlung* [Death as a transformation of life] (GA 182), lecture of 16 October 1918.
24. *Grundelemente der Esoterik* [Basic elements of esotericism] (GA 93a), lecture of 8 October 1905.
25. *Kunstgeschichte als Abbild innerer geistiger Impulse* [Art history as an image of inner spiritual impulses] (GA 292), lecture of 5 October 1917.
26. Ibid.
27. For example: Karl Ruh, *Geschichte der abendländischen Mystik* [History of Western mysticism], Vol. 1, *Die Grundlegung durch die Kirchenväter und die Mönchstheologie des 12. Jahrhunderts* [Founding through the Church Fathers and monastic theology in the twelfth century] (Munich, 1990).
28. Dionysius Areopagita, *Himmlische Hierarchie* [Heavenly hierarchy], trans. Josef Stiglmayr (Kempten and Munich, 1911).

Lecture 3

1. *Christus und die geistige Welt: Von der Suche nach dem heiligen Gral* [Christ and the spiritual world: On the quest for the Holy Grail] (GA 149), lecture of 28 December 1913.

2. *Anthroposophische Leitsätze* [Anthroposophical guiding principles] (GA 26), chapter on 'Gnosis and Anthroposophy'.
3. *Der innere Aspekt des sozialen Rätsels* [The inner aspect of the social question] (GA 193), lecture of 4 November 1919.
4. *Die geistige Vereinigung der Menschheit durch den Christus-Impuls* [The spiritual union of humanity through the Christ impulse] (GA 165), lecture of 28 December 1915.
5. *Zeitgeschichtliche Betrachtungen, Das Karma der Unwahrhaftigkeit, Erster Teil* [Contemporary studies; the karma of untruthfulness, Part One] (GA 173), lecture of 21 December 1916.
6. See Werner Foerster (ed.), *Die Gnosis, Koptische und mandäische Quellen* [The Gnosis: Coptic and Mandaic sources], introduced, translated and annotated by Martin Krause and Kurt Rudolf (Zürich, 1995).
7. *Lied von der Perle* [Song of the pearl], in *Die Gnosis, Zeugnisse der Kirchenväter* [The Gnosis, testaments of the Church Fathers], introduced, translated, and annotated by Werner Foerster with Martin Krause and Kurt Rudolf (Zürich, 1995).
8. *Das Sonnenmysterium und das Mysterium von Tod und Auferstehung* [The sun Mystery and the Mystery of death and resurrection] (GA 211), lecture of 26 March 1922.
9. *Pistis Sophia*, in Erich Schmitt, *Die Gnosis: Grundlage der Weltanschauung einer edleren Kultur* [The Gnosis: Foundation of the world view for a more noble culture], Vol. 1 (Leipzig, 1903).
10. Ibid.
11. Ibid.
12. Thomas Maurer, 'Gnostische Verse' [Gnostic verses], *Das Goetheanum*, Vol. 15, no. 7 (1936).
13. *Okkultes Lesen und okkultes Hören* [Occult reading and occult hearing] (GA 156), lecture of 26 December 1914. Note by the editor of GA 156: 'The original text is found in the tenth chapter of Book V of *Philosophumena* by the opponent of the Gnosis, Hippolytos. It was not found until the middle of the nineteenth century in a monastery on Mount Athos. In the edition by P. Wendland in *Die griechischen christlichen Schriftsteller der ersten drei Jahrhunderte* [The Greek Christian writers of the first three centuries], Vol. 26 (Leipzig, 1916), p. 102. This translation of the Greek text is faithful to its meaning, and comes from Rudolf Steiner.'
14. *Die geistige Vereinigung* (GA 165), lecture of 2 January 1916.
15. On Clement of Alexandria, see Schmitt.

Lecture 4

1. Manfred Schmidt-Brabant, *Sternenwege: Von den alten zu den neuen Mysterien, Die Hintergründe des Camino nach Santiago de Compostela* [Star paths: From the

old to the new Mysteries, the background of the Camino to Santiago de Compostela] (Dornach, 1996); this book is currently only available in German.

2. These translations currently have a limited availability.
3. *Aus den Inhalten der esoterischen Stunden* [From the contents of the esoteric lessons] (GA 266/1), lecture of 13 July 1924.
4. *Der Orient im Lichte des Okzidents: Die Kinder des Luzifer und die Brüder Christi* [The Orient in the light of the Occident: The children of Lucifer and the brothers of Christ] (GA 113), lecture of 23 August 1909.
5. *Perspektiven der Menschheitsentwickelung* [Perspectives in the development of humanity] (GA 204), lecture of 16 April 1921.
6. *Das christliche Mysterium* [The Christian mystery] (GA 97), lecture of 29 July 1906.
7. *Perspektiven* (GA 204), lecture of 16 April 1921.
8. Ibid.
9. Ilona Schubert, *Selbsterlebtes im Zusammensein mit Rudolf Steiner und Marie Steiner* [What I experienced while with Rudolf Steiner and Marie Steiner] (Basel, 1977), see note 80.
10. Walter Johannes Stein, *Weltgeschichte im Lichte des Heiligen Gral: Das neunte Jahrhundert* [World history in the light of the Holy Grail: The ninth century] (Stuttgart, 1986).
11. Sigrid Hunke, *Allahs Sonne über dem Abendland: Unser arabisches Erbe* [Allah's sun over Europe: Our Arabic heritage] (Frankfurt a. M., 1997).
12. Ibid.
13. *Perspektiven* (GA 204), lecture of 16 April 1921.
14. Ibid.
15. Ibid.
16. *Aus den Inhalten* (GA 266/1), lesson of 27 August 1909, record C.
17. Heb. 7:3.
18. Heb. 7:17.
19. Heb. 7:3.
20. Jakob Petuchowski, *Melchisedek* [Melchizedek] (Freiburg, 1972), p. 78.
21. *Das Matthäus-Evangelium* [The Gospel of Matthew] (GA 123), lecture of 4 September 1910.
22. *Aus den Inhalten* (GA 266/1), lesson of 27 August 1909, record C.
23. *Die Mysterien des Morgenlandes und des Christentums* [The Mysteries of the East and of Christianity] (GA 144), lecture of 7 February 1913.
24. Ibid.
25. Wolfram von Eschenbach, *Parzival* [Parzival], trans. Karl Pannier, based on the original edition by Karl Lachmann (Leipzig, 1926), Book 9: 479.
26. *Mysterienwahrheiten und Weihnachtsimpulse: Alte Mythen und ihre Bedeutung* [Mystery truths and Christmas impulses: Old myths and their meaning] (GA 180), lecture of 15 January 1918.

27. *Die Mysterien des Morgenlandes und des Christentums* [The Mysteries of the East and of Christianity] (GA 144), lecture of 7 February 1913.
28. Ibid.
29. See Friedrich Schiller, 'Das verschleierte Bild zu Sais' [The veiled image at Sais] (1795).
30. *Perspektiven* (GA 204), lecture of 16 April 1921.
31. *Esoterische Betrachtungen karmischer Zusammenhänge* [Esoteric studies of karmic connections] Vol. 4 (GA 238), lecture of 14 September 1924.
32. Ilona Schubert, *Selbsterlebtes im Zusammensein mit Rudolf Steiner und Marie Steiner* [What I experienced while with Rudolf Steiner and Marie Steiner] (Basel, 1977), see note 80.
33. *Aus den Inhalten* (GA 266/1), lesson of 27 August 1909, record C.
34. Chréstien de Troyes, *Perceval oder die Geschichte vom Gral* [Perceval, or the history of the Grail], trans. Konrad Sandkühler (Dornach, 1991), Book 11.
35. Wolfram von Eschenbach, *Parzival* [Parzival], trans. Karl Pannier, based on the original edition by Karl Lachmann (Leipzig, 1926), Book 5.
36. *Aus den Inhalten* (GA 266/1), lesson of 1 November 1906.
37. *Parzival*, Book 16.
38. *Das Prinzip der spirituellen Ökonomie in Zusammenhang mit Wiederverkörperungsfragen* [The principle of spiritual economy in connection with questions of reincarnation] (GA 109), lecture of 11 April 1909.
39. *Parzival*, Book 9: 479.
40. Dion Fortune, *Glastonbury* (Munich, 1993).
41. *Christus und die geistige Welt: Von der Suche nach dem heiligen Gral* [Christ and the spiritual world: On the quest for the Holy Grail] (GA 149), lecture of 2 January 1914.
42. Ibid.
43. Ibid.

Lecture 5

1. *Das Lukas-Evangelium* [The Gospel of Luke] (GA 114), lecture of 26 September 1909.
2. Ludwig Koenen and Cornelia Römer, eds., *Mani: Auf der Spur einer verschollenen Religion* [Mani: On the trail of a lost religion] (Freiburg, 1993), 'The Cologne Mani Codex'.
3. *Die Tempellegende und die Goldene Legende* [The Temple Legend and the Golden Legend] (GA 93), lecture of 11 November 1904.
4. Ludwig Koenen and Cornelia Römer, eds., *Mani: Auf der Spur einer verschollenen Religion* [Mani: On the trail of a lost religion] (Freiburg, 1993), note 2, p. 50.
5. *Tempellegende* (GA 93), lecture of 11 November 1904.
6. *Die Gnosis, Der Manichäismus* [The Gnosis, Manichaeism], introduced,

translated, and annotated by Alexander Böhlig with Jens Peter Asmussen (Zürich, 1995).

7. Cf. *Zur Geschichte und aus den Inhalten der ersten Abteilung der Esoterischen Schule von 1904 bis 1914* [On the history of the first section of the Esoteric School 1904–1914, and from its contents] (GA 264), 1984 ed., p. 240.
8. *Das Prinzip der spirituellen Ökonomie in Zusammenhang mit Wiederverkörperungsfragen* [The principle of spiritual economy in connection with questions of reincarnation] (GA 109), lecture of 31 March 1909.
9. Wilhelm Pelikan, *Lebensbegegnung mit Leonardos 'Abendmahl'* [A vital encounter with Leonardo's 'Last Supper'] (Dornach, 1988), pp. 66 ff.
10. *Esoterische Betrachtungen karmischer Zusammenhänge* [Esoteric studies of karmic connections] Vol. 3 (GA 237), lecture of 8 July 1924.
11. Déodat Roché, *Die Katharer-Bewegung* [The Cathar movement], trans. Erich von Houwald with Konrad Sandkühler (Stuttgart, 1992).
12. Ibid., p. 427.
13. On Esclarmonde de Foix see Krystel Maurin, *L'Esclarmonde: La femme et la féminité dans l'imaginaire du catharisme* [L'Esclarmonde: the woman and femininity in the imagery of Catharism] (Toulouse, 1995).
14. *Die Gnosis, Der Manichäismus* [The Gnosis, Manichaeism], introduced, translated and annotated by Alexander Böhlig with Jens Peter Asmussen (Zürich, 1995).
15. Cf. Michel Roquebert, *Die Religion der Katharer* [The religion of the Cathars], trans. Rosi Hoffmann (Portet-sur-Garonne, n.d.).
16. Eugen Roll, *Die Welt der Troubadours und das Reich der Minne* [The world of the troubadours and the realm of courtly love] (Stuttgart, 1977).
17. *Meditative Betrachtungen und Anleitungen zur Vertiefung der Heilkunst* [Meditative studies and indications for the deepening of the healing arts] (GA 316), lecture of 23 April 1924 (Dornach).
18. Following Virginia Sease's lecture, there was an opportunity for those in attendance to listen to tape recordings of troubadour songs. The songs were performed by Bénédicte Primault with a *viéle à archet* (Bow-viola) she had constructed according to a sculpture from the twelfth century. She was accompanied with song and flute by Pascal Caumont. Both artists live in Toulouse.

Lecture 6

1. Emil Bock, *Die drei Jahre* [The three years] (Stuttgart, 1998), p. 119; and Emil Bock, *Cäsaren und Apostel* [Caesars and Apostles] (Stuttgart, 1978), p. 281.
2. Helmut Gebelein, *Alchemie* [Alchemy] (Munich, 1996), p. 111.
3. Jakobus de Voragine, *Legenda Aurea* [The Golden Legend], trans. Richard Benz (Jena, 1925), p. 442. In a voluminous work (*Jesus und die Urchristen, Die Qumran-Rollen entschlüsselt* [Jesus and the first Christians, The Qumran scrolls deciphered] (Munich, 1995) about James, the brother of Jesus,

Robert Eisenmann recently wrote: 'Since a James who was the brother of John probably never existed—and we also know with certainty that a foundation stone bearing the name of James even existed centuries before this reburial—it was easily possible that the relics kept in northern Spain since that time are, in reality, the bones of "our" James, the brother of Jesus.' (p. 771.)

4. *Esoterische Betrachtungen karmischer Zusammenhänge* [Esoteric studies of karmic connections] Vol. 3 (GA 237), lecture of 13 July 1924.
5. Ibid.
6. Ibid.
7. *Die Menschheitsentwickelung und Christus-Erkenntnis* [The development of humanity and knowledge of the Christ] (GA 100), lecture of 20 November 1907.
8. Salcia Landmann, *Jesus starb nicht in Kaschmir* [Jesus did not die in Kashmir] (Munich, 1996).
9. Heinz Kaminsky, *Sternstrassen der Vorzeit* [Star routes of prehistory] (Munich, 1996), pp. 321 f.
10. Ibid.
11. Ibid.
12. *Wie kann die Menschheit den Christus wiederfinden?* [How can humanity find the Christ again?] (GA 187), lecture of 29 December 1918.
13. Ibid.
14. Ibid.
15. *Mysterienwahrheiten und Weihnachtsimpulse: Alte Mythen und ihre Bedeutung* [Mystery truths and Christmas impulses: Old myths and their meaning] (GA 180), lecture of 17 January 1918.
16. Pseudo-Turpin, *Historia Karoli Magni* [History of Charlemagne], cited in: Yves Bottineau, *Der Weg des Jakob-Pilgers* [The path of the James pilgrim] (Bergisch-Gladbach, 1987).
17. *Mysterienwahrheiten* (GA 180), lecture of 15 January 1918.
18. *Erdensterben und Weltenleben: Anthroposophische Lebensgaben* [Earthly death and cosmic life: Anthroposophical gifts] (GA 181), lecture of 16 July 1918.
19. Andrew Welburn, *Das Buch mit den vierzehn Siegeln und die Christus-Offenbarung* [The book with fourteen seals and the Christ revelation] (Stuttgart, 1995).
20. *Das Geheimnis der Trinität* [The mystery of the Trinity] (GA 214), lecture of 23 July 1922.
21. Lars-Ivar Ringbom, *Gralstempel und Paradies* [Grail temple and Paradise] (Stockholm, 1951), p. 262.
22. Ibid.
23. *Der Orient im Lichte des Okzidents: Die Kinder des Luzifer und die Brüder Christi* [The Orient in the light of the Occident: The children of Lucifer and the brothers of Christ] (GA 113), lecture of 31 August 1909.

24. *Drei Perspektiven der Anthroposophie* [Three perspectives of anthroposophy] (GA 225), lecture of 6 July 1923.
25. Helmut Gebelein, *Alchemie* [Alchemy] (Munich, 1996), p. 182.
26. Basilius Valentinus, *Chymische Schriften* [Alchemical writings] (Hildesheim, 1976).
27. *Die Mission einzelner Volksseelen im Zusammenhang mit der germanisch-nordischen Mythologie* [The mission of individual folk souls in connection with Germanic-Nordic mythology] (GA 121), lecture of 16 June 1910.
28. Ibid., lecture of 12 June 1910.
29. *Der Zusammenhang des Menschen mit der elementarischen Welt* [The human connection with the elemental world] (GA 158), lecture of 14 November 1914.
30. *Anthroposophische Leitsätze* [Anthroposophical guiding principles] (GA 26), no. 1.
31. John 14:6.

Lecture 7

1. *Grundelemente der Esoterik* [Basic elements of esotericism] (GA 93a), lecture of 30 September 1905.
2. Reinhold Hammerstein, *Die Musik der Engel: Untersuchungen zu Musikanschauung des Mittelalters* [The music of the angels: Research on the musical view of the Middle Ages] (Bern, 1990), p. 118.
3. Rev. 4:4.
4. Rev. 5:8–9.
5. Bishop Victorinus of Pettau; cited in Eugenio Romero Pose, 'O Pórtico do cántico novo' [O portico of the new song], (German trans. by V. Sease), in *El Pórtico de la Gloria: Musica, Arte y Pensamiento* [The Portico de la Gloria: Music, art and thought] (Santiago de Compostela, 1988), trans. K. Ammerman, M. Malin and A. Miller, p. 247.
6. Rudolf Steiner to a member, Berlin, 20 January 1905; cited in *Bilder okkulter Siegel und Säulen: Der Münchner Kongress Pfingsten 1907 und seine Auswirkungen* [Images of occult seals and columns: The Whitsun, 1907, Munich Congress and its consequences] (GA 284), 1993 ed., p. 182.
7. See Carl Schmidt, *Pistis Sophia: Ein gnostisches Originalwerk* [Pistis Sophia: An original work of the Gnosis] (Leipzig, 1925), chapter 83.
8. See José López-Calo, *Coordination: Los Instrumentos del Pórtico de la Gloria* [Coordination: The instruments of the Pórtico de la Gloria], 2 vols. (La Coruña, 1993).
9. Pierre A. Riffard, *L'Ésotérisme: Qu'est-ce que l'Ésotérisme?* [Esotericism: What is esotericism?] (Paris, 1990).

Lecture 8

1. Reinhold Hammerstein, *Die Musik der Engel: Untersuchungen zur Musikanschauung des Mittelalters* [The music of the angels: Investigations into the musical view of the Middle Ages] (Bern, 1990), p. 39.
2. Ibid., p. 50.
3. See Ismael Fernández de la Cuesta, *Historia de la música espanola* [History of Spanish music], Vol. 1, *Desde Los orígenes hasta el 'ars nova'* [From its origins to the 'new art'] (Madrid, 1983), p. 100.
4. Ibid., p. 92.
5. Sigrid Hunke, *Allahs Sonne über dem Abendland: Unser arabisches Erbe* [Allah's sun over Europe: Our Arabic heritage] (Frankfurt a. M., 1997).
6. *Esoterische Betrachtungen karmischer Zusammenhänge* [Esoteric studies of karmic connections] Vol. 4 (GA 238), lecture of 19 September 1924.
7. *Die geistige Vereinigung der Menschheit durch den Christus-Impuls* [The spiritual union of humanity through the Christ impulse] (GA 165), lecture of 27 December 1915.
8. The song was in the public domain and is now available on many tape recordings. A song sung for more than a thousand years—pilgrims still sing it today—can be understood as a kind of Mystery impulse. In 1993, a small conference was arranged in Compostela by the Anthroposophical Society in Spain. It was also a 'holy year', meaning that the birthday of St James (July 25) fell on a Sunday. Visitors from all over the world—almost 5000 people from many different religions—sang this song in the cathedral several times a day.
9. *Kunst im Lichte der Mysterienweisheit* [Art in the light of Mystery wisdom] (GA 275), lecture of 2 January 1915.
10. See Ismael Fernández de la Cuesta, *Historia de la música espanola* [History of Spanish music], Vol. 1, *Desde Los orígenes hasta el 'ars nova'* (Madrid, 1983).
11. On the passage through the planets after death, see Rudolf Steiner, *Das Leben zwischen dem Tode und der neuen Geburt im Verhältnis zu den kosmischen Tatsachen* [Life between death and a new birth in relationship to cosmic facts] (GA 141), lectures of 5 and 20 November 1912.
12. *Okkulte Untersuchungen über das Leben zwischen Tod und neuer Geburt* [Occult research on life between death and a new birth] (GA 140), lecture of 27 October 1912.
13. Ibid., lecture of 3 November 1912.
14. *Esoterische Betrachtungen*, Vol. 4 (GA 238), lecture of 18 September 1924.
15. *Das Initiaten-Bewusstsein* [Initiate consciousness] (GA 243), lecture of 22 August 1924.
16. At the close of Virginia Sease's lecture, the participants sang several songs of the Camino.

Lecture 9

1. Rudolf Steiner, *Über die Wanderung der Rassen* [On the migrations of the races] (Berlin, 1904); reprinted in *Gäa Sophia* [Gaia Sophia], ed. Guenther Wachsmuth, Vol. 3 (Stuttgart/Den Haag/London, 1929), pp. 19 ff.
2. Ibid.
3. *Innere Entwicklungsimpulse der Menschheit: Goethe und die Krisis des neunzehnten Jahrhunderts* [Inner impulses in the development of humanity: Goethe and the crisis of the nineteenth century] (GA 171), lecture of 25 September 1916.
4. *Aus den Inhalten der esoterischen Stunden* [From the contents of the esoteric lessons] (GA 266/1), lecture of 27 August 1909.
5. Ibid.
6. Walter Johannes Stein, *Weltgeschichte im Lichte des Heiligen Gral: Das neunte Jahrhundert* [World history in the light of the Holy Grail: The ninth century] (Stuttgart, 1986).
7. J. Fleckenstein and M. Hellmann, eds., *Die geistlichen Ritterorden Europas* [The spiritual knightly orders of Europe] (Sigmaringen, 1980).
8. Alexander von Thymus, *Das harmonikale System des Altertums* [The harmonic system of antiquity] (Cologne, 1868).
9. Hermann Beckh, *Die kosmischen Rhythmen im Markusevangelium* [The cosmic rhythms in the Gospel of Mark] (Stuttgart, 1997).
10. *Zur Geschichte und aus den Inhalten der erkenntniskultischen Abteilung der Esoterischen Schule von 1904 bis 1914* [On the history of the cognitive-cultic section of the Esoteric School 1904–1914, and from its contents] (GA 265), p. 95.
11. *Innere Entwicklungsimpulse* (GA 171), lecture of 25 September 1916.
12. *Die Tempellegende und die Goldene Legende* [The Temple Legend and the Golden Legend] (GA 93), lecture of 22 May 1905.
13. *Wanderung der Rassen.*
14. *Innere Entwicklungsimpulse* (GA 171), lecture of 25 September 1916.
15. Ibid.
16. *Wanderung der Rassen.*
17. *Die Geheimwissenschaft im Umriss* [Occult science in outline] (GA 13), chapter on 'The Present and Future of Cosmic and Human Evolution'.
18. *Innere Entwicklungsimpulse* (GA 171), lecture of 25 September 1916.
19. *Erdensterben und Weltenleben: Anthroposophische Lebensgaben* [Earthly death and cosmic life: Anthroposophical gifts] (GA 181), lecture of 16 July 1918.
20. Emil Bock, *Urgeschichte* [Primal history] (Stuttgart, 1978), pp. 34 f.
21. *Das Verhältnis der verschiedenen naturwissenschaftlichen Gebiete zur Astronomie* [The relationship of the various scientific areas to astronomy] (GA 323), lecture of 10 January 1921.
22. Ibid.
23. *Mythen und Sagen: Okkulte Zeichen und Symbole* [Myths and sagas: Occult signs and symbols] (GA 101), lecture of 28 December 1907.

24. Ibid., lecture of 14 September 1907.
25. *Das Hereinwirken geistiger Wesenheiten in den Menschen* [How spiritual beings work into the human being] (GA 102), lecture of 11 June 1908.
26. Helmut Gebelein, *Alchemie* [Alchemy] (Munich, 1996), p. 111.
27. Ibid.
28. *Innere Entwicklungsimpulse* (GA 171), lecture of 25 September 1916.
29. Ibid.
30. Hildgard Wiegand, *Der Kampf gegen den Tarnhelm* [The battle against the Tarnhelm] (Stuttgart/Den Haag, 1930).
31. *Zeitgeschichtliche Betrachtungen: Das Karma der Unwahrhaftigkeit, zweiter Teil* [Contemporary studies; the karma of untruthfulness, Volume Two] (GA 174), lecture of 15 January 1917.
32. *Innere Entwicklungsimpulse* (GA 171), lecture of 25 September 1916.
33. Ibid.

Lecture 10

1. *Der Orient im Lichte des Okzidents: Die Kinder des Luzifer und die Brüder Christi* [The Orient in the light of the Occident: The children of Lucifer and the brothers of Christ] (GA 113), lecture of 31 August 1909.
2. Ibid.
3. *Zur Geschichte und aus den Inhalten der erkenntniskultischen Abteilung der Esoterischen Schule von 1904 bis 1914* [On the history of the cognitive-cultic section of the Esoteric School 1904–1914, and from its contents] (GA 265), lesson of 15 April 1908.
4. Ibid., pp. 416 f.
5. *Das esoterische Christentum and die geistige Führung der Menschheit* [Esoteric Christianity and the spiritual guidance of humanity] (GA 130), lecture of 27 September 1911.
6. Ibid.
7. *Der Orient im Lichte des Okzidents* (GA 113), lecture of 31 August 1909.
8. *Esoterische Betrachtungen karmischer Zusammenhänge* [Esoteric studies of karmic connections] Vol. 4 (GA 238), Supplementary Comments.
9. Arthur Koestler, *The Yogi and the Commissar* (New York, 1945).
10. *Mysterienwahrheiten und Weihnachtsimpulse: Alte Mythen und ihre Bedeutung* [Mystery truths and Christmas impulses: Old myths and their meaning] (GA 180), lecture of 5 January 1918.
11. *Die Mission einzelner Volksseelen im Zusammenhang mit der germanisch-nordischen Mythologie* [The mission of individual folk souls in connection with Germanic-Nordic mythology] (GA 121), lecture of 17 June 1910.
12. *Die Geheimwissenschaft im Umriss* [Occult science in outline] (GA 13), chapter on 'The Evolution of the Cosmos and the Human Being' (Leipzig, 1910).
13. *Die Geheimwissenschaft im Umriss* [Occult science in outline], p. 376.

14. Charles IV.
15. *Seelenübungen* [Soul exercises], Vol. 1 (GA 267), 1997 ed., p. 362.
16. *Mysterienstätten des Mittelalters* [Mystery sites of the Middle Ages] (GA 233a), lecture of 6 January 1924.
17. Ibid.
18. *Die Tempellegende und die Goldene Legende* [The Temple Legend and the Golden Legend] (GA 93), lecture of 23 May 1904.
19. *Initiationswissenschaft und Sternenerkenntnis* [Initiation science and star knowledge] (GA 228), lecture of 15 September 1923.
20. *Die Sendung Michaels* [The mission of Michael] (GA 194), lecture of 13 December 1919.

Lecture 11

1. *Individuelle Geistwesen and ihr Wirken in der Seele des Menschen* [Individual spirit beings and their work in the human soul] (GA 178), lecture of 16 November 1917.
2. Barry Fell, *America BC, Ancient Settlers in the New World* (New York 1976).
3. In the summer of 1999, I had a long conversation with the park ranger—who was half Native American—in Peterborough, right where the petroglyphs are located. I was told essential facts about the insights of the Native Americans, the 'First Nation', in regard to the origins of the petroglyphs and their symbolism. However, a fuller elaboration would go beyond the framework of this presentation. The important thing is that the sun symbolism has a deep meaning and is interpreted by the Native Americans on many levels.
4. *Individuelle Geistwesen and ihr Wirken in der Seele des Menschen* [Individual spirit beings and their work in the human soul] (GA 178), lecture of 16 November 1917.
5. See Virginia Sease, 'Das frühe Amerika und der Ostseeraum' [Early America and the Baltic area] in *Die Ostsee-Mysterien im Werdegang der Menschheitsgeschichte* [The Baltic Mysteries in the course of human history], publication of the Anthroposophische Gesellschaft in Deutschland, Arbeitszentrum Ost (1991).
6. *Exkurse in das Gebiet des Markus-Evangeliums* [Excursus into the realm of the Gospel of Mark] (GA 124), lecture of 10 June 1911.
7. *Ursprungsimpulse der Geisteswissenschaft* [Original impulses of spiritual science] (GA 96), lecture of 8 October 1906.
8. *Vor dem Tore der Theosophie* [At the gate of theosophy] (GA 95), lecture of 22 August 1906.
9. *Initiations-Erkenntnis* [Initiation knowledge] (GA 227), lecture of 25 August 1923; and *Initiationswissenschaft und Sternenerkenntnis* [Initiation science and star knowledge] (GA 228), lecture of 15 September 1923.
10. *Mysterienstätten des Mittelalters* [Mystery sites of the Middle Ages] (GA 233a), lecture of 6 January 1924.

11. King Charles II owed William Penn £16,000, money which Admiral Penn (William's father) had lent him. Seeking a haven in the New World for persecuted Friends, Penn asked the King to grant him land in the territory between Lord Baltimore's province of Maryland and the Duke of York's province of New York. With the Duke's support, Penn's petition was granted. The King signed the Charter of Pennsylvania on 4 March 1681, and it was officially proclaimed on 2 April. The King named the new colony in honour of William Penn's father. (http://www.legis.state.pa.us/WU01/VC/visitor_info/pa_history/pa_history.htm)
12. *Die soziale Grundforderung unserer Zeit—in geänderter Zeitlage* [The basic social demand of our time—in a changed condition of the age] (GA 186), lecture of 12 December 1918.
13. Rudolf Steiner, lecture of 5 May 1904, manuscript.
14. *Rudolf Steiner/Marie Steiner-von Sivers: Briefwechsel und Dokumente 1901–1925* [Rudolf Steiner/Marie Steiner-von Sivers: Correspondence and documents 1901–1925] (GA 262), 1967 ed., p.16.

Lecture 12

1. *Die Theosophie des Rosenkreuzers* [The theosophy of the Rosicrucian] (GA 99), lecture of 22 May 1907.
2. Karl Stockmeyer cited in *Bilder okkulter Siegel und Säulen: Der Münchner Kongress Pfingsten 1907 und seine Auswirkungen* [Images of occult seals and columns: The Whitsun 1907 Munich Congress and its consequences] (GA 284); written for *Mitteilungen aus der anthroposophischen Arbeit in Deutschland* (Christmas, 1949).
3. Rudolf Steiner, 'Der theosophische Kongress in München' [The Theosophical Congress in Munich] in *Lucifer-Gnosis* [Lucifer Gnosis] (GA 34).
4. *Mein Lebensgang* [The course of my life] (GA 28), chapter 38.
5. See Marie Steiner, 'Aus der Geschichte unserer Gesellschaft vor vier mal sieben Jahren' [From the history of our Society four times seven years ago] (1935) in *Bilder okkulter Siegel und Säulen: Der Münchner Kongress Pfingsten 1907 und seine Auswirkungen* [Images of occult seals and columns: The Whitsun, 1907, Munich Congress and its consequences] (GA 284).
6. On the 'Masters' see *Zur Geschichte und aus den Inhalten der ersten Abteilung der Esoterischen Schule von 1904 bis 1914* [On the history of the first section of the Esoteric School 1904–1914, and from its contents] (GA 264), 1984 ed., pp. 205, 229 and 246.
7. *Kunst und Kunsterkenntnis* [Art and art knowledge] (GA 271), lecture of 28 October 1909.
8. Christian Morgenstern to Friedrich Kayssler, 24 August 1913, in Hella Wiesberger, *Marie Steiner-von Sivers, Ein Leben für die Anthroposophie, Eine biographische Dokumentation* [Marie Steiner-von Sivers, a life for anthroposophy: a biographical documentation] (Dornach, 1988), p. 300.

9. *Zur Geschichte* (GA 264), 1984 ed., p. 421.
10. Ibid., p. 435.
11. Magdalene Siegloch and Lory Maier-Smits, *Die erste Eurythmistin und die Anfänge der Eurythmie* (Dornach 1993) [*How the New Art of Eurythmy Began: Lory Maier-Smits, The First Eurythmist*, Temple Lodge Publishing, 1997].
12. *Eurythmie als sichtbare Sprache* [Eurythmy as visible speech] (GA 279), lecture of 26 August 1923.
13. Rudolf Steiner, *Anthroposophischer Seelenkalender* [Anthroposophical calendar of the soul] (Dornach, 1987).
14. *Erfahrungen des Übersinnlichen: Die drei Wege der Seele zu Christus* [Experiences of the supersensible: The three paths of the soul to Christ] (GA 143), lecture of 7 May 1912.
15. *Vier Mysteriendramen* [Four mystery plays] (GA 14).
16. Rudolf Steiner to Marie Steiner-von Sivers, 13 October 1924, in *Rudolf Steiner/Marie Steiner-von Sivers: Briefwechsel und Dokumente 1901–1925* [Rudolf Steiner/Marie Steiner-von Sivers: Correspondence and documents 1901–1925] (GA 262), 1967 ed.
17. *Von Jesus zu Christus* [From Jesus to Christ] (GA 131), lecture of 14 October 1911.
18. *Wahrspruchworte* [Verses and meditations] (GA 40).
19. *Das Initiaten-Bewusstsein* [Initiate consciousness] (GA 243), lecture of 22 August 1924.

Lecture 13

1. *Die Geheimwissenschaft im Umriss* [Occult science in outline] (Leipzig, 1910), p. 376.
2. *Exkurse in das Gebiet des Markus-Evangeliums* [Excursus into the realm of the Gospel of Mark] (GA 124), lecture of 10 June 1911.
3. *Esoterische Betrachtungen karmischer Zusammenhänge* [Esoteric studies of karmic connections], Vol. 6 (GA 240), lecture of 20 July 1924.
4. Ibid., lecture of 18 July 1924.
5. *Der Orient im Lichte des Okzidents: Die Kinder des Luzifer und die Brüder Christi* [The Orient in the light of the Occident: The children of Lucifer and the brothers of Christ] (GA 113), lecture of 31 August 1909.
6. *Mysterienwahrheiten und Weihnachtsimpulse: Alte Mythen und ihre Bedeutung* [Mystery truths and Christmas impulses: Old myths and their meaning] (GA 180), lecture of 6 January 1918.
7. *Der Orient im Lichte des Okzidents* (GA 113), lecture of 31 August 1909; and *Geisteswissenschaftliche Menschenkunde* [Spiritual scientific knowledge of the human being] (GA 107), lecture of 22 March 1909.
8. *Perspektiven der Menschheitsentwickelung* [Perspectives in the development of humanity] (GA 204), lecture of 16 April 1921.
9. *Zur Geschichte und aus den Inhalten der erkenntniskultischen Abteilung der*

Esoterischen Schule von 1904 bis 1914 [On the history of the cognitive-cultic section of the Esoteric School 1904–1914, and from its contents] (GA 265), 1987 ed., pp. 46f., 68 and 94.

10. Ibid.
11. Ibid., p. 158. English translation by V. Sease.
12. *Esoterische Betrachtungen karmischer Zusammenhänge* [Esoteric studies of karmic connections], Vol. 2 (GA 236), lecture of 22 June 1924.
13. Ibid.
14. See *Die Geheimwissenschaft im Umriss* [Occult science in outline] (GA 13), chapter on 'The Present and Future of Cosmic and Human Evolution'.
15. *Bilder okkulter Siegel und Säulen: Der Münchner Kongress Pfingsten 1907 und seine Auswirkungen* [Images of occult seals and columns: The Whitsun 1907 Munich Congress and its consequences] (GA 284), lecture of 21 May 1907.
16. Rev. 17:1–6, Emil Bock, trans. (Stuttgart, 1980).
17. *Perspektiven* (GA 204), lectures of 16 and 17 April 1921.
18. *Zur Geschichte und aus den Inhalten der erkenntniskultischen Abteilung der Esoterischen Schule von 1904 bis 1914* [On the history of the cognitive-cultic section of the Esoteric School 1904–1914, and from its contents] (GA 265), 1987 ed., p. 418.

Bibliography of Cited Materials from the Collected Works of Rudolf Steiner Available in English

(Where a GA [Gesamtausgabe] number is absent, the work is currently unavailable in English.)

GA Volumes Available in English

GA No.	Title of Volume in English, Publisher, Date(s) of Lecture(s) Cited
13	*Occult Science* (Rudolf Steiner Press, 1962/3); *An Outline of Esoteric Science* (Anthroposophic Press, 1997).
14	*The Four Mystery Dramas* (Rudolf Steiner Press, 1997), 'The Portal of Initiation', 'The Soul's Probation', 'The Guardian of the Threshold', and 'The Soul's Awakening'.
26	*Anthroposophical Leading Thoughts* (Rudolf Steiner Press, 1973).
28	*The Course of My Life* (Anthroposophic Press, 1970).
93	*The Temple Legend* (Rudolf Steiner Press, 1985), 20 lectures, Berlin, 23 May, 4 and 11 November 1904, 22 May 1905.
93a	*Foundations of Esotericism* (Rudolf Steiner Press, 1983), Berlin, 30 September and 8 October 1905.
95	*Founding a Science of the Spirit* (Rudolf Steiner Press, 1999), Stuttgart, 22 August 1906.
97	*The Christian Mystery* (Completion Press, 2000), 29 July 1906.
99	*Rosicrucian Wisdom* (Rudolf Steiner Press, 2000), 14 lectures, Munich, 22 May and 6 June 1907.
103	*The Gospel of St John* (Anthroposophic Press, 1940), 12 lectures, Hamburg, 19 May 1908.
109	*The Principle of Spiritual Economy* (Anthroposophic Press and Rudolf Steiner Press, 1986), 11 lectures, Heidelberg, 31 March and 11 April 1909.
112	*The Gospel of St John* (Anthroposophic Press and Rudolf Steiner Press, 1948), 14 lectures, Kassel, 28 June 1909.
113	*The East in the Light of the West* (Garber Communications Inc., 1986), 9 lectures, Munich, 23, 28 and 31 August 1909.
114	*The Gospel According to Luke* (Anthroposophic Press, 2001), 10 lectures, Basel, 26 September 1909.
121	*The Mission of the Individual Folk Souls* (Rudolf Steiner Press, 1970), 11 lectures, Christiania (Oslo), 12, 16 and 17 June 1910.
123	*The Gospel of St Matthew* (Rudolf Steiner Press, 1965), 12 lectures, Berne, 4 September 1910.

124 *Background to the Gospel of St Mark* (Rudolf Steiner Press, 1985), 13 lectures, Berlin, 10 June 1911.

130 *Esoteric Christianity* (Rudolf Steiner Press, 2000), 23 lectures, 27 September 1911.

131 *From Jesus to Christ* (Rudolf Steiner Press, 1991), 11 lectures, Karlsruhe, 14 October 1911.

137 *Man in the Light of Occultism, Theosophy and Philosophy* (Rudolf Steiner Publishing Co. and Anthroposophic Press, 1945), 10 lectures, Christiania (Oslo), 12 June 1912.

141 *Between Death and Rebirth* (Rudolf Steiner Press, 1975), 10 lectures, Berlin, 5 and 20 November 1912.

144 *The Mysteries of the East and of Christianity* (Rudolf Steiner Press, 1972), 4 lectures, Berlin, 7 February 1913.

149 *Christ and the Spiritual World and The Search for the Holy Grail* (Rudolf Steiner Press, 1963), 6 lectures, Leipzig, 28 December 1913 and 2 January 1914.

173 *The Karma of Untruthfulness* (Rudolf Steiner Press, 1988), 13 lectures, Basel, 21 December 1916.

174 *The Karma of Untruthfulness* (Rudolf Steiner Press, 1992), 12 lectures, Dornach, 15 January 1917.

187 *How Can Mankind Find the Christ Again?* (Anthroposophic Press, 1984), 8 lectures, Dornach, 29 December 1918.

204 *Materialism and the Task of Anthroposophy* (Anthroposophic Press, 1987), 17 lectures, Dornach, 15, 16 and 17 April 1921.

227 *The Evolution of Consciousness* (Rudolf Steiner Press, 1991), 13 lectures, Penmaenmawr, 25 August 1923.

233a *Rosicrucianism and Modern Initiation* (Rudolf Steiner Press, 1965), 6 lectures, Dornach, 6 and 13 January 1924.

237 *Karmic Relationships* (Rudolf Steiner Press, 1977), 11 lectures, Dornach, 8 and 13 July 1924.

243 *True and False Paths in Spiritual Investigation* (Anthroposophical Publishing Co., 1927), 11 lectures, Torquay, 22 August 1924.

262 *Correspondence and Documents 1901–1925* (Rudolf Steiner Press and Anthroposophic Press, 1988).

264 *From the History and Contents of the First Section of the Esoteric School 1904–1914* (Anthroposophic Press, 1998), ed. Hella Wiesberger.

275 *Art as Seen in the Light of Mystery Wisdom* (Rudolf Steiner Press, 1984), 2 January 1915.

284 *Occult Seals and Columns* (Anthroposophical Publishing Co., 1924) Photogravure and half-tone reproductions, with introductory text (1907).

286 *Architecture as a Synthesis of the Arts* (Rudolf Steiner Press, 1999), Berlin, 12 December 1911.

316	*Course for Young Doctors* (Mercury Press, 1994), 13 lectures, Dornach, 23 April 1924.
323	*The Relationship of the Diverse Branches of Natural Science to Astronomy* (Rudolf Steiner Research Foundation, 1989), 18 lectures, Stuttgart, 10 January 1921.
346	*Book of Revelation* (Rudolf Steiner Press, 1998), conversations and question-and-answer sessions with the priests of the Christian Community, Dornach, 9 September 1924.

Additional Cited Works by Rudolf Steiner Available in English

From GA No.	Volume Title, Publisher, and Date(s) of Lecture(s) Cited
(40)	*Truth-Wrought Words* (Anthroposophic Press, 1979).
(101)	*Occult Signs and Symbols* (Anthroposophic Press, 1972), 4 lectures, Stuttgart, 14 September 1907.
(102)	*The Influence of Spiritual Beings upon Man* (Anthroposophic Press, 1961), 11 lectures, Berlin, 11 June 1908.
(107)	*The Deed of Christ and the Opposing Spiritual Powers* (Steiner Book Centre, 1976), 2 lectures, Berlin, 22 March 1909.
(109)	*The Principle of Spiritual Economy* (Anthroposophic Press and Rudolf Steiner Press, 1986), 11 lectures, Rome, 31 March 1909.
(156, 165)	*Festivals of the Seasons* (Anthroposophical Publishing Co. and Anthroposophic Press, 1928), 19 lectures, Dornach, 26 December 1914 and 2 January 1916.
(171)	*Inner Impulses of Evolution* (Anthroposophic Press, 1984), 7 lectures, Dornach, 25 September 1916.
(175)	*Building Stones for an Understanding of the Mystery of Golgotha* (Rudolf Steiner Press, 1972), 10 lectures. Berlin, 27 March 1917.
(178)	*Geographic Medicine* (Mercury Press, 1986), 2 lectures, St Gallen, 16 November 1917.
(180)	*Ancient Myths* (Steiner Book Centre, 1971), 7 lectures, Dornach, 5, 6 and 15 January 1918.
(182)	*How Do I Find the Christ?* (Rudolf Steiner Publishing Co. and Anthroposophic Press, 1941), 1 lecture, Zürich, 16 October 1918.
(186)	*Social and Anti-Social Forces in the Human Being* (Mercury Press, 1982), 1 lecture, Bern, 12 December 1918.
(193)	*Influences of Lucifer and Ahriman* (Rudolf Steiner Book Centre, 1984), Bern, 4 November 1919.
(194)	*The Mysteries of Light, of Space and of the Earth* (Anthroposophic Press and Rudolf Steiner Publishing Co., 1945), 4 lectures, Dornach, 13 December 1919.

(214) *The Mystery of the Trinity* (Rudolf Steiner Publishing Co. and Anthroposophic Press, 1947), 4 lectures, Dornach, 23 July 1922.

(228) *Man in the Past, the Present and the Future. The Evolution of Consciousness.* (Rudolf Steiner Press, 1966), 3 lectures, Stuttgart, 15 September 1923.

(236) *Karmic Relationships* (Rudolf Steiner Press, 1974), 16 lectures, Dornach, 22 June 1924.

(238) *Karmic Relationships* (Rudolf Steiner Press, 1997), 10 lectures, Dornach, 14, 18 and 19 September 1924.

(240) *Karmic Relationships* (Rudolf Steiner Press, 1971), Arnhem, 18 and 20 July 1924.

(271) *The Nature and Origin of the Arts* (Anthroposophical Society/ H. Collison, n.d.), 1 lecture, Berlin, 28 October 1909.

For more information on the works of Rudolf Steiner in English and German please contact these libraries:

The Rudolf Steiner Library
65 Fern Hill Road
Ghent, New York 12075
Phone: 518 672 7690
Fax: 518 672 5827
Email: rsteinerlibrary@taconic.net

The Library
Rudolf Steiner House
35 Park Road, London NW1 6XT
England
Phone/Fax: 020 7224 8398
Email: RSH-Library@anth.org.uk